SATIE REMEMBERED

Satie
Remembered

ROBERT ORLEDGE

with translations from the French
by ROGER NICHOLS

faber and faber
LONDON · BOSTON

First published in 1995
by Faber and Faber Limited
3 Queen Square London WC1N 3AU

Phototypeset by Intype, London
Printed in England by Clays Ltd, St Ives Plc

A CIP record for this book
is available from the British Library

ISBN 0–571–17271–7
0–571–17272–5 (pbk)

2 4 6 8 10 9 7 5 3 1

For Charles McFeeters

Although our information is false, we do not vouch for it.

Erik Satie

Contents

Illustrations

Acknowledgements

As with all my work on Satie, I owe a special debt of gratitude to Ornella Volta, who placed the invaluable resources of the Archives de la Fondation Erik Satie at my disposal and gave me much helpful advice in the preparation of this book. I should also like to thank Frédéric Caby, who sent me copies of documents in the collection of his father, the late Robert Caby, and allowed me to cite extracts from them. I also gained much useful information from interviews with Jacques Guérin, Madeleine Milhaud and Robert Caby, and from other interviews undertaken by Roger Nichols and by the BBC. For help with translations, I should like to thank Louisa Kerr, Caroline Potter and Dr Ian Williamson, and for other help of various kinds I should like to thank the staffs of the Bibliothèque Nationale, Paris (Département de la Musique) and the Harry Ransom Humanities Research Centre (University of Texas at Austin), Thierry Bodin, Margaret Cobb, Dr Patrick Gowers, Dr Roy Howat, Madeleine Li-Koechlin, Charles McFeeters, Sarah Nichols, Ian Qualtrough, Pierre Joseph-Lafosse-Satie, Richard Hoo Wing Tsang, Dr Steven Moore Whiting and Stephen Wyatt. I need hardly say that this book could never have appeared in its present form without the invaluable advice of Roger Nichols at every stage.

I am also grateful for permission to quote from the following copyright material (detailed source references are given at the end of each extract):

George Auriol, Pierre Bertin, Robert Caby, René Chalupt, Jean Cocteau, Gabriel Fournier, Stanislas Fumet, Valentine Hugo, Moïse Kisling, Charles Koechlin, Fernand Léger, Pierre de Massot, E. L. T. Mesens, Francis Poulenc, Roland-Manuel, Henri Sauguet, *La Revue Musicale* (*ReM*, now Éditions Hermann); Georges Auric, *Quand j'étais là* (Grasset, 1979); André Beucler, *Poet of Paris* (Chatto & Windus, 1955); Blaise Cendrars, Interview (1950) (*Cahiers Blaise Cendrars*) (Éditions de la Baconnière, 1989); René Clair (trans. Richard Jacques and Nicola Hayden), *À Nous la Liberté* (Lorrimer Publishing, 1970); Germaine Everling, *L'anneau de Saturne* (Fayard, 1970); Augustin Grass-Mick, 'Le souvenir d'Erik Satie' (*Les Arts*); Vladimir Golschmann, 'Golschmann Remembers Erik Satie' (*Musical America*); Jacques Guérin, 'Un dimanche à Luzarches' (*L'Optimiste*); Harry Halbreich, *Arthur Honegger* (Fayard, 1992, and Amadeus Press); Francis Jourdain, *Né en 76* (Éditions du Pavillon, 1951); Louis Laloy, *La musique retrouvée* (Librairie Plon, 1928); Contamine de Latour, 'Erik Satie intime' (*Comoedia*); Darius Milhaud, *Notes Without Music* (Calder & Boyars, 1967); René Peter, *Claude Debussy* (Gallimard, 1944); Francis Poulenc (trans. and ed. Sidney Buckland), *Echo and Source: Selected Correspondence 1915–1963* (Gollancz, 1991); Henri-Pierre Roché, *Carnets 1920–21* (André Dimanche, 1990); Pierre-Daniel Templier, *Erik Satie* (Éditions Rieder/Éditions d'Aujourd'-hui); Jean Wiéner, *Allegro appassionato* (Belfond, 1978).

For permission to reproduce illustrations I am grateful to the Archives de la Fondation Erik Satie (3, 9–11, 14 (photo Cocteau), 18 (photo Waléry), 19); the Bibliothèque Nationale (2); Frédéric Caby (from the collection of Robert Caby) (cover, 8, 13, 15, 16, 20); Jacques Guérin (17, photo taken by his mother Mme Jeanne Louise Guérin); Paul Laxton (1). Illustrations 4–7 and 12 are from the collection of Robert Orledge (photo 7 by Claude Noyer).

Every effort has been made to contact the copyright holders of material reproduced in this book, but in some cases without success. The publishers will be pleased to hear from anyone I have not acknowledged above. In general, extracts of 500 words or less have been reused under the standard copyright permissions rule.

Note

Since a large number of extracts come from *La Revue Musicale* this has been abbreviated as *ReM* in the source details given at the end of each piece. Material supplied by Ornella Volta from the Archives de la Fondation Erik Satie, 56 rue des Tournelles, Paris 3, is credited as *AFS*.

Introduction

Uncovering the truth about Satie from behind his carefully cultivated public image is a hard task, and it should come as no surprise that this prickly, eccentric and apparently irrational man provoked conflicting souvenirs from those who knew him. For even his public image contained contradictions: the dapper bourgeois functionary in dress was at the same time an anarchic, uncompromising iconoclast in his art – the jester's mask concealing a serious, painstaking professional composer. Given Satie's infinite capacity for bearing grudges, his seemingly childish behaviour and explosive temperament, his excessive consumption of alcohol, and his continual requests to borrow money (which he usually squandered on umbrellas or handkerchiefs), it is surprising that he had many friends at all. Yet, by all accounts, he got on equally well with plumbers, poets and princesses, was a stimulating conversationalist, and genuinely appeared to many as charming, courteous and excessively polite and moral. His uncanny awareness of real talent in all branches of art led him to become close friends with seminal figures as diverse as Apollinaire and Cocteau, Derain and Picasso, Man Ray and Brancusi. While he remained principally attracted to young composers like Milhaud, Auric and Poulenc, and disliked discussing his music with his peers (or listening to the music of others), he nonetheless got on well with the conservative Dukas and maintained a close friendship with the equally secretive Debussy that lasted over a quarter of a century. Indeed, one of the most unfortunate gaps in this book is any sort of testimony from Debussy himself, for however deferential Satie appeared to others in his distinguished company, their private conversations were almost certainly one of the only outlets Satie allowed himself to discuss his musical and personal problems in any depth. He did discuss them on occasions with his brother Conrad, but he was not a musician.

While Satie undoubtedly varied his responses depending on the social status of the company involved, and some of his outbursts can be attributed to drink, his strange logic, or to annoyance at being distracted from work in hand, there is another, more plausible explanation for his apparent eccentricities. Recent research by Sarah Nichols (the wife of the translator of this book) suggests that many of the conflicting traits in Satie's bizarre personality fit in with a picture of his being a higher order dyslexic or imagist, and in this he has many distinguished artistic predecessors from Lewis Carroll and Hans Christian Andersen to Rodin (all of whom Satie admired). Satie was fascinated by his own thought processes and explored them deliberately, as Lewis Carroll did. Typically, his exceptional intelligence and different logical approach made him easily frustrated with what he saw as the inadequacies of others (especially music critics), and this led to frequent 'explosions'. He experienced periods of elated bonhomie alternating with others of almost embarrassing shyness and timidity; he was anti-authoritarian and saw himself as having 'come to this world very young in a very old age'; and he was sensitive to others, yet volatile when he felt himself threatened in any way. He liked making jokes, but hated it when the joke was turned on him – as Pierre Bertin discovered to his cost when he mimicked Satie during a performance of *Le piège de Méduse*. Most important, he seems to have conceptualised his ideas in a three-dimensional way, which made the two-dimensional concept of writing extremely laborious and led him to mask these difficulties through his slow and elaborate calligraphy. At the same time, his higher order dyslexia gave him a spatial approach to music (which explains his fascination with Cubism and sculpture) and made him attracted to transformational thinking, magic and the potentials of formal mirroring. Characteristically, he was obsessed with making lists (often of a fantastical nature which would have struck him as extremely funny), and like many higher order dyslexics his frustration with early learning led to repeated reports of idleness at the Paris Conservatoire and of his inability to sight-read music with any degree of adequacy. His dislike of playing or even discussing his own music in public is symptomatic of this. While the spelling difficulties we normally associate with dyslexia applied more to Debussy than Satie, this hypothesis explains so much that it must be given serious credence. It should in no way be regarded as dismissive or condescending, for in his determination to overcome the unusual perspectives and difficulties it presented lies an important key towards understanding Satie's far-sighted creative genius.

The concept of being like a 'sad child' recurs in several reminiscences of Satie and there can be no doubt that his chosen life of continual poverty and self-denial in the interests of his art made his existence profoundly unenviable. Much of his life was spent on foot, trekking back and forth from his hermetic isolation in the dingy suburb of Arcueil to the lights and attractions of Paris. His one real delight lay in stopping to drink at his favourite cafés *en route* and it is no surprise that, despite his robust health, he died of cirrhosis of the liver at the relatively early age of 59. When his friends finally entered his miserable room for the first time in 1925 it was as if they had 'penetrated his brain', for Satie had never thrown anything out (or cleaned the room) in over a quarter of a century. The principal remaining mystery is how he emerged from it every day impeccably dressed – 'like an actor stepping out from the wings' – and how the manuscripts he copied there remained, like Satie, so virginal. There has been speculation that he lived some sort of double life: even that he had a mistress who was a laundress. But there is no evidence to support this theory, and in the final analysis the reader must make up his/her own mind about Satie from the evidence presented here.

In the following text, irrelevant or uninteresting passages have been omitted without notice. Preference has been given in each section to the accounts of people who actually knew Satie during the relevant period, though in the first section (in particular) the scarcity of first-hand accounts has meant that retrospective memories have had to be used. The ordering is broadly chronological and no excuse is made for conflicting testimonials or the occasional repetition. Well over half of the extracts appear here in English for the first time.

ROBERT ORLEDGE
Liverpool, July 1994

Chronology

Satie's Life and Works
Contemporary Figures and Events

Additional information [in square brackets] comes from Conrad Satie's 'Chronologie de la vie et de l'oeuvre d'Erik Satie', prepared for use in Pierre-Daniel Templier's biography of Satie around 1928 (from the collection of Robert Caby, Paris). Satie signed himself 'Erik' on all his compositions (from 1884 onwards), though he still used the 'Eric' form on documents up to 1906.

1866 *17 May* Eric-Alfred-Leslie Satie born in Honfleur, Normandy

1866   Busoni, Kandinsky born
    Rückert (78) dies
    First performances of *The Bartered Bride* (Smetana), *Mignon* (Thomas), Symphony No. 1 (Bruckner)
    Prussia defeats Austria
    Alfred Nobel invents dynamite

1867   Bonnard, Granados, Koechlin, Pirandello born
    Baudelaire (46) dies
    First performances of *Roméo et Juliette* (Gounod), *La Grande-Duchesse de Gérolstein* (Offenbach), *Don Carlos* (Verdi)
    Exposition Universelle in Paris
    Dominion of Canada established
    USA buys Alaska from Russians
    Sholes invents the typewriter

1868 *17 June* Louise-Olga-Jeannie Satie born. Summer holiday in Brighton

1868   Stefan George, Scott Joplin, Vuillard born
    Rossini (76) dies
    First performances of *Die Meistersinger von Nürnberg* (Wagner), Piano Concerto (Grieg), Piano Concerto No. 2 (Saint-Saëns)
    Trade Union Congress founded

1869 *21 October* Conrad Satie born

1869   Gide, Lugné-Poe, Matisse, Pfitzner, Roussel, Frank Lloyd Wright born
    Berlioz (66), Dargomizhsky (56) die
    First performance of *Das Rheingold* (Wagner)
    Suez Canal opened
    Mendelyev devises the periodic table

1870 Satie family moves to 3 Cité Odiot, Paris 8

1870   Lenin, Florent Schmitt born
        Dickens (58), Mercadante (75) die
        First performance of *Die Walküre* (Wagner)
        Franco-Prussian War
        Proclamation of Third French Republic
        Negro suffrage enforced in USA
        Papal infallibility asserted by First Vatican Council

1871   Proust, Rouault, Valéry born
        Auber (89), Serov (51) die
        First performances of *Aida* (Verdi), *Le rouet d'Omphale* (Saint-
        Saëns)
        Société Nationale de Musique founded
        Paris Commune
        Treaty of Frankfurt
        Trade unions legalised in Britain

1872   Jane Satie (mother) dies. Eric and Conrad sent to live with
        paternal grandparents in Honfleur. Eric enters Collège d'Hon-
        fleur

1872   Diaghilev, Mondrian, Skryabin, Vaughan Williams born
        Théophile Gautier (61) dies
        First performances of *L'arlésienne*, *Djamileh* (Bizet), *La princesse
        jaune* (Saint-Saëns)
        Secret ballot introduced in Britain

1873   Rakhmaninov, Reger, de Séverac born
        John Stuart Mill (67) dies
        First performances of *Jeux d'enfants* (Bizet), *Rédemption* (Franck),
        Cello Concerto No. 1 (Saint-Saëns), Symphony No. 2 (Tchai-
        kovsky)
        Ashanti War
        End of German Occupation of France

1874   Begins music lessons (solfège, Gregorian chant) with M. Vinot,
        organist at Église St-Léonard and pupil of Niedermeyer

1874   Holst, Ives, Schoenberg, Suk born
        Cornelius (50) dies
        First performances of *Boris Godunov* (Mussorgsky), *Danse
        macabre* (Saint-Saëns), *Die Fledermaus* (Strauss)
        Monet's *Impression, Sunrise* exhibited
        Bourbons recalled in Spain
        Disraeli begins last term of office

1875   Reynaldo Hahn, Thomas Mann, Ravel, Rilke, Roger-Ducasse,
            Ricardo Viñes born
            Bizet (37), Corot (79) die
            First performances of *Carmen* (Bizet), *Symphonie espagnole*
            (Lalo), Piano Concerto No. 4 (Saint-Saëns)
            Third Republic founded in France
            Disraeli wins control of Suez Canal for Britain

1876   Brancusi, Casals, Falla, Fargue, Monteux, Vlaminck born
            First performances of *Der Ring des Nibelungen* (Wagner), *Sylvia*
            (Delibes), *The Kiss* (Smetana), Symphony No. 1 (Brahms)
            First legislative elections in France
            End of Second Carlist War in Spain
            Alexander Graham Bell patents the telephone
            Custer's last stand

1877   Dohnányi, Cortot, Dufy, van Dongen born
            First performances of *L'étoile* (Chabrier), *Samson et Dalila* (Saint-
            Saëns), Symphony No. 2 (Brahms), Symphony No. 2 (Borodin)
            Queen Victoria proclaimed Empress of India
            Russia declares war on the Turks
            Edison invents the phonograph

1878   *Summer* Grandmother drowns. Eric rejoins father in Paris. End
            of formal education. [On Sundays, dinner with Albert Sorel at
            Château de Versailles]

1878   Caplet, Augustus John, Masefield born
            First performances of *Polyeucte* (Gounod), Symphony No. 4
            (Tchaikovsky)
            Exposition Universelle in Paris
            Bulgaria established as separate principality under Turkey

1879   *21 January* Alfred Satie marries Eugénie Barnetche, a piano
            teacher

            8 November Eric enters preparatory piano class of Émile Des-
            combes at Paris Conservatoire

1879   Beecham, Bridge, Delage, E. M. Forster, Grovlez, Ireland,
            Klee, Picabia, Respighi, Cyril Scott born
            Viollet-le-Duc (65) dies
            First performances of *Eugene Onegin* (Tchaikovsky), *Une édu-
            cation manquée* (Chabrier)
            Jules Grévy elected President of the French Republic

1880   *January* Described as 'gifted but lazy' after performance of Hiller's Piano Concerto (Op. 69) in Paris Conservatoire exams. [Frequent visits to organist Alexandre Guilmant. Lessons in Latin and Greek from M. Mallet]

1880   Apollinaire, Bloch, Derain, Epstein, Inghelbrecht, Medtner, Pizzetti born
George Eliot (61), Flaubert (59), Offenbach (61) die
First performances of *A May Night* (Rimsky-Korsakov), *The Pirates of Penzance* (Sullivan)
Gladstone becomes Prime Minister for the second time
Amnesty for French Communards

1881   [Moves to 70 rue de Turbigo, Paris 2, 5th floor. Reads Voltaire, Alexandre Dumas *père*, Eugène Chavette]

1881   Bartók, Enescu, Gleizes, Léger, Miaskovsky, Picasso born
Carlyle (86), Dostoevsky (60), Mussorgsky (42) die
First performances of *Hérodiade* (Massenet), *Les contes d'Hoffmann* (Offenbach), Piano Concerto No. 2 (Brahms), Symphony No. 4 (Bruckner), *Ballade* (Fauré)
Treaty of Bardo and French Occupation of Tunisia
French laws on public meetings and press
First Irish Home Rule Bill
Canadian Pacific Railway Company formed

1882   *June* Eric again fails to impress Conservatoire examiners with his piano playing and is dismissed under Article 60 by Thomas

1882   Braque, Joyce, Kodály, Malipiero, Stravinsky, Szymanowski, Turina, Virginia Woolf born
Raff (60) dies
First performances of *The Snow Maiden* (Rimsky-Korsakov), *Parsifal* (Wagner)
Ferry Laws on French Educational Reform
Founding of the French League of Patriots
Britain fighting in Egypt; Cairo occupied

1883   *4 December* Admitted as auditor in Conservatoire harmony class of Antoine Taudou. Father establishes himself as publisher of salon music. [Move to 6 rue de Marseilles, Paris 10. Reads Alphonse Karr, Hans Andersen, Joseph Méry, Alfred de Musset. Plays Bach, Chopin, Schumann, Bernica [sic], Messager]

1883	Ansermet, Bax, Casella, Kafka, Maurice Utrillo, Webern born Manet (51), Wagner (70) die First performances of *Lakmé* (Delibes), Symphony No. 3 (Brahms)

1884 *9 September* First composition, a brief Allegro for piano, written on holiday in Honfleur. [Hears César Franck at Sainte Clotilde]

1884	Modigliani, van Dieren born Smetana (60) dies First performances of *Manon* (Massenet), *Le villi* (Puccini), *L'enfant prodigue* (Debussy – as winner of Prix de Rome), Symphony No. 4 (Brahms), Symphony No. 7 (Bruckner) Trade unions legalised in France Third Reform Bill Invention of Maxim machine-gun

1885 *6 November* Accepted into intermediate piano class of Georges Mathias (who had also taught his stepmother Eugénie). Writes *Valse-ballet*, *Fantaisie-valse*, his only salon pieces

1885	Berg, Klemperer, D. H. Lawrence, Pound, Varèse, Wellesz born Victor Hugo (83) dies First performances of Symphony No. 7 (Dvořák), *The Mikado* (Sullivan), *Le Cid* (Massenet) Khartoum captured: General Gordon killed Canadian Pacific Railway completed

1886 Meets Spanish-born poet Contamine de Latour. [Moves to 66 boulevard Magenta, Paris 9.] Interest in mysticism, Gothic art develops. Composes four *Ogives* for piano
9 December Leaves Conservatoire by volunteering for military service (with 33rd Infantry Regiment at Arras, Pas-de-Calais). [Meets Isidore Philipp, Charles Levadé]

1886	Alain-Fournier born Ponchielli (52), Liszt (75) die First performances of *Khovanshchina* (Mussorgsky), *Variations symphoniques* (Franck), *Le carnaval des animaux* and Symphony No. 3 'Organ' (Saint-Saëns) First conference of National Federation of Trades Unions (Lyons)

Daimler produces his first motor-car
Statue of Liberty unveiled

1887   [*April* Bronchitis. Two months' convalescence. Writes three
Gymnopédies and Latour songs, *Élégie*, *Les anges* and *Sylvie*]
September Trois sarabandes for piano
November/December Released from military service. Leaves
home for room at 50 rue Condorcet, Montmartre. Adopts
bohemian life-style and dandified appearance. Frequents Chat
Noir cabaret and meets Rodolphe Salis, Alphonse Allais,
[George Auriol, Maurice Donnay, Jules Jouy, Henri Rivière,
Albert Tinchant]

1887   Rupert Brook, Chagall, Le Corbusier, Arthur Rubinstein, Edith
Sitwell, Villa-Lobos born
Borodin (53) dies
First performances of *Le roi malgré lui* (Chabrier: seen by Satie
on 18 May), *Otello* (Verdi)
Sadi Carnot elected as President of Third French Republic
First inter-capital phone link established (Paris–Brussels)
Queen Victoria's Jubilee

1888   *February–April Trois gymnopédies* completed and copied out

1888   Irving Berlin, Durey, T. S. Eliot, T. E. Lawrence born
Alkan (75), Heller (74) die
First performances of *Le roi d'Ys* (Lalo), Symphony No. 5
(Tchaikovsky), *Requiem* (first version) (Fauré)
Pasteur Institute established in Paris
Pneumatic tyre invented

1889   Frequents Edmond Bailly's Librairie de l'Art Indépendant where
he meets esoteric writers. Visits Exposition Universelle
8 July Gnossienne (known as No. 5)

1889   Chaplin, Cocteau born
Gerard Manley Hopkins (45), Villiers de l'Isle-Adam (51) die
First performances of *Don Juan* (Strauss), *Esclaramonde* (Mas-
senet), *Shylock* (Fauré)
Exposition Universelle (Paris): Eiffel Tower completed
Maeterlinck's *La Princesse Maleine* published
Death of Crown Prince Rudolf of Austria (Mayerling, near
Vienna)

1890   *?Spring* Moves to smaller room at 6 rue Cortot, Montmartre, to escape creditors. Meets Joséphin Péladan, self-appointed leader of the Ordre de la Rose-Croix Catholique, du Temple et du Graal (for which he becomes official composer and chapelmaster in 1891–2)
Gnossiennes (known as Nos 1–3)
5 December Danse for small orchestra
?Meets [Van Gogh, Gauguin]

1890   Ibert, Frank Martin, Martinů, Nijinsky, Pasternak born
               Van Gogh (37), Franck (68) die
               First performances of *Prince Igor* (Borodin), *Cavalleria rusticana* (Mascagni), *The Queen of Spades* (Tchaikovsky), Symphony No. 8 (Dvořák), *Ode à la musique* (Chabrier)
               Parnell's divorce scandal splits Irish Nationalists
               Charles de Gaulle born

1891   Quarrels with Salis and leaves Chat Noir to become second pianist at Auberge du Clou. Friendship with Debussy develops
21 January Gnossienne (known as No. 4)
2 November Salut Drapeau! (from Péladan's play *Le Prince du Byzance*)
?December Incidental music for Péladan's 'Pastorale Kaldéenne' *Le fils des étoiles*

1891   Bliss, Ernst, Migot, Prokofiev, Roland-Manuel born
               Delibes (55), Rimbaud (37), Seurat (32) die
               First performances of Clarinet Trio and Quintet (Brahms)
               Verlaine's *Bonheur*, *Chansons pour elle*, *Mes hôpitaux* published
               Hardy's *Tess of the D'Urbervilles* published

1892   *?February Trois sonneries de la Rose +Croix*
May Applies for election to Académie des Beaux-Arts
June Two *Préludes du Nazaréen* for play by Henri Mazel
14 August Breaks with Péladan in open letter to *Gil Blas*
27 October Debussy dedicates copy of *Cinq poèmes de Baudelaire* to 'Erik Satie, a gentle medieval musician lost in this century'
November–December Two versions of *Uspud* ('Ballet chrétien' in three acts with Contamine de Latour). [Meets Utrillo, Valadon, de Feure]

December Challenges Eugène Bertrand, director of the Paris Opéra, to a duel to persuade him to consider *Uspud* for performance

1892   Honegger, Milhaud, Tailleferre born
            Lalo (69) dies
            First performances of *Werther* (Massenet), *I pagliacci* (Leoncavallo), Symphony No. 8 (Bruckner)
            Maeterlinck's *Pelléas et Mélisande* published
            Founding of the National Federation of Bourses de travail (Paris)
            Panama scandal

1893   *14 January–20 June* Only known affair with painter (and neighbour) Suzanne Valadon. Meets Ravel at Café de la Nouvelle Athènes
            March Nine *Danses gothiques* for piano
            ?mid-1893 Vexations; Eginhard, Prélude
            October Founds Église Métropolitaine d'Art de Jésus Conducteur, in which he assumes roles of Parcier and Maître de Chapelle [Visits Salon des Impressionistes. Makes acquaintance of Paul Signac. Reads Maurice Beaubourg, Hugues Rebell. Portrait painted by Comte Antoine de La Rochefoucauld (*June*)]

1893   Mayakovsky, Wilfrid Owen born
            Gounod (75), Maupassant (43), Tchaikovsky (53) die
            First performances of *La damoiselle élue* (Debussy), *Hänsel und Gretel* (Humperdinck), *Manon Lescaut* (Puccini), *Falstaff* (Verdi), Symphony No. 6 (Tchaikovsky)
            Maeterlinck's *Pelléas et Mélisande* first performed in Paris, on Satie's birthday (*17 May*)
            French entente with Russia
            Foundation of the Independent Labour Party in Britain

1894   *March Prélude à La porte héroïque du ciel* (play by Jules Bois)
            30 April Second application for election to Académie des Beaux-Arts after death of Gounod. Angry letter to Saint-Saëns published in *Le ménestrel* (*17 May*) after application is again rejected

1894   Jean Borlin, e.e. cummings, Huxley, Piston, James Thurber born
            Chabrier (53), Anton Rubinstein (64) die
            First performances of *Prélude à l'après-midi d'un faune* (Debussy),

Thaïs (Massenet), Symphony No. 5 (Bruckner), Symphony No. 1 (Mahler)
Dreyfus convicted of treason
Assassination of President Sadi Carnot
French laws against anarchists passed (Lois scélérates)
Japan declares war against China

1895   With a small inheritance Satie publishes extracts from his compositions, and attacks on his critical and theatre enemies. Buys seven identical velvet corduroy suits at the store 'La Belle Jardinière'. Rose+Croix period gives way to 'Velvet Gentleman' period
[Portrait painted by Georges de Feure (*April*)]
Completes *Messe des pauvres* (begun in 1893)

1895   Éluard, Robert Graves, Hindemith born
First performances of *Till Eulenspiegel* (R. Strauss), Symphony No. 2 (Mahler)
Felix Faure elected French President
Promenade Concerts inaugurated by Henry Wood
Oscar Wilde imprisoned
First commercial showing of moving pictures by Lumière brothers
Röntgen discovers X-rays
Gillette invents the safety razor

1896   *30 April* Third unsuccessful application for election to the Académie des Beaux-Arts after death of Ambroise Thomas
25 July Moves to tiny 'placard' at 6 rue Cortot as inheritance exhausted. End of Église Métropolitaine d'Art

1896   Gerhard, Massine, Scott Fitzgerald, Sessions born
Bruckner (72), Ambroise Thomas (85), Verlaine (52) die
First performances of *Andrea Chénier* (Giordano), *La bohème* (Puccini), *Der Corregidor* (Wolf)
French annexe Madagascar
Gold discovered in Klondike

1897   *January Gnossienne* (known as No. 6)
20 February Première of *Gymnopédies* Nos 3, 1 (orchestrated by Debussy in 1896) at Salle Érard, conducted by Gustave Doret
March Pièces froides (*Airs à faire fuire*; *Danses de travers*)

1897   William Faulkner, Korngold, Thornton Wilder born
      Brahms (64) dies
      First performances of *Fervaal* (d'Indy), *Sapho* (Massenet)
      Queen Victoria's Diamond Jubilee

1898   *October* ['Escapes'] to room at 22 (now 34) rue Cauchy in
      Arcueil and begins daily routine of 10-kilometre walks to and
      from Paris (with frequent stops in cafés *en route* to drink and
      compose). Closes door on world outside

1898   Brecht, René Clair, Eisenstein, Gershwin, Hemingway, Henry
      Moore born
      Aubrey Beardsley (26), Lewis Carroll (66), Mallarmé (56) die
      First performances of *Véronique* (Messager), *Sadko* (Rimsky-
      Korsakov), *Pelléas et Mélisande* (Fauré)
      Founding of the Action Française
      The Curies discover radium
      Zeppelin invents rigid airship

1899   To gain money, starts accompanying Vincent Hyspa in
      Montmartre cabarets. Writes popular songs (like *Un dîner à
      l'Élysée*) and theatrical collaborations with Jules Dépaquit (*Jack-
      in-the-Box*) and Latour (*Geneviève de Brabant*)
      19 October Witness at Debussy's marriage to Lilly Texier

1899   Auric, Noël Coward, Duke Ellington, Alfred Hitchcock, Lorca,
      Vladimir Nabokov, Poulenc born
      Chausson (44), Johann Strauss (74) die
      First performances of *Enigma Variations* (Elgar), *The Tsar's Bride*
      (Rimsky-Korsakov), *Cendrillon* (Massenet)
      Émile Loubet elected French President
      Dreyfus retried and again convicted
      Aspirin first marketed
      Boer War begins

1900   Writes first article on 'Les musiciens de Montmartre' for tourist
      guide. Settles down in Arcueil, though locals regard him as
      enigma
      5 August Verset laïque & somptueux (for collection published for
      Exposition Universelle)
      9 December Introduced to Ricardo Viñes by Ravel at Concerts
      Chevillard

1900   Antheil, Copland, Křenek, Kurt Weill born
               Fibich (49), Nietzsche (56), Sullivan (58) die
               First performances of *Nuages*, *Fêtes* (Debussy), *Louise* (Charpen-
               tier), *Tosca* (Puccini), *The Dream of Gerontius* (Elgar), *Prométhée*
               (Fauré), *Finlandia* (Sibelius)
               Opening of Paris Métro
               Inauguration of Vincent d'Indy as president of Schola Cantorum
               Boer War: relief of Kimberley and of Mafeking
               Boxer Rebellion in China
               Publication of Freud's *The Interpretation of Dreams*
               Gamma rays discovered

1901   *The Dreamy Fish*, *The Angora Ox* – music for stories by Lord
            Cheminot (alias Contamine de Latour)

1901   Giacometti, Malraux, Rubbra, Sauguet born
               Toulouse-Lautrec (37), Verdi (87) die
               First performances of *Sirènes* (Debussy), *Rusalka* (Dvořák),
               Feuersnot (Strauss), Piano Concerto No. 2 (Rakhmaninov), Sym-
               phony No. 4 (Mahler)
               First Congress of the Socialist and Radical–Socialist Party in
               France
               Universal Edition established in Vienna
               Death of Queen Victoria
               Marconi transmits radio signals across the Atlantic
               Nobel Prizes inaugurated

1902   Waltzes *Tendrement*, *Poudre d'or* registered with Société des Aut-
            eurs. Paulette Darty ('Queen of the Slow Waltz') takes an interest
            in his songs, especially *Je te veux*

1902   Marlene Dietrich, Ogden Nash, Walton born
               Samuel Butler (67) dies
               First performances of *Pelléas et Mélisande* (Debussy: Satie is
               'absolutely astounded' by this), *Pour le piano* (Debussy), *Jeux
               d'eau* (Ravel), Symphony No. 2 (Sibelius), Symphony No. 3
               (Mahler)
               End of Boer War

1903   *November* Completes *Trois morceaux en forme de poire* for piano
            duet (based on works from 1890–91 and more recent cabaret
            songs). Thinks he has found his way forward as a serious com-
            poser

1903   Khachaturian, Nicolas Nabokov, Radiguet, Simenon, Waugh
        born
        Gauguin (55), Wolf (43) die
        First performances of *The Apostles* (Elgar), Symphony No. 9
        (Bruckner), *L'étranger* (d'Indy)
        First controlled flight by Wright brothers
        Pope Pius X sanctions the restoration of Gregorian chant as sung
        by the Benedictine monks at Solesmes

1904   *La diva de l'"Empire'* (song for Darty); *Le Piccadilly* (March for
        piano with early Ragtime influence). Darty popularises his songs
        in Paris (after they have proved successful on provincial tours)

1904   Balanchine, Count Basie, Dali, Dallapiccola, Graham Greene,
        Horowitz, Kabalevsky, Petrassi, Skalkottas born
        Chekov (44), Dvořák (62), Hanslick (79) die
        First performances of *Madama Butterfly* (Puccini), String Quar-
        tet (Ravel), *Estampes* (Debussy), Symphony No. 5 (Mahler)
        Russo-Japanese War (1904–5)
        Entente Cordiale between France and Britain
        First British car registration plate (A1) issued

1905   *October* Enrols at Schola Cantorum, against Debussy's advice.
        Takes counterpoint course with Roussel (1905–8) and parts of
        Vincent d'Indy's ten-year *Cours de composition musicale* (analysis,
        form, sonata construction, orchestration) till November 1912

1905   Greta Garbo, Jolivet, Constant Lambert, Sartre, Rawsthorne,
        Tippett born
        First performances of *La mer* (Debussy), *Le palais hanté*
        (Schmitt), *Pelléas et Mélisande* (Schoenberg), *Salome* (Strauss),
        The Merry Widow (Lehár)
        Press scandal after Ravel is disqualified after preliminary round
        of Prix de Rome competition
        Fauré appointed director of Paris Conservatoire
        Founding of French Socialist Party
        Law of Separation of Church and State passed in France
        Einstein publishes his *Special Theory of Relativity*
        Revolution in Russia

1906   Replaces 'Velvet Gentleman' look with final appearance as bour-
        geois functionary (bowler hat, wing collar, black suit, umbrella).
        Still writes cabaret songs plus many experimental spin-offs from

Schola studies (*Fugue-Valse*; *Chanson médievale*; *Passacaille*; *Prélude en tapisserie* – with complex motivic construction)

1906   Samuel Beckett, Betjeman, Shostakovich born
Arensky (45), Cézanne (67), Ibsen (78), Stassov (83) die
First performances of *Miroirs* (Ravel), *Images* (1st set: Debussy), *The Kingdom* (Elgar), Symphony No. 6 (Mahler)
Exoneration of Alfred Dreyfus
Vitamins discovered
San Francisco earthquake

1907   Completes *Nouvelles 'Pièces froides'* for piano (summer), experimenting with styles of Fauré and Debussy

1907   Auden, Moravia born
Grieg (64), Joachim (76) die
First performances of *Histoires naturelles* (Ravel), String Quartet, Op. 7 (Schoenberg), *Ariane et Barbe-bleue* (Dukas), *A Village Romeo and Juliet* (Delius)
Strauss's *Salome* banned in New York, Boston and London
Picasso paints *Les demoiselles d'Avignon* (first signs of Cubism)
Publication of Bergson's *Creative Evolution*
First helicopter flight

1908   *June 15* Obtains counterpoint diploma at Schola Cantorum
August–September Writes *Choral* and *Fugue* of *Aperçus désagréables* as piano duets to play with Debussy
Attends Radical–Socialist meetings in Arcueil and participates in charitable activities of its Patronage Laïque

1908   Elliott Carter, Messiaen born
MacDowell (46), Rimsky-Korsakov (64) die
First performances of *Rapsodie espagnole* (Ravel), *Children's Corner* (Debussy), Symphony No. 1 (Elgar), Symphony No. 7 (Mahler)
Belgium annexes Congo
First Model T Ford
First aeroplane flight in Britain

1909   Intensifies activities in Arcueil with humorous newspaper articles and performances of cabaret works in concerts with Paulette Darty and Vincent Hyspa. Studies orchestration with d'Indy

1909   Albéniz (48), Bordes (47), Catulle Mendès (67) die
            First performances of *The Golden Cockerel* (Rimsky-Korsakov),
            Elektra (Strauss), *Gaspard de la nuit* (Ravel), Piano Concerto
            No. 3 (Rakhmaninov)
            Marinetti publishes first Futurist Manifesto in Paris
            Proust begins *À la recherche du temps perdu*
            Joan of Arc beatified
            Blériot flies across English Channel
            Bakelite invented

1910   Resigns from Patronage Laïque and all local involvement in
        Arcueil

1910   Anouilh, Samuel Barber, Genet born
            Balakirev (73), Edouard Colonne (72), Reinecke (86), Tolstoy
            (82) die
            First performances of *Ibéria*, *Rondes de printemps* (Debussy), *La
            fanciulla del West* (Puccini), *The Firebird* (Stravinsky), Violin
            Concerto (Elgar), Symphony No. 8 (Mahler)
            First concert of Société Musicale Indépendante in Paris
            Diaghilev's Ballets Russes take Paris by storm
            Jaques-Dalcroze founds Institute of Eurhythmics in Hellerau
            Union of South Africa
            Britain opens first Labour Exchanges

1911   *16 January* Ravel plays some early Satie piano pieces at SMI
        concert
        25 March Debussy conducts his *Gymnopédie* orchestrations at
        Salle Gaveau. Satie is dismayed that Debussy should be surprised
        at their success. Discovery of Satie begins at last. He renounces
        his earlier cabaret work and begins his championship of younger
        composers (with Roland-Manuel)
        June–September En habit de cheval, the culmination of '8 years'
        work' to arrive at new 'modern fugue'. This and other pieces are
        published by Rouart-Lerolle and his friendship with Stravinsky
        begins

1911   Mahler (50), Guilmant (74) die
            First performances of *Prometheus* (Skryabin), Symphony No. 4
            (Sibelius), *L'heure espagnole* (Ravel), *Le martyre de Saint Sébastien*
            (Debussy), Symphony No. 2 (Elgar), *Petrushka* (Stravinsky),
            Das Lied von der Erde (Mahler), *Der Rosenkavalier* (Strauss)

Thomas Mann writes *Death in Venice*
Ballets Russes make first London appearance
Nationalist Republic set up in China under Sun Yat-sen
Amundsen reaches South Pole
Vitamins classified

1912   Ironical writings begin, including 'Mémoires d'un amnésique'
Begins humorous piano pieces with *Préludes flasques (pour un chien) (July)* and *Véritables préludes flasques (pour un chien) (August)*. Demets rejects the first set but accepts the second for publication and a partnership begins which increases Satie's productivity and notoriety

1912   Cage, Françaix, Markevitch, Ionesco born
Coleridge-Taylor (37), Massenet (70) die
First performances of *La péri* (Dukas), *Evocations* (Roussel), *Daphnis et Chloé* (Ravel), Symphony No. 9 (Mahler), *Der ferne Klang* (Schreker), *Pierrot lunaire* (Schoenberg), *Ariadne auf Naxos*, first version (Strauss), *Prélude à l'après-midi d'un faune*, ballet (Debussy)
Sinking of the *Titanic*
China becomes a republic
Scott's last expedition to the South Pole

1913   *February–March Le piège de Méduse*, comedy in one act which prefigures Surrealism and uses prepared piano in its seven Monkey Dances
Numerous piano pieces including *Descriptions automatiques (April)*, *Embryons desséchés (June–July)*, *Chapitres tournés en tous sens (August–September)* and three sets of children's pieces *(Enfantines) (October)*.
November Les pantins dansent written for Metachoric Festival of Valentine de Saint-Point (performed *18 December*)
December Friendship with Auric (14) begins

1913   Britten, Camus, Lutosławski born
First performances of *Gurrelieder* (Schoenberg), *Pénélope* (Fauré), *La vida breve* (Falla), *Le sacre du printemps* (Stravinsky), *Jeux* (Debussy)
Raymond Poincaré elected President of France
Lili Boulanger becomes first woman to win Prix de Rome

Russolo publishes Manifesto on the Art of Noises (Milan) and gives first demonstration of noise instruments (Modena)
Treaty of Bucharest

1914 *January Choses vues à droite et à gauche (sans lunettes)* for violin and piano
March–May Sports et divertissements written for Lucien Vogel with texts by Satie and drawings by Charles Martin (published 1923)
June–July Heures séculaires et instantanées for piano. Forbids texts to be read aloud during performance
June 28 Meets Diaghilev *chez* Misia Edwards. Acts as Corporal in Home Guard in Arcueil
July Trois valses distinguées du précieux dégoûté
August 1 Joins Socialist Party after assassination of Jean Jaurés
November–December Trois poèmes d'amour to own 'magic' texts (modern equivalents of 13th-century French troubadour poetry)

1914 Panufnik, Dylan Thomas, Tennessee Williams born
Alain-Fournier (28), Lyadov (59), Magnard (49) die
First performances of *A London Symphony* (Vaughan Williams), *Josephslegende* (Strauss), *Le rossignol* (Stravinsky)
Opening of Panama Canal
Archduke Franz Ferdinand of Austria assassinated at Sarajevo
Outbreak of First World War
Battle of the Marne

1915 *March–April* Writes *Cinq grimaces* for forthcoming Cocteau production of *A Midsummer Night's Dream* at Cirque Médrano
August–October Avant-dernières pensées, dedicated to Debussy, Dukas, Roussel
18 October Meets Cocteau *chez* Valentine Gross. Shakespeare production does not materialise

1915 Saul Bellow, Arthur Miller, Orson Welles born
Rupert Brooke (28), Goldmark (84), Skryabin (43) die
First performances of Piano Trio (Ravel), Symphony No. 5, first version (Sibelius), *Alpine Symphony* (Strauss)
Chaplin's film *The Tramp*
Henry Ford develops the first farm tractor
Einstein publishes his *General Theory of Relativity*
Sinking of the *Lusitania*

1916 *April–May Trois mélodies* (Fargue/Godebska/Chalupt)
2 May Receives Cocteau's initial plans for *Parade*, but composition gets under way only after Picasso joins team on *24 August*
2 November First public lecture: 'Les animaux dans la musique'
Interest in contemporary art develops

1916 Babbitt born
George Butterworth (31), Granados (49), Henry James (73), Reger (43) die
First performances of *Goyescas*, opera (Granados), *Savîtri* (Holst)
Tristan Tzara invents word 'Dada' and mounts first Dadaist exhibition in Zurich
Battles of Verdun, the Somme, Jutland

1917 *6 January* First work on *Socrate* (Plato, trans. Victor Cousin), to commission from Princesse Edmond de Polignac
8 March Breaks with Debussy over derogatory opinions of *Parade*
8 May Finishes orchestration of *Parade* just in time for scandalous Ballets Russes première on *18 May* (without *Choral* and *Final* which were added in *April–May 1919*)
30 May Sends insulting postcard to critic Jean Poueigh (Octave Séré) who had complimented Satie after *Parade* première but then published a hostile review (*27 May*). Poueigh wins libel case against Satie, who escapes a prison sentence only after an appeal (*27 November*). He is helped to pay his fine and damages by the Princesse de Polignac
6 June Auric, Durey and Honegger organise homage to Satie in Salle Huyghens (Montparnasse) from which emerges the loose affiliation of young radical composers known as the Nouveaux Jeunes (from which Les Six in turn emerge in 1920)
July Sonatine bureaucratique (anticipating neo-classicism)
Mid–late 1917 First 'musique d'ameublement' and formulation of compositional aesthetic

1917 Robert Lowell, Yehudi Menuhin, Sidney Nolan born
Degas (83) dies
First performances of *Turandot* and *Arlecchino* (Busoni), *Palestrina* (Pfitzner), *La rondine* (Puccini), Violin Sonata (Debussy)
First jazz recordings by Victor Company in America
Bolshevik Revolution in Russia
Balfour Declaration

1918   *5 February* First Nouveaux Jeunes concert, introduced by Satie
        March Reconciliation with Debussy shortly before his death on
        25 March
        August Reaches depths of poverty and despair
        October Completes orchestration of *Socrate*
        November 1 Breaks links with Nouveaux Jeunes
        December Proposes concert tour of America to be arranged by
        his author friend Henri-Pierre Roché
        Cocteau publishes *Le Coq et l'Arlequin* which deifies Satie as the
        musical leader of the post-war *esprit nouveau*. Satie claims he
        owes his 'return to classical simplicity with a modern sensibility'
        to his Cubist painter friends (like Picasso and Braque)

1918   Apollinaire (38), Boito (76), Lili Boulanger (24), Cui (83),
                Debussy (55), Klimt (56), Lecocq (86), Wilfrid Owen (25),
                Parry (70) die
                First performances of *The Miraculous Mandarin* (Bartók), *His-*
                toire du soldat (Stravinsky), *Pause del silenzio* (Malipiero), Classi-
                cal Symphony (Prokofiev)
                First American jazz band performs in Paris
                Publication of Spengler's *The Decline of the West*
                End of First World War

1919   *August–November* Five *Nocturnes* for piano mark return to sys-
        tematic approach to composition
        November–December Trois petites pièces montées for orchestra
        Refuses to write article on Ravel for Jean-Aubry. Involvement
        with Tzara and Dada movement increases. Begins to move in
        high society circles and delights in shocking them with his
        Bolshevist views. Concern grows to make music new, chic and
        Parisian

1919   Leoncavallo (61), Renoir (78) die
                First performances of *The Three-Cornered Hat*, ballet (Falla),
                Die Frau ohne Schatten (Strauss), Cello Concerto (Elgar), *Fenni-*
                more and Gerda (Delius), *Le tombeau de Couperin* (Ravel)
                Paris Peace Conference and Treaty of Versailles
                Alcock and Brown make first transatlantic flight

1920   *8 March Musique d'ameublement* (with Milhaud) at Galerie Bar-
        bazanges

June Premier menuet for piano
7 June Première of *Socrate* (with orchestra) by Marya Freund as part of Festival Erik Satie organised by Cocteau
July–October La belle excentrique written for dancer Caryathis
September–December Quatre petites mélodies, including *Élégie* for Debussy and their 'friendship of 30 years' to a poem by Lamartine
22 November Hears reading of *Paul & Virginie* by Cocteau and Radiguet. Work on this *opéra-comique* continues till 1923 though little is achieved

1920   Maderna born
Bruch (82), Modigliani (36) die
First performances of *La valse* (Ravel), *Le Boeuf sur le Toit* (Milhaud), *Pulcinella* (Stravinsky), *La légende de Saint-Christophe* (d'Indy), *The Adventures of Mr Brouček* (Janáček), *The Planets*, complete (Holst)
Alexandre Millerand elected President of France
Henri Rabaud appointed director of Paris Conservatoire
Music and Letters and *La revue musicale* founded
First meeting of League of Nations
Congress of Tours
Prohibition begins in America
First commercial radio broadcast in Detroit

1921   *April* Visits Brussels and Ghent for performances of *Socrate*
24 May Première of *Le piège de Méduse*
30 August Sonnerie pour réveiller le bon gros Roi des Singes
December Joins Communist Party. Helps Man Ray construct his first French 'ready-made' sculpture. Friendship with Brancusi develops

1921   Caruso (48), Déodat de Séverac (47), Humperdinck (67), Saint-Saëns (86) die
First performances of *Le Roi David* (Honegger), *Katya Kabanova* (Janáček), *Chout*, *The Love of Three Oranges* and Piano Concerto No. 3 (Prokofiev), Symphonies of Wind Instruments (Stravinsky), *Les mariés de la Tour Eiffel* (Les Six, minus Durey)
Varèse founds International Composers' Guild (New York)
First Congress of the French Communist Party
Polish Agreement

1922   *17 February* Presides at public trial and condemnation of André
        Breton at Closerie des Lilas (after Breton challenged Tzara's
        leadership of Dada movement in Paris at Congrès de Paris).
        Movement comes to an end after Soirée du Coeur à Barbe (*July*)
        July–November Articles on Stravinsky (2) and Debussy. Journal-
        istic work increases (1922–4)

1922   Kingsley Amis, Philip Larkin, Xenakis born
                Pedrell (81), Proust (51) die
                First performances of *Mavra* and *Renard* (Stravinsky), *Pastoral
                Symphony* (Vaughan Williams), Symphony in Bb (Roussel),
                Colour Symphony (Bliss)
                James Joyce's *Ulysses* and T. S. Eliot's *The Waste Land* published
                International Society for Contemporary Music founded
                BBC formed and first regular radio programmes begin
                Tutankhamun's tomb discovered

1923   *January* Formation of École d'Arcueil (Cliquet-Pleyel, Désorm-
        ière, Maxime Jacob, Sauguet) by Satie and Milhaud
        May Song-cycle *Ludions* (Fargue)
        30 May Divertissement (*La statue retrouvée*) performed *chez*
        Comte Étienne de Beaumont as final collaboration between
        Picasso, Satie, Cocteau and Massine
        July–December Sets spoken dialogue from Gounod's opera *Le
        médecin malgré lui* for Diaghilev's production in Monte Carlo
        (*January 1924*)

1923   First performances of *The Perfect Fool* (Holst), *Les noces* (Stravin-
                sky), *Padmâvatî* (Roussel), *El Retablo de Maese Pedro* (Falla),
                La brebis égarée (Milhaud)
                First ISCM Festival in Salzburg
                First Labour government in Britain
                Hitler attempts first *coup d'état* in Bavaria

1924   *February* Breaks with Auric, Poulenc and Cocteau after events
        in Monte Carlo in January (opium-smoking, homosexuality).
        Moves further to left in music and ideas. Ballet plans with
        Derain, Braque etc. continue (as they have done since 1921)
        February–May Writes ballet *Mercure* with Picasso and Massine
        for de Beaumont's Soirées de Paris (première *15 June*)
        June–October Writes 'ballet instantanéiste' *Relâche* with Picabia

and Borlin for Rolf de Maré's Ballets Suédois (this grew out of the scenario for *Après-dîner* by Blaise Cendrars of *November 1923*)

October–November Composes *Cinéma* to accompany Surrealist film shot by René Clair in June (as interval feature in *Relâche*)

5 December Scandalous (twice delayed) première of *Relâche* at Théâtre des Champs-Élysées. Satie makes last stage appearance with Picabia at end in conductor Roger Désormière's 5CV car

1924	Nono born

Busoni (58), Joseph Conrad (67), Fauré (79), Anatole France (80), Kafka (41), Lyapunov (64), Puccini (65), Cecil Sharp (55), Stanford (71) die

First performances of *Les biches* (Poulenc), *Rhapsody in Blue* (Gershwin), Symphony No. 7 (Sibelius), *Pacific 231* (Honegger), *Salade* and *Le train bleu* (Milhaud), *Erwartung* and *Die glückliche Hand* (Schoenberg), *Intermezzo* (Strauss), *The Cunning Little Vixen* (Janáček)

Occupation of the Ruhr continues

Gaston Doumergue elected President of France

Breton publishes first *Surrealist Manifesto*

Birds Eye starts commercial production of frozen food

1925 *January* Rapid decline in health due to cirrhosis of liver and pleurisy. Jean Wiéner arranges room at Grand Hôtel, place de l'Opéra, but Satie dislikes it and moves to Hôtel Istria, Montparnasse

20 February Comte Étienne de Beaumont arranges private room in Hôpital St-Joseph, rue Pierre-Larousse. Health deteriorates rapidly and Satie refuses to see friends he had quarrelled with, remaining intransigent to the end

1 July Death of Satie (8 p.m.), aged 59

1925 Berio, Boulez born

First performances of *Wozzeck* (Berg), *L'enfant et les sortilèges* (Ravel), Symphony No. 2 (Prokofiev), *Les matelots* (Auric), Piano Concerto (Gershwin), *Sinfonia semplice* [No. 6] (Nielsen)

Eisenstein films *Battleship Potemkin*

First French Fascist groups formed

Electric recording introduced

I
Youth and student years

Eric Satie was born on 17 May 1866 in Honfleur, a busy Normandy seaport at the mouth of the Seine estuary. His father, Alfred, was a shipping broker who also wrote poetry and salon music, liked travel and spoke seven languages fluently. His mother, Jane Leslie Anton, was born in London of Scottish parents and was also cultivated: she is 'a good musician, and draws well', Alfred told his friend Albert Sorel during their whirlwind courtship in 1865. They were married in St Mary's Church in Barnes and Eric was conceived during their honeymoon in Scotland. After the births of Olga and Conrad, the family moved to Paris in 1870, where Sorel helped Alfred find work as a translator. After Jane's death in 1872, Eric and Conrad were sent back to live with Alfred's parents in Honfleur, where Eric studied music with the local organist, M. Vinot. After his grandmother's death in 1878, Eric rejoined his father in Paris. Shortly after this, in January 1879, Alfred married a piano teacher and fellow salon composer, Eugénie Barnetche, and it was probably due to her persuasion that Eric entered the preparatory piano class of Émile Descombes at the Paris Conservatoire that November, at the age of 13. His career there was undistinguished and in November 1886 he volunteered for military service to escape its tyrannies. In 1887, Alfred (who was now a music publisher) brought out four of Erik's early songs, but at the end of this year Erik left home for a Bohemian life among the cabarets of Montmartre.

As there are no contemporary accounts of Satie's early years, I have included some secondary source material in this section, and expanded it to include Satie's period as a mature student at the Schola Cantorum which was altogether more serious and deeply motivated for being voluntary. Between October 1905 and June 1908 he studied counterpoint with Albert Roussel, and he continued to study other parts of Vincent d'Indy's ten-year composition course (including fugue

3

and orchestration) until November 1912, when his independent career as a composer began to take off following his rediscovery by Ravel in 1911.

PIERRE-DANIEL TEMPLIER
(1905–87)

Pierre-Daniel Templier was the son of the the architect Pierre-Alexandre Templier (1867–1932), the editor of the Radical–Socialist journal *L'avenir d'Arcueil-Cachan*, to which Satie contributed humorous reviews of local events in 1909–10. Pierre-Alexandre also became President of the Patronage Laïque in 1910 and Satie helped with their philanthropic work by taking poor local children on outings to the country. Pierre-Daniel wrote the first biography of Satie in 1932, with a great deal of help from Satie's brother Conrad, and it is from this source that most of our knowledge of Satie's early life derives.

Families

Satie's great-grandfather was a sea-going captain under the Empire. From his battles and victories over the English he gained trophies and a deep hatred of the island race. His son, Jules, became a shipbroker, a firemen's leader and was given the Légion d'Honneur. He was noted for his integrity and his profound intransigence; intransigence being the great vice – or the great virtue – of the Saties.

Jules married a girl from Alsace (not enough notice has been taken of this stock in considering the make-up of the composer's family), and by her he had three children: Alfred, Adrien and Marguerite. The two brothers had opposite characters: Alfred was studious and docile, Adrien undisciplined. They became boarders at the college in Honfleur, but soon managed to find a way out; Adrien didn't go on with his studies, but Alfred went on to the college in Lisieux, where he passed his baccalaureate. He was an excellent pupil, and was a friend of his brilliant fellow student Albert Sorel,* who also came from Honfleur.

The two brothers then went off to England, where they stayed with a

---

*Sorel (1842–1906) became a distinguished historian, noted for his studies of the French Revolution, and a member of the Institut de France.

clergyman. Adrien, known as *Sea-Bird*,* shocked the congregation by making jokes during the services and was banned from the church. He proceeded to scandalise the village; shut up in his cottage, he seduced the maids.

The two then made a second journey to Norway, before Jules Satie bought each of them jobs as shipbrokers. Sea-Bird lacked enthusiasm and displayed a deplorable wealth of imagination, but out of the obedience and respect he owed his father he was obliged to keep his post. As for Alfred, he took his duties very seriously.

Jane-Leslie Anton was born in London of Scottish parents. Her father died when she was young. Her mother, left with very little money, lived as a companion to a rich sister, married to a Mr MacCombay, a virtuous Anglican. During a visit to Paris, Mr MacCombay distributed moralising tracts, while his nephew's son did the same at the doors of concert halls. Jane Anton was sent to board in Honfleur, Alfred met her, they liked each other and got married. The respectable Saties, Catholics and anglophobes, and the worthy Antons examined each other in silence, frostily.

The young newly-weds went on their honeymoon and Jane showed her delighted husband all that Scotland had to offer. On their return, they announced the impending arrival of a young Satie.

Childhood

Eric Alfred Leslie arrived on 'this earthly, earthy earth' on 17 May 1866 at 9 o'clock in the morning. 'Was I sent here to amuse myself? To afford myself a little distraction? To forget the miseries of a beyond which I can no longer remember? Am I not an intruder here?' M. Cocteau assures us that French and English fairies surrounded his cradle. And seeing that Satie has been compared to the Sleeping Beauty, I may add that the old sorceress appeared and said: 'My gift is of a judgement so sure as to dishearten you!'

In 1867 [1868] and 1869 a sister, Olga, and a brother, Conrad, joined him. The three of them were baptised as Anglicans – murmurings in the Satie clan! The children were too close to their grandparents; Alfred began to worry about a growing split in the family. After the war of

---

*The 1932 biography gives 'See-Bird', but the 1969 translation (MIT Press) gives the more likely 'Sea-Bird'. As this edition was approved by Templier, I have adopted the later version here.

1870, he sold his shipbroking business and the five of them moved to Paris. Here Jane died in 1872.

Eric barely knew his mother. Here, perhaps, lay the roots of that tendency to solitary reflection and of that independence of spirit which were to characterise him. The two boys were entrusted to their paternal grandparents and were baptised a second time, as Roman Catholics. The Antons, dignified as ever, wished them well and departed. Eric, aged 6, was sent as a boarder to the College of Honfleur and stayed there until 1878. As a true nephew of Sea-Bird, he was not over-docile and gained only moderate esteem from his teachers.

After his wife died, Alfred became more studious and started learning foreign languages. He travelled, too, spending a year in Lübeck and another in Milan. On his return to Paris, he followed courses at the Sorbonne and the Collège de France. On Sundays he used to go and have dinner with Albert Sorel, the Secretary-General of the Senate, at Versailles, and there he met various Establishment figures, members present and future of the Académie Française. Sorel also found him a job as a translator.

In Honfleur, the young Eric grew apace, surrounded by his old miscreant of a grandfather, his pious, high-minded grandmother and his thoughtful, well-behaved brother Conrad. He saw a lot of his Uncle Sea-Bird and felt strangely drawn to him. His uncle divided his enthusiasm between a love of boats and a love of horses. He owned a superbly decorated carriage which nobody dared climb into, in case they damaged it – like the famous staircase later invented by Erik.*

Sea-Bird would sit down in front of his favourite horse and smoke in silence. He also had a magnificent boat built for him, called 'The Wave', which was all the more precious because it was useless; the owner used to go on board to smoke a pipe or two, but very rarely put out to sea. On great occasions, he'd leave the harbour, with a sailor rejoicing in the Shakespearian name of *Ass's Jaw*, go for a little cruise and come back. When troupes of visiting actors put on plays at the Honfleur theatre, he used to take Eric and smuggle him into the wings. This immoral uncle gave up shipbroking on his father's death, bought a bookshop which was

---

*In the 'Marche du grande escalier', the third of the *Enfantillages pittoresques* of 1913. Satie's accompanying story tells us it had over 1000 ivory steps. Even the king was forbidden to use it, having to 'jump out of the window' instead!

looked after by an old female shop assistant, and spent all his time and energy on horseracing and boats.

Eric learnt the piano with an organist of the church of St Catherine called Vinot, who no doubt had a considerable influence on him. Vinot had been a pupil of Niedermeyer, and perhaps he introduced the boy to the old Gregorian modes and to plainchant. Did Eric show any startling aptitude? No evidence from this period has survived.

In 1878 his grandmother died in strange circumstances while bathing on the little beach at Honfleur. Her husband then became a convert and a devout parishioner, and used to take a curious devotional book to church: *Harmonies de la nature* by Bernardin de Saint-Pierre. After his first communion, Eric rejoined his father in Paris.

It was a happy time for him. Alfred Satie had become bitterly disillusioned by formal education and took him out of school for good, though Eric's freedom was still subject to his father's control. Instead of school, he took lectures and classes at the Collège de France. On Sundays, Eric would go with his father to visit Albert Sorel. Here Alfred had met a young lady, a piano teacher, and in 1879 he married her, much to the annoyance of *Crin-Crin* (as Eric was known). Unfortunately, with Mlle Barnetche came a tiresome mother, and young Eric found two stepmothers hard going!

Both ladies had a real passion for music – Mme Satie had been a pupil of Alexandre Guilmant and Georges Mathias, and had imbibed Conservatoire attitudes. Satie's hatred of these dated from this first contact.

Music

Eric took a liking to the piano which, 'like money, is pleasant only for the person who handles it'. His parents decided to get him to work at it seriously. Was he enthusiastic? Later on he was to state that a musical career had been forced on him, and it's true that his parents' proselytism knew no boundaries. The concierge's daughter in the rue de Constantinople, where the Saties were living, was to join the Opéra-Comique. Either from admiration or in obedience to his stepmother, Eric went to hear the organist Alexandre Guilmant at the Trinité church and was a regular at the concerts at the Trocadéro.

His father, wanting to round out his education, found him a teacher of Latin and Greek. M. Mallet had once taught in a Jesuit college and was now running a stationer's in the rue de Rome. He had a daughter,

so a neat exchange took place by which Mlle Mallet would learn the piano
and Crin-Crin would learn Latin – or not. M. Mallet used to come to
the Saties' to give his lessons and master and pupil would install themselves
in the drawing-room. Eric learnt nothing. Père Mallet would say, 'On
with your revision, dear boy,' and immediately drop off to sleep. The
young latinist wouldn't move, wouldn't breathe until the old man woke
up. Progress was rather slow.

It wasn't much quicker at the Conservatoire, to which Eric went in
1879. All his life he had unpleasant memories of that 'vast, highly
uncomfortable and rather ugly building; a sort of local penitentiary without any redeeming internal features – nor external, come to that'. He
weathered the classes of Descombes for basic piano technique and of
Lavignac for solfège.

Eric spent a lot of his time reading – a family vice. The authors he
read were those favoured by his father: *Le siècle de Louis XIV*, novels by
Dumas *père* and Chavette, and a little later Alphonse Karr, Méry, Musset.
And he discovered Hans Christian Andersen, a lifelong passion. His
musical enthusiasms were of the highest class: first and foremost Bach, to
which he was introduced by Vinot and Guilmant, then Chopin and Schumann. He was already making fun of grand opera and preferred the
operettas of Messager. He entered Mathias's piano class in 1884 [1885]
and in 1885 [1883] Taudou's harmony class. Satie claimed that Taudou
used to say, 'You should devote yourself to the piano,' while Mathias
would insist, 'You're a born composer.'

His songs *Les anges*, *Les fleurs* and *Sylvie* were published by Alfred
Satie, [66] boulevard Magenta, Paris; *copyright for all countries*. Erik's
father had tried to make his fortune but without success. With the Barnetche family he started music classes in the rue Turbigo, a risky enterprise
which didn't promise well. After Jules Satie's death he bought a stationer's
in the boulevard Magenta with the little his father left him. The old
Mme Barnetche, Erik's long-time enemy, served on the counter. They
introduced music as a sideline – Euterpe once more! Alfred then gave up
the stationery and became a music publisher, bringing out café-concert
ditties, songs by his son and one or two works by a young composer-
friend of Erik's, Charles Levadé. Bit by bit he ran through the whole of
his modest inheritance.

Under the combined influences of Contamine de Latour, his reading
and Gregorian chant, Satie developed an ingenuous and slightly joky

mysticism. He talked endlessly about 'his religion', the strict commandments of which were meticulously followed. He affected a great humility, and was nicknamed 'Monsieur le pauvre'. He spent his time either in the reverie-inducing gloom of Notre-Dame or else in the Bibliothèque Nationale, passionately thumbing through Viollet-le-Duc's* weighty tomes on Gothic art. It was at that time [1886] that he composed four *Ogives*, a clumsy, charming souvenir of the naive enthusiasms of the period.

These accesses of melancholy left him little time for the Conservatoire and he was eager to be free of official tuition. He had applied to study with Taudou only so he could legally opt out of his military service, and on 15 November 1886 he set out, as keen as mustard, for Arras and the 33rd Infantry Company. But he was soon tired of this new life in which the teaching was just as formal and boring as that of false relations, and to escape the barracks he took drastic steps.

One winter evening he lay out under the stars with no shirt on. Serious bronchitis ensued, followed by convalescence and further convalescence; he was left in peace for nearly three months. He read and reread Flaubert's *Salammbô*, which sent him into ecstasies, and the *Tentation de Saint Antoine*, which amused him and seized his imagination. He discovered Péladan.† No doubt he enjoyed works by the Sâr such as *Le vice suprême* and *L'androgyne*, but he was more attracted by the mysterious character who was reviving the medieval brotherhoods in his Rose-Croix movement.

During his convalescence he sketched out the wonderful *Gymnopédiès*, which he claimed were inspired by *Salammbô*, but they are infinitely purer than Flaubert's evocations and seem to be extremely exact musical representations of the paintings of Puvis de Chavannes, which he adored. During his sick-leave, the Opéra-Comique put on a prophetic work, Chabrier's *Le roi malgré lui*. Satie went overboard for Chabrier the liberator and left with the master's concierge one of his own compositions, complete with a superb dedication, in red ink, naturally. The excellent Chabrier did not think it worth acknowledging.

*Eugène-Emmanuel Viollet-le-Duc (1814–79) was the controversial architect and medievalist who restored the Cathedral of Notre-Dame and the Abbey of Saint-Denis.

†Joséphin Péladan (1859–1918), the flamboyant and prolific author of risqué, pseudo-religious texts. He founded the Ordre de la Rose-Croix Catholique, du Temple et du Graal in 1888, and Satie became its official composer in 1891–2. Péladan adopted the royal Assyrian title of Sâr (Priest-King) early in his career, posing as a spiritual descendant of the Babylonian–Assyrian monarchy. He sometimes styled himself 'Sâr Mérodack', after the biblical Babylonian king Mérodack-Baladan.

In September 1887 he wrote his three charming *Sarabandes* with, as an epigraph, some words by Contamine de Latour:

> *Soudain s'ouvrit la nue et les maudits tombèrent . . .*
> (Suddenly all was revealed and the damned fell . . .)

The words were old-fashioned, but not the music. On his demobilisation in November he left the Conservatoire, without regret. Montmartre was calling him. To begin with, he became a regular at the Chat Noir where he met his fellow townsman Alphonse Allais* – a family link, because Allais the pharmacist and the Satie family had known each other for years.

Young Satie's general education had been neglected. His father's ideas about teaching, the freedom he allowed him and Erik's instinctive horror of everything 'academic' were not designed to give him a wide general culture. But we should remember that at this period of his life Satie was a voracious reader, and would spend complete nights in front of a book. He had a good memory that registered everything he read, including his apparently useless studies at the Bibliothèque Nationale into the liturgy or Gothic art. In this way he acquired a curious, fragmentary erudition which had a considerable influence on his mind and his style. Later on he read nothing except Andersen and animal stories – the same stories and the same pages.

Pierre-Daniel Templier
Erik Satie (Paris, Éditions Rieder, 1932), pp. 6–14, 58

PARIS CONSERVATOIRE REPORTS
(1880–86)

Satie loathed his time at the Conservatoire, where his step-mother had enrolled him in November 1879. She obviously hoped he would become a respectable concert pianist, but Satie preferred reading to practising and had little aptitude for sight-reading. His attendance record at the classes of Émile Descombes (1879–82) was poor (though not the worst) and in June 1882 he was dismissed from the Conservatoire

---

*Allais (1854–1905) was one of France's most inventive humorists. His surreal sense of the absurd and his penchant for alcohol made him a natural ally for Satie. He is best remembered for his short stories.

under Article 60, which the director, Ambroise Thomas, had been ordered to enforce strictly by the Ministry of Fine Arts in September 1881. This rule of 1878 meant automatic dismissal for any student 'who had not gained a prize or an honourable mention' after presenting himself for examination in three consecutive years. In November 1885 Erik was persuaded to try again, and after performing a Chopin *Ballade* he was admitted to the intermediate piano class of Georges Mathias. Mathias had previously taught his stepmother and Erik's attendance improved in 1885–6 (though not his results). He must have had some respect for Mathias for he originally dedicated his third *Gymnopédie* to him in 1888. The concertos Satie performed indicate that he must have been quite an accomplished pianist, and the reports of gifted indolence rather reflect his hatred of the Conservatoire and its methods. As he explained in 1892 in a typically curious open letter to the institution: 'despite my extreme youth and my delicious agility, through your unintelligence you made me detest the coarse art that you teach, by your inexplicable harshness you made me despise you for a long time'. Besides the director and opera composer Ambroise Thomas (1811–96), the professors concerned in the following selected reports are Émile Descombes, Victor Duvernoy (1842–1907), M. Sauzay, Louis Diémer (1843–1919), Henry Fissot and Georges Mathias.

January 1880 Ferdinand Hiller (1811–85): Piano Concerto in f# minor (Op. 69, 1861)

Descombes: Has tone-quality – little sense of timing – should work extremely hard. Very gifted student but also very lazy.

Thomas: Has tone-quality – can be fluent. Lazy.

Duvernoy: Could have studied harder.

June 1880 Henri Herz (1803–88): Piano Concerto No. 5 in f minor (Op. 180)

Descombes: Very beautiful hands, beautiful sonority, no lack of grace or natural talent, but *the only student* in the class who doesn't work hard enough.

Thomas: Should do well but doesn't work hard enough.

Duvernoy: Ordinary performance. Sight-reading very poor.

Sauzay: Rather feeble, lazy. Poor sight-reading.

January 1881 Ignaz Moscheles (1794–1870): Piano Concerto No. 5 in C
major (Op. 87, 1826)

Descombes: At last beginning to study better. But rather heavy –
                 pleasing sound. Will do well by working hard.
Thomas: Passable.
Sauzay: Ordinary.
Duvernoy: Didn't do badly.
Diémer: Feeble.
Fissot: Ordinary.

June 1881 Mendelssohn (1809–47): Piano Concerto No. 2 in d minor
(Op. 40, 1837)

Descombes: The laziest student in the Conservatoire. Pleasing sound.
                 Splendid touch. Has excellent qualities that hard work
                 alone could develop. Sight-reads laboriously.
Thomas: Should have a good technique if he works. Feeble sight-
                 reading.
Sauzay: Lacks colour. Bad. Reads badly.
Duvernoy: Some good things. Sight-reading feeble.
Diémer: Flabby – ordinary. Sight-reading very feeble.
Fissot: Ordinary.

January 1882 Mendelssohn: Characteristic Piece *[possibly Op. 7 no. 4 in*
A major, which we know Satie was practising at the time as his '1881'
Peters edition of Mendelssohn's piano works has survived in the Fuld
Collection, New York]

Descombes: Satie has finally decided to get down to work. He has great
                 physical qualities, a good, strong and very flexible hand,
                 and an attractive sound. If he continues to work, he will
                 surely succeed.
Thomas: Thin sound.
Souzay: Uneven and flabby.
Duvernoy: Variable. Does not strike the keys hard enough.
Diémer: Feeble.
Fissot: Flabby fingers. [Sight-reading] *bad.*

15 June 1882 Beethoven: Sonata in Ab major (Op. 26, 1800–1). Finale: Allegro

Descombes: Has worked better this year. Plays somewhat automatically. Good hands. Attractive sound.

Thomas: Passable. Pretty ordinary. Feeble sight-reading.

Sauzay: Colourless but good enough performance. Feeble sight-reading.

Duvernoy: Not bad. Feeble sight-reading.

Diémer: Feeble. Feeble sight-reading.

January 1886 Mendelssohn: Rondo capriccioso in E major (Op. 14, 1824)

Mathias: Very insignificant. He is laborious.

Sauzay: Little lightness or skill.

Duvernoy: Ordinary as regards technique and style.

June 1886 Mendelssohn: Prelude in D major [probably Op. 104a No. 3, 1836]

Mathias: Worthless. Three months just to learn the piece. Incapable of sight-reading.

Thomas: Very poor. Sight-reading passable.

Sauzay: Passable. Sight-reading ditto.

Duvernoy: Sight-reading passable.

Fissot: Sight-reading feeble.

Diémer: Mendelssohn Prelude not bad. Sight-reading feeble.

From the Conservatoire records in the Archives Nationales, Paris
translated by Robert Orledge from Patrick Gowers: *Erik Satie: His Studies, Notebooks and Critics* (Ph.D. diss., University of Cambridge, 1966), Vol. 1, pp. 10–22

RENÉ PETER

(1872–1947)

René Peter was an aspiring playwright who published several light comedies and farces written in association with Georges Feydeau, Robert Danceny and others from 1894 onwards. His acquaintance with Debussy and Satie began in the 1880s, though jealousy of their more intimate relationship coloured his later reminiscences. Between 1896 and 1901, Debussy gave Peter 'theatre lessons' and they collaborated on a 'roman à clef' entitled *Les Frères en Art* and on other projects.

Even before Debussy came across him, I'd known Satie personally. Our acquaintance went back to the earliest days of my youth. My teacher, M. Mallet, had a daughter and Satie had a mother, a piano teacher and a very dignified lady. She gave the daughter lessons and in return the girl's father inculcated into her son, not the elementary principles of Latin – that would certainly have been a waste of time – but simply handwriting and the basic elements of arithmetic. Young Erik, who was at that time a large beardless boy of 18 or 20, showed so little aptitude in these areas that the excellent M. Mallet would have thrown in the towel straight away, had it not been for the friendly ties between the two families. He used to sigh: 'Ah well, I'll have another go at licking this poor devil into shape!' And Satie, whose left nostril was slightly deformed by a lump of cartilege (later to be hidden by his moustache), would give a gentle, respectful sniff and express his gratitude, not that it helped his progress much. He admitted he'd certainly not forgotten his encounters with the noisy kid I'd been in those days and seemed to derive considerable inner amusement from my surprise at finding how he'd turned out.

René Peter
Claude Debussy (Paris, Gallimard, 1931; 2/1944), pp. 69–70

CHARLES LEVADÉ
(1869–1948)

Charles Levadé became friends with Satie in the 1880s when he was a composition student in Massenet's class at the Paris Conservatoire. He also made settings of the poetry of Contamine de Latour, one of which ('Sonnet') was published by Alfred Satie, who also brought out three of his piano pieces (Op. 27) in 1887. Satie dedicated his third *Gymnopédie* to him instead of Mathias when it was privately published in 1888. Levadé went on to win the Prix de Rome in 1899 with his cantata *Callirhoé* and is best known for his successful comic opera *La rôtisserie de la Reine Pedauque*. Unlike his 'pupil', Levadé never managed to shed the Massenet style he so much admired.

I knew Satie very well. It was I who corrected his earliest songs, which were grateful compositions in the style of Massenet. I gave him harmony lessons – not for long, though, because he soon felt the need to work in his own way.

That was in 1887. At that time Satie was not the picturesque Bohemian most people remember, but a kind of dandy, all spick and span. I then lost sight of him for a couple of years before meeting him again, completely transformed, at the Auberge du Clou. He was fond of saying, 'You were the one who encouraged me to compose.' And as a mark of his gratitude, he dedicated one of his characteristic *Gymnopédies* to me.

Charles Levadé
Article in *Liberté*, 13 January 1932, p. 2

J. P. CONTAMINE DE LATOUR
(1867–1926)

Patrice Contamine, as he was known to close friends like Satie, was in reality José Maria Vicente Ferrer, Francisco de Paula, Patricio Manuel Contamine, as Ornella Volta has discovered. He was born in Tarragona in Spain and was a prolific writer of poems, plays, short stories and newspaper articles, which he rather grandly signed 'J. P. Contamine de Latour' or, around the turn of the century, 'Lord Cheminot'. He claimed to be related to Napoleon, but in reality he was as poor as Satie in the 1880s when they discovered the delights of the Chat Noir together. Satie's earliest dedication to Contamine was the *Fantaisie-valse* and it is Latour's apocalyptic verses that appear on the manuscript of the first *Sarabande* in 1887. They continued to collaborate until about 1905 and shared a love of provocative practical jokes, esoteric sects, mysticism and deliberate eccentricity. Satie called him 'Le Vieux Modeste' and Patrice's sister, Barbara, married another of Satie's collaborators, Henry Pacory. Latour's verses are often sentimental and platitudinous, sometimes bizarre, but

he was exactly the sort of catalyst Satie needed at the outset of
his career.

When we were young – under 20 – Erik Satie often used to say to me:
'When I'm dead, you'll write *Erik Satie, His Life and Works.*' And he'd
burst into fits of loud, honest laughter, so preposterous did the idea seem
to him. He even spoke of dying at 25, like the sick romantic hero in the
works of the poet Millevoye:* 'They'll put me in a little invalid carriage
and you'll take me for walks in the sun.' A simple joke, designed to elicit
my protestations (which amused him hugely) against this forthcoming
role as nurse.

He did not die at 25, happily for him, for those of us who loved him
and for music, which he served with a courageous loyalty; and I never
thought I would one day have the melancholy task of fulfilling the duty
which he self-mockingly laid upon me.

We were joined in a fraternal friendship. I don't know how it began:
probably through one of those vague channels which chance makes use of
to unite two beings with the same affinities, and which continue to exercise
a considerable influence on our life even after they're no longer part of
it.

We were inseparable, spending our days and part of our nights
together, exchanging ideas, planning ambitious projects, dreaming of
sensational successes, growing drunk on crazy hopes and laughing at our
own poverty. I could say we lived out the final episodes of Murger's *La
bohème*, transplanted from the Latin Quarter to Montmartre. We didn't
eat every day, but we never missed an aperitif: I remember a particular
pair of trousers and a pair of shoes which used to pass from one to the
other, and which we had to mend every morning before going off in
search of the hypothetical publisher who would set the seal on our genius
and open up the avenues of riches and fame. It was a happy life.

Even so, Satie could have spared himself these struggles and privations.
He came from an excellent family who refused him nothing, and he
himself, in the first years of our friendship, proved sensible, level-headed,
and inclined to favour elegance and good manners. But his instinct was
calling him away from this path. If he had gone on living in this milieu,

---

*Charles-Hubert Millevoye (1782–1816), a consumptive poet, whose work was often
melancholic in a manner later associated with Romanticism.

his personality would never have broken free. It was Rodolphe Salis's Chat Noir which revealed his vocation to him and transformed him completely.

He entered the Conservatoire at the age of 12, going into Georges Mathias's [Émile Descombes'] piano class. To be a pianist, giving lessons and concerts, seemed to him then to be the most enviable of positions. He worked hard at Beethoven and J. S. Bach, at Schumann and Chopin, at Liszt and César Franck: but in so working he remained the slave of an essentially whimsical temperament. When all is said, he was a fairly mediocre student. His teacher, recognising that he had his serious side, used to deplore this lack of application. He would tell him frequently, 'You're a thoroughgoing delinquent!'

Satie couldn't have cared less. The most striking feature of his studies at the time was that they would allow him to get away with one year in the reserves instead of the prescribed five years of military service: and that, for him, was enough.

At that time Massenet was the idol of the young at the Conservatoire, where he was a professor of composition. His pupils saw everything through his eyes and did their best to imitate his style. Satie underwent his influence and, without any study of fugue or counterpoint, of which he was totally ignorant, composed a few songs (*Élégie*, *Sylvie*, *Complainte**) which were entirely after Massenet's manner. These were his first attempts at composition, the babblings of a talent which was to develop markedly in the course of time – the kind of pale, beginner's efforts which one disavows in one's maturity.

P. Contamine de Latour
'Erik Satie intime: souvenirs de jeunesse', *Comoedia*, 3 August 1925, p. 2

ALBERT ROUSSEL

(1869–1937)

Albert Roussel was born into a wealthy family in Tourcoing and first pursued a naval career. He resigned his commission in 1894 to devote his life to music and enrolled as a student at Vincent d'Indy's newly created Schola Cantorum in Paris

*This early Latour setting has since disappeared, like the orchestral song *Roxane* (mentioned in a letter to Conrad Satie in June 1893).

in 1898. He was appointed professor of counterpoint there in 1902, though he did not finish his own ten-year composition course until 1908 — the same year that Satie gained his diploma in counterpoint. But by that time he had composed several major works, including his First Symphony (*Le poème de la forêt*), and it was fortunate for Satie that Roussel had such a strongly developed interest in music education and such liberal attitudes.

I wonder what his motivation was when, in 1905, he turned up at the rue Saint-Jacques with the intention of studying counterpoint and fugue? Was it that he'd seen someone else successfully realising the artistic ideal he'd imagined, and so wanted to go in a diametrically opposite direction? Or did he already foresee that the furious pursuit by Debussy's imitators of more and more complex chords could end only in a sterile impasse?

The fact is that one day, to my great amazement, he mentioned to me his intention to come and study at the Schola. I may say that, to begin with, I tried to dissuade him, imagining him to be well enough up in contrapuntal writing and not seeing really what practical application he could make of a study of four-part writing. But he insisted, and that majestic institution on the rue Saint-Jacques never had a more punctilious and disciplined pupil. I confess that to begin with, while I was reading through the pupils' exercises at the piano, I was a bit disconcerted by the presence behind me of this strange pupil who was so unlike all the others and whose ironic smile seemed to say: 'Ah! So that's not allowed? Really? What a significant improvement you've just made! Now there's a bit of counterpoint without a wrinkle on it!'

But no, there was no irony. With the most serious and committed expression, Satie would bring me counterpoint that was impeccable, in an amazing calligraphic hand, and his enthusiasm for Bach chorales would have singled him out even in an organ class! The result was that in June 1908 he was awarded a superb diploma, stating that the pupil Satie had been judged competent to practise his art. And I should be very surprised if he hadn't carefully preserved this precious document among his papers.

Albert Roussel
'À propos d'un récent festival', *Le Gaulois*, 12 June 1926, p. 3

CHARLES KOECHLIN
(1867–1950)

Like Roussel, Koechlin was a major French composer with a personal vision. Both of them shared a love of exotic subjects and expressed themselves best through the medium of the post-Romantic symphony orchestra. Koechlin first met Satie around 1896 and they soon established a mutual respect which sprang from their similar desire for artistic independence and refusal to compromise their ideals. Koechlin is best known for his symphonic fresco *Le livre de la jungle* (based on Kipling's *Jungle Book* stories), and within this Satie particularly admired the *Berceuse phoque*. In turn, Koechlin was one of the few immediately to realise the importance of Satie's *Socrate*, and he continued to defend Satie's genuine classicism and simplicity to the end of his life.

For some years he was to be found in the classrooms of the Schola Cantorum. What would he become under M. d'Indy's tutelage? Would he be fixed in the uniform mould in which so many composers were ossified? Would he write cyclic sonatas – with two themes, one masculine, the other feminine – boring sonatas, such as the rue Saint-Jacques produces all too often? No. As you will have guessed, he remains free and *himself*, providing the example of a unique pupil of M. d'Indy (for whom he retains the affectionate respect that d'Indy inspires in his pupils) – a pupil who is independent and who is not by and large subject to the theories propounded by the Schola's 'Cours de composition'. But his labours have not been in vain. Four-, five- and six-part counterpoint has clarified his style, animated his melodic lines and enlivened his rhythms. And it has, on the other hand, given him the desire to prune.

Charles Koechlin
'Erik Satie', *ReM*, 5, March 1924, p. 195

II

The Bohemian and mystic
in Montmartre

Like the heroine of Charpentier's opera *Louise*, Satie found the lure of bohemian Montmartre irresistible. In truth, he moved only about a mile up the road from his parents' home in the boulevard Magenta and the nearest he got to 'free love' was a rather traumatic affair with the painter Suzanne Valadon in early 1893, but the call of liberty was just as great, and for Satie it lasted over a decade (1887–98). During this time, Satie secured occasional employment as a musician in the Chat Noir cabaret, moving on to become a house-pianist at the Auberge du Clou in 1891 after he fell out with the Chat Noir's phlegmatic Master of Ceremonies, Rodolphe Salis. He also frequented Edmond Bailly's bookshop, the Librairie de l'Art Indépendant, where he met esoteric writers like Victor-Émile Michelet, Villiers de l'Isle-Adam, as well as Claude Debussy (with whom he developed a lifelong friendship). Probably through Bailly, his interest in mysticism and the occult grew and in 1891–2 he became official composer to Joséphin Péladan's Ordre de la Rose-Croix Catholique, du Temple et du Graal, a spurious breakaway sect whose main use to Satie lay in the publicity it brought him. Publicity was also the aim behind the bizarre apocalyptic ballet *Uspud* that he wrote with Contamine de Latour in 1892: through it Satie enhanced his reputation in Montmartre circles by challenging the director of the Paris Opéra to a duel in order to gain a hearing for his impractical creation. After breaking with Péladan, Satie founded his own sect in 1893, the Église Métropolitaine d'Art de Jésus Conducteur, which lasted till early 1896 and provided him with the necessary cover to launch critical attacks on his artistic enemies through self-sponsored publications.

During his Montmartre period, Satie first adopted the persona of the dandified (but rather scruffy) man-about-town, complete with top hat and frock-coat. Then in 1895, with a small legacy, he purchased seven identical velvet corduroy

suits to create his better known 'Velvet Gentleman' look. This
he replaced with his final persona as a bourgeois functionary
around 1906.

J. P. CONTAMINE DE LATOUR

We'd been introduced to the Chat Noir by a charming humorist, now
dead, called Vital Hocquet,* who used the pseudonym Narcisse Lebeau.
It was he who claimed that it's always a bad idea to drown oneself directly
after a meal. Satie was already thinking of his *Gymnopédies*. Truth to tell,
he had so far found nothing beyond the title; but the strangeness of the
word already gave it a kind of halo. The first evening that we went to
the cabaret on the rue Victor-Massé – 'This is the rue de Laval' the posters
defiantly proclaimed – Vital Hocquet announced imposingly: 'Erik Satie,
gymnopedist!' To which Rodolphe Salis, bowing as low as he could,
replied: 'That's a very fine profession!'

Satie at once found himself on home ground, thanks to Alphonse Allais
who was, like him, a native of Honfleur. Their shared upbringing and
the love they both had for their beautiful native city soon sealed their
friendship. Although Allais was considerably older, they had memories
in common, notably of a certain M. Boudin, the principal of the college
they'd both been to, on the subject of whom their animation was inexhaust-
ible.

Those who didn't know the Chat Noir at this period cannot be aware
what that famous establishment was like. It was nothing like what are
nowadays called 'Montmartre joints' and the reconstructions that were
tried out for a few weeks at the Théâtre de l'Odéon gave only a faint
flavour of the original. There was none of Aristide Bruant's vulgarity,
nor of the trivialities which often attract a simple-minded public. The
tone was caustic, witty, but within certain limits. Clients were made fun
of and mystified, but not molested. Indeed, an entertaining form of
etiquette was observed: a magnificent Swiss guard announced the patrons
with three thumps of his gleaming halberd, and Rodolphe Salis came to

*A local plumber, turned poet, who also frequented the Chat Noir in the later 1880s.

meet them, addressing them ceremoniously as 'Monseigneur' and 'Noble Dame' . . .*

It was in these surroundings, so different from the ones in which he had grown up, that Satie, who until then had been timid and reserved, gave free rein to the treasure-house of mad gaiety which lay within; the contrast between this free, unbuttoned life and the bourgeois correctness of his own showed him the silliness of certain prejudices and the hypocrisy of certain conventions, and awoke in him a distrust of platitudes and received ideas, of superficial boasting and bloated reputations. He cast aside everything that he'd loved out of habit; he waxed enthusiastic over the beauty of free, bold, untrammelled effort, which does not encumber itself with rules or methods, and recognizes no criticism but its own; he gave his admiration to those companions on his journey who showed him the way and who, heedless of the present or of future difficulties, with head held high, with empty pockets and a swooning soul, plunged joyfully and wildly in pursuit of their ideal. Impulsive by nature, he gave himself to them entirely: and as he grew into their cast of mind, he broke with all the polite forms of his early education in a bid to be yet more like them.

One day he took his clothes, rolled them into a ball, sat on them, dragged them across the floor, trod on them and drenched them with all kinds of liquid until he'd turned them into complete rags; he dented his hat, broke up his shoes, tore his tie to ribbons and replaced his fine linen with fearful flannelette shirts. He stopped trimming his beard and let his hair grow.

At the same time he forged a personal artistic style for himself. His musical education was decidedly incomplete, but he put together the things he knew and out of them manufactured a formula of his own, maintaining that all other techniques were non-existent and even a barrier to true musical expression. He was in the position of a man who knows only thirteen letters of the alphabet and decides to create a new literature using only these, rather than admit his own insufficiency. For sheer bravado, it was unparalleled at the time, but he made it a point of honour to succeed with his system. He admitted to me:

'I have to commit *tours de force* to get one bar to stand up.'

*Satie sometimes adopted the same exaggerated degree of politeness in later life, just as he copied phrases from Vincent Hyspa's speeches.

We must agree that he didn't come out of it too badly, because his originality soon made itself felt. Whether natural or contrived, it remained the dominant note in his work, and even made an impression on that of Debussy who, despite his profound technique, nonetheless held Satie in high regard.

Satie's behaviour caused a certain amount of scandal among those close to him, and there were some fairly lively family discussions. Satie left the paternal home to 'live his own life', in the phrase used these days by rebellious young girls. He had 1600 francs to his name. It was a respectable sum at the time, especially for a young bachelor accustomed to living on 100 sous a week, and it looked as though it would last for ever. He rented a mezzanine apartment [at 50 rue Condorcet, Paris 9] and filled it with expensive furniture. Then he had to start retrenching. The furniture disappeared piece by piece, as his capital declined. Soon he had to leave this apartment and look for more modest lodgings, on the summit of the Butte, in an uncomfortable room [6 rue Cortot], but with a superb view – he used to claim, as far as the Belgian frontier.

This was the real bohemian life, with its uncertainties and expedients, but free and happy, as he had intended. The Butte of Montmartre was not yet disfigured by six-storey apartments, by night-clubs, wide streets or motor-cars. In living memory, no horse-drawn cab had ever ventured into its twisting alleyways – it was a real village, almost unknown to the uninitiated. Once you'd climbed its rough steps, you felt as though you were hundreds of miles away from the capital, its uproar and its complications. You felt, as Satie put it, above your creditors. Everything about it was rustic and peaceful. Streams ran down the middle of the streets, almost naked children played around in a gaggle of dogs, cats, chickens, sheep and goats, and birds twittered in the luxuriant greenery that covered the old, ruined walls.

Jules Dépaquit, the future mayor of the free commune of Montmartre, would be sitting outside a wine merchant's in the place du Tertre, with his head on one side and his tongue hanging out, like a schoolboy in class, drawing pictures for the less serious newspapers. The painter Zuloaga lived in the Moulin de la Galette, where he could be seen washing and dressing through the gaps in the floorboards. One day in the street, when it was raining torrents, he made a remarkable portrait of Satie which was shown in the Salon of the Académie Nationale. The engraver Marcellin Desboutin often used to climb up to see us, when it was time for an apéritif, with his son André Mycho. His pockets were always stuffed with a collection of innumerable pipes of every size. To the accompaniment of his fist pounding on the table, he would tell tales in his earthy voice of when he was a young man in Venice, in the time of George Sand and Alfred de Musset. Aristide Bruant would draw, on the pink walls of his house, his tall figure in green velvet, his postillion's boots, his large, black felt hat and his famous red scarf. Jean-Baptiste Clément, the author of those charming stories *La chanson des blés d'or* and *Le temps des cerises*, used to glide along the walls like a shadow, clutching a little jug of milk – we never knew whether it was for him or his cat, because he never spoke. And under the tall, silent woods of the Château des Brouillards lived a veritable colony of artists, models and writers. Suzanne Valadon used to make enormous pieces of furniture out of old lumps of wood and Léon Bloy, lurking in his lair, would sink his teeth into his contemporaries, particularly his fellow Roman Catholics.

Satie and I lived close to one another, he in the rue Cortot, I in the rue de l'Abreuvoir. Whoever got out of bed first in the morning would visit the other and we'd spend the rest of the day together.

Our lives were brightened by small incidents, but even so we did work. Satie set about substituting for the Italian terms like *piano, pianissimo, dolce, mezzo-forte*, others of his own invention, of a far less classical character, such as *while watching oneself approach*, *with a fear of the obscure* or *astonishing and convenient*. He used to amuse himself hugely with his own inventions, or else he would draw pictures, although he had absolutely no talent for it. I've seen him spend hours on end tracing on a stave an organ pipe which he felt was indispensable to the understanding of his musical text. There was a good deal of the mystic in him. Although brought up as a Protestant, he adored the Middle Ages and their fervour, the paintings of the Primitives, Gothic churches and their tombstones, the lives of the saints and Christian legends. I believe that at the end of his life he wholeheartedly adopted Catholicism, since it was to the Catholic Church that he made the request for prayers to be said over his coffin.

As to the 1600 francs I mentioned, these had gone long since. He owed several months' rent to his landlord, until the latter finally got angry and spoke of throwing him out. A terrible threat! He was going to find himself homeless, and he had a suite of furniture he needed to save, which had been made specially for him for the modest sum of 60 francs! – a table, a seat, a chest, a wardrobe and a bed made of three planks resting on trestles, with a straw mattress and a woollen blanket, all in pale wood, stained with walnut juice and carefully polished to make it look like oak.

The fatal day arrived and the landlord appeared. Satie had been able to rustle up a few louis, which he held out in the palm of his hand. He moved towards his creditor, saying:

'Monsieur, I am in debt to you and you have the right to eject me; but that's not in your interest. Here's all the money I possess. If you insist on my leaving your house, I'll take this money to the hotelier on the corner, as I can't sleep in the street; but if you agree to go on being my landlord, then you will be the one to get it.'

The landlord, who was a decent sort, proposed a deal. He needed the room, for which he could charge 200 francs a year. But if Satie would pay him 20 francs a quarter, he could give him a small room where, he was sure, he'd be perfectly comfortable.

The 'small room' had to be seen! It was a cranny three metres high, two metres long and one and a half metres across. There was no window, only, up by the ceiling, a tiny triangular opening through which you could see a patch of sky. There was just room for the bed, jammed up against a piano which Satie religiously preserved through all his comings and goings, and which he never used. The whole tightly packed ensemble prevented you opening the door. When you wanted to get in, you had to slide through the crack between the door and the doorpost, and stand on the bed. Satie could only stay in the room lying down. In summer he sweltered, in winter he froze; then he would add his clothes to the blankets, even his socks, for added warmth. He used to wear half a dozen shirts one on top of the other and, as they didn't have any buttons, he used to do them up with a long hatpin, with a cork on the end so as not to prick himself.

He called his new room 'le placard'. He covered the walls with pictures from the Middle Ages, with sketches and paintings. He was happy there. It was there he wrote the works which gave him his early reputation: the *Sarabandes*, the *Gymnopédies*, the *Ogives* and the *Gnossiennes*. He even started on the *Sonneries de la Rose-Croix* and the *Prélude de La porte héroïque du ciel*.

We had more or less abandoned the Chat Noir for the Auberge du Clou, in the avenue Trudaine. There too, in the basement, thrived the intellectual life of Montmartre, but the clientele was more mixed: rich young men, financiers, shopkeepers, businessmen with artistic pretensions, with whom we had only limited sympathy. They regarded Satie as a phenomenon. He got his revenge by taking part in their discussions and mystifying them totally.

One evening they were talking about La Fontaine. Someone quoted from the story called 'The Blind Man and the Paralytic'. Satie objected: it wasn't 'The Blind Man and the Paralytic' but 'The Blind Man and the one with Tuberculosis'. General protest.

'What! You don't know the story of the blind man who takes the paralytic on his shoulders and walks while the paralytic guides him?'

'You're talking rubbish,' argued Satie vigorously. 'There's nothing out of the way about a paralytic guiding the steps of a blind man, you can see that any day of the week! But the combination of a blind man and one with tuberculosis, that's more poetical and absolutely in the La Fontaine manner!'

They were all wrong, because the story in question isn't by La Fontaine, but by Florian. No matter. It was the custom in these surroundings to get heated over the slightest thing. Satie kept to his viewpoint with some asperity. The argument turned sharper, and rude words were exchanged. The more moderate participants tried to calm things down.

'Can't you see, he's shooting a line?'

'You mean, he thinks we're a load of a———holes!'

In short, the discussion degenerated into fisticuffs, which spilled out on to the pavement and round a gas lamp in the rue des Martyrs.

Similar scenes took place frequently, much to Satie's delight. Happily, they never went any further and the next day everyone was good friends again. But this kind of joke eventually palled, and something else had to be thought of.

Together we wrote a ballet in three acts called *Uspud*, a conglomeration of every extravagance likely to astonish the public. On this scenario Satie had composed half a dozen musical phrases, which he called grandly 'his score'. He had it printed and for the cover Suzanne Valadon designed an inset of our two profiles juxtaposed.

As soon as it came out, all Montmartre knew about it, and I may say it produced the desired effect. Passionate discussions ensued, some saying it was a masterpiece, others declaring it was a disgraceful hoax. One evening at the Clou, Satie played his score on the piano. Opinions were very much divided. He roused wild approbation and violent reprobation. To those who found it incomprehensible, he stated categorically that they were nothing but bourgeois ignoramuses, that he would insist on the Opéra producing it, and that he would be proved right and everybody else wrong.

'In any case,' he added with the utmost seriousness, 'I'm far superior to you, but my well-known modesty prevents me from saying so.'

In the middle of the tumult brought about by this rendition, one man remained impassive. Beneath his stubborn, bulging forehead, two little dark eyes shone like carbuncles; with his arms crossed, he smiled silently under his faun-like beard. It was Claude Debussy. He had realised at once what a fund of seriousness, of boldness and sensitivity lay under Satie's outrageous clowning. He appreciated the quality of his unquiet, restless spirit, eager for contrasts and discoveries, and searching for its true nature even while laughing at itself. He was the first to defend Satie. Soberly, without excitement or self-satisfaction and with the authority that was already his, he explained the curious stamp of Satie's musical personality and the hopes that it gave rise to for the future . . . That was the beginning of a friendship which never failed and which was profitable to both parties. From Debussy, Satie got invaluable advice and the sort of encouragement which went straight to his heart; and Debussy drew from Satie those innovations which, grafted on to his profound musical knowledge, were to constitute his second manner, that of *Pelléas et Mélisande*.

When the initial hubbub caused by *Uspud* had subsided, Satie said to me: 'Next, we must go to the Opéra.' The following day found us striding importantly along the corridors of that building. The director then was Bertrand, who'd come directly from the Variétés. We asked to see him.

'What for?' asked the reception clerk, in that elegant language that characterises the government employee.

'We would like to hand in a work,' replied Satie.

We only just escaped being thrown out. We were given to understand that the director could not see people just like that, at the drop of a hat, and that there would be no point in coming back. We had expected as much. Satie began to rub his hands:

'Splendid, splendid! We shall have some fun!'

And he wrote to Bertrand asking him, in a threatening manner, for an interview within the week. The week passed without a reply. Another letter from Satie:

'I cannot believe,' he wrote, 'that your silence is the result of inefficiency or bias; if it were, your attitude would invite punishment. In your capacity as a functionary charged with watching over the interests of music, you are not permitted to refuse a work without seeing it. If indeed your silence were due to the above reasons, I should be compelled to report the matter to the Minister for Education and the Arts, and your persistent refusal to give me a reply would take on the character of a personal insult, for which I should be obliged to ask satisfaction by force of arms.' He gave Bertrand a further week to make up his mind.

In Montmartre, this time, all the wags were on Satie's side. The tone of his letters was admired – and he was not slow in handing out copies. He gained considerable approval for waging war on those miserable exploiters of artists who put on a hackneyed repertoire and reserve their favours for authors and composers who have made their name. He was seen as the swashbuckling antagonist of the profiteers and of the 'official art' which was always the *bête noire* of the up-and-coming and the avant-garde. Satie himself found the role of knight-errant highly congenial. The week went by as before. Another missive from Satie to Bertrand:

'The good will which, despite everything, I bear you disposes me to allow you a further week's grace, after which I shall, with regret, be forced to apprise the minister of my righteous indignation and to send two of my friends to call upon you.'

Clearly, the director of the Opéra was treating *Uspud* with disdain. When the week was over, Satie instructed André Mycho and myself to go and seek the famous satisfaction by force of arms which the director was certainly not expecting.

'Above all, be energetic!' he exhorted us.

Bertrand lived a long way out, in Levallois or some such place. It was a fine morning and we went on foot, slowly so as to assure ourselves of the importance of our mission, and with a strong desire to stop off in every café we passed. Satie came with us. He was in an emotional state. Just think, if things followed their course! If the duel took place! What a success, and what a triumphal return there would be to the bosom of his friends!

Mycho and I arrived at the apartment block where M. Bertrand lived. A servant came to the door:

'Monsieur has gone out, and will not be back until this evening.'

'What?' Mycho and I exclaimed, with as much energy as we could summon. 'M. Bertrand has gone out? He should have waited for our arrival. Kindly tell him that we came on behalf of our friend Satie,

Monsieur Erik Satie, that is, and that we shall not be coming back. He
will know what that means.'

And with a dignified gesture we handed him our cards, leaving him
completely speechless.

'I understand,' said Satie with a serious expression, when we rejoined
him to give an account of our exploits, 'he's afraid.'

We concurred. 'Yes, he's afraid.'

And we went off to have lunch, as one does after an emotional encoun-
ter. For the first time in my life, I ate snails, and they sat on my stomach
for about seven years.

Satie waited several days for Bertrand's seconds. He was beginning to
give up waiting when one night – it must have been about 2 o'clock in
the morning – I was woken up by fists violently banging on my door.
Outside was Satie, shouting at the top of his voice:

'Ch'ti mi!* Ch'ti mi! (This was his nickname for me.) Open up! I've
had a letter from Bertrand!'

He burst into my room doubled up with laughter. The director of the
Opéra begged to be excused. He claimed he'd written before but had got
the wrong address. He gave us a rendez-vous for the following afternoon
at 3 o'clock, with our manuscript.

'We can't show it to him like this,' Satie said; 'you must help me copy
it out.' And we spent the rest of the night† giving human form – so to
speak – to our lucubration.

The next day we were at the Opéra at the appointed time. The director
received us with great amiability, standing in the middle of his room.
He immediately took in the sight of the manuscript, which Satie was
holding and which was no larger than a pad of writing paper.

'Gentlemen,' he said, 'I understand the impatience of youth and I
should be delighted to help young talent to make itself known. And please
believe that this delay in seeing you has not been intentional. But running
a theatre like the Opéra is a time-consuming business; added to which,
my remit from the ministry imposes certain obligations on me, as a result
of which I cannot put on as many works as I should like. However, I
shall be very happy to examine yours . . .'

I admit, we weren't terribly proud of our position. But one thing

*This means 'Cher ami' ('Dear friend') in the dialect of Arras, where Satie did his military
service in 1886–7.
†Of 16–17 November 1892.

strengthened our will. If we had made up our mind not to leave our manuscript with him, so as not to uncover our ruse, we realised that he for his part was only concerned to get rid of us politely. Satie seized the opportunity.

'Monsieur,' he answered seriously, 'the work we're offering you is not of the banal variety, destined to make a lot of money. I must in all honesty warn you that it won't bring in a penny. But it is an artistic manifestation of the highest calibre and we thought that the Opéra would make it a point of honour to produce it with all the care and magnificence it calls for.'

M. Bertrand raised his arms towards the ceiling.

'Alas, gentlemen!' he groaned. 'I should be delighted to give you that satisfaction, but the limited budget at my disposal, which is already used up for the whole season, prevents me from thinking of such sacrifices.'

'And furthermore,' continued Satie imperturbably, 'a work like ours cannot be appreciated instantly and without the support of the most highly qualified practitioners. So I should have to insist on the appointment of a jury of forty musicians, half chosen by the minister and yourself, and half by us.'

This time the director exploded. 'Impossible, gentlemen! Impossible! The rules forbid it and the minister would not allow me to disobey them!'

'In that case,' we retorted, assuming a highly offended tone, 'there is nothing left for us to do except take our leave.' And we descended the directorial staircase faster than we had climbed it, such was our desire to pass on to other matters.

Shortly after that Satie inherited the sum of 7000 francs. It was a fortune. He didn't know what to do with it.

He paid his debts and ordered seven grey velvet suits, with hats to match, which were the sensation of Montmartre. Wherever you were, you were sure of seeing him as soon as he put a foot out of doors. From the rue Caulaincourt to the avenue Trudaine, from the place Clichy to the boulevard Barbès, his silhouette soon became a familiar sight. He deposited the rest of his money in a branch of the Société Générale where he soon became their best customer, because he came to take out money every day, and sometimes twice a day, depending on the state of his prodigality.

He was the soul of munificence with his friends, offering free meals at restaurants and being the centre of a circle at the brasserie. As he tipped regally, the waiters treated him with the utmost respect.

At the same time, he founded an order of chivalry, on the model of those of the Middle Ages, which never had a definite name, still less definite rules, but had as its centre the Église Métropolitaine d'Art of which he appointed himself 'parcier' and *maître de chapelle*. He was also the only member.

'Parcier' is an old French word, meaning 'he who has a part or portion of something'. I don't know what meaning Satie gave it, but he regarded it as being very important and from now on he was known only as the 'parcier'. As for the Église Métropolitaine d'Art, placed under the protection of Jesus, leader of the people, it was situated on the ground floor of the house in the rue Cortot where he lived. It was an unimposing, square, tiled room, through which the pipe carrying dirty water from the house inopportunely passed. There was no altar nor any ceremonial objects, nothing to give it the air of a religious sanctuary; just the pale wooden suite, which he'd brought down from the loft where it had been rotting for months, and which now gave the room the look of a monk's cell or a non-commissioned officer's bedroom.

He'd had printed some beautiful writing paper, adorned with two interlocking crosses and a superb red seal. On this paper, in Gothic script and with a touching concentration, he would write manifestos about art and aesthetics. He heaped anathemas on the heads of the infidels, heretics and miscreants who spurned the Ideal, condemning them to the secular branch of an imaginary Inquisition. He exhorted Massenet, who was a candidate for the Académie des Beaux-Arts, to retire from the world and do penitence for his numerous sins. He even published a 'cartulaire', which ran to no more than eight or ten numbers,* and which it would be interesting to read in its entirety. He had entered so fully into this character that he ended up by exchanging punches with a fashionable critic in the middle of one of the Colonne concerts,† and beating him with his stick, because he'd made some joke that Satie found intolerable. That was the final outburst of his mocking, somewhat morbid whimsicality.

*Actually, only two issues appeared: No. 1–63 in May 1895, and No. 2–63 in June 1895.
†Henry Gauthier-Villars, known as 'Willy', the first husband of the writer Colette. This event actually took place at a Chevillard concert on 10 April 1904, from which Satie was escorted by the police.

Circumstances came between us, and we saw each other more and more rarely. One evening he told me that the 7000 francs had all gone and that he'd had to go back to the Chat Noir and accept a job as pianist, which gave him bed and board. He'd left Montmartre for Arcueil and he used to cross Paris every night on foot, starting on the stroke of 2 a.m., to reach his distant lodging.

He struck me as solemn, anxious and disenchanted. This rather sudden transformation has been attributed to a number of factors, but it's wrong to think there was any drama or romance in Satie's life. He'd simply found his way, after a slow, difficult evolution. He was tired of insincere gaiety and of living from day to day, especially as the face of Montmartre had changed and he no longer felt at one with the latest arrivals. For another thing, Debussy had introduced him to the publishers Baudoux and Bellon, who had just set up their business on the boulevard Haussmann. They were preparing an edition of his works and he'd engaged Joséphin Péladan and Jules Bois as collaborators, so he felt the need to devote himself entirely to work and study. At the same time, his mysticism, which contained a large contemplative element, encouraged him to seek solitude. So he shut himself up in his den in Arcueil, from which he never moved and would open the door, slightly and grudgingly, only for very particular friends.* Perhaps some part in this was played by Flaubert's *La tentation de Saint Antoine*, which was his bedside reading, and by *L'histoire de Port-Royale*,† which he used to read as a form of meditation.

I never attempted to breach his solitude, knowing how much he disliked it. But he often used to come and see me. He'd renounced grey suits, long hair, eccentricity and boisterousness and gone back to looking formal and to his natural air of distinction. He spoke slowly, in a low voice, with a sort of intentness, as though he were afraid of damaging his internal dream. But his remarks were full of wit and original humour.

I won't speak of Satie the composer – others who are expert in the field will take care of that. But I believe that Erik Satie was a very great artist who was understood only by an élite, and to whom the passage of time will do justice. I wanted to pay this affectionate tribute, over his recently closed coffin, to one who was the dear and intimate companion of my

---

*In fact, Satie never admitted anyone, as we shall see.
†One of many historical studies of the city of Paris, which Satie loved to read.

youth, and whose memory recalls so many hours of carefree happiness
and glittering dreams that are no more.

P. Contamine de Latour
'Erik Satie intime: souvenirs de jeunesse', *Comoedia*, 3, 5, 6 August 1925

STANISLAS FUMET

Stanislas Fumet was the son of the composer Dynam-Victor
Fumet (1867–1949), who knew Satie in both a personal and
a professional capacity at the Chat Noir between 1887 and
1890, when Satie took over from him as conductor of the
orchestra that accompanied Henri Rivière's shadow theatre
spectacles. As Dynam-Victor enrolled at the Paris Conservatoire in 1885, their friendship may have begun then. It
almost certainly continued after 1890, for Fumet had an
active interest in alchemy and the occult: he also had strong
anarchist sympathies, from which his nickname Dynam[ite]
derived. During the 1880s he was a follower of the Russian
Peter Kropotkin and he also contributed to the anarchist
journal *La révolte*. Both Fumet and Satie founded their own
religious sects, yet both died within the Catholic faith. Fumet
was a far more virtuosic pianist than Satie and was renowned
for his improvisations. His own music never shook off the
harmonic legacy of Liszt and Wagner, but the static, quasi-
religious, chordal opening of a work like *Les enlisements d'en-
haut* (?1885) suggests that some inter-influence with Satie may
have been possible.

Satie remained apart, thanks to his poverty. Instead of refusing it, he
coaxed it, knowing that this poverty would cause him to sin less than the
lucky ones of this world, the kept women, the 'poules de luxe'. In 1887
and 1888, perhaps earlier, he had a friend: my father. He would take
his place at Rodolphe Salis's Chat Noir when my father refused to conduct,
on an evening when the manager, at the request of one of the customers
in his 'beer-pump', had asked him to play some fatuous tune. My father
was already the soul of intransigence. He was about 20, and Satie a year
older. My father was officially, like Debussy, a composition pupil of
Guiraud's at the Conservatoire (where he never set foot any more) and

César Franck was his organ teacher. He was already an excellent pianist and an extraordinary improviser.

Satie was at this time infatuated with my father's music. All my father could remember was that Satie imitated him. It's quite possible that my father's improvisations at that time were (no doubt with a greater show of virtuosity) quite close to the *Gymnopédies* and the *Sarabandes*, to judge by the few written-out pieces he kept, which are undoubtedly of the same sort, though written with more technique. The characteristic of Dynam-Victor Fumet's music at that time, like Satie's, was purity, nakedness. Both of them were to remain faithful to these ideals, but in different directions. This uprightness was to gain each of them a rejection from official music circles and an almost total lack of performances.

Satie's music aimed at being almost colourless: perhaps that's why he claimed to eat nothing but 'white food'. He loved Puvis de Chavannes's painting.* My father too, even though he was not searching for truth in a lack of colour or in the single, unadorned line. He discovered it in the heart of things, in the mystery of being and in the questions his philosophy was to ask of 'Him who is before Being', as he used to say. He derived his music from the 'Impersonal' and from 'Absolute Silence'. These were not attitudes shared by his fellow composers of the period. Erik Satie shows, in the *Pièces froides* of 1897 even more than in his other works, that the idea of a composition does not need to stray outside itself.

Stanislas Fumet
'Eironeia', *ReM*, 214, June 1952, pp. 20–22

FRANCIS JOURDAIN
(1876–1958)

Francis Jourdain began his career as a painter, later turning towards the decorative arts. His name is mainly associated with a simple, sparse style of furniture inspired by the rational use of space in architecture. He was also an art historian who published essays and books on Cézanne, Utrillo, Toulouse-Lautrec and Rodin (among others). He moved in the same bohemian artistic circles as Satie in the Montmartre of the

---

*Pierre Puvis de Chavannes (1824–98) was a master of decorative art, responsible for the murals in the Sorbonne and the Panthéon.

1890s, sharing Satie's love of good food and popular entertainment, and presumably his wayward sense of humour.

Erik Satie could not fail to be seduced by the all-embracing paradoxicality
of Ubuesque cynicism,* but he was without cruelty or bitterness and his
gaiety always retained traces of its origins in the Chat Noir. This did not
affect his interest as an observer of the evolution of Ubuism, in which he
took part with a continuing enthusiasm, because jokes were for a long
time the only things he took absolutely seriously. He sacrificed the best
part of his talent to them.

Around 1895 Satie was better known as a clown than as a composer.
If he presented himself as a candidate for the Institut [the Académie des
Beaux-Arts], it was merely to make fun of the Establishment. He composed very little. The titles of his works gave a clear idea – in fact, too
clear an idea – of how tendentious they were, stuffed with double meanings
that one was never quite sure of catching. One listened to Satie's music –
very, very occasionally – with a carefulness that was so close to mistrust
as to count almost as embarrassment. One was afraid of being taken in,
and attributed to every bar such delicately humorous intentions that one
was unwilling to let the allusions which they might contain – which they
certainly did contain – go by without the support of a complicitous smile.

I was never one of Satie's close friends. I doubt whether anybody was
entrusted with the favour of a heartfelt outburst from him; I doubt
whether he ever stopped being witty, precise, a joker, or whether he ever
allowed himself suddenly to be nothing but a poor devil who has a serious
pain or petty anxieties, a corn on his foot, or a desire to lower his defences,
to confide in someone, to cry, to be comforted, to ask, like Bovary's first
wife,† for 'a drink of some sort and a little more love'.

I've heard hundreds of stories about Satie and I've known many of his
friends; none of them has ever referred to any gesture of resignation made
in a moment of weakness or disgust by this curiously inaccessible man, a
prisoner of mystification, as the mystic is a prisoner of his dream. Perhaps
he lay under the mystique of mystification. He fooled himself by going
to live in Arcueil at a time when he was still, with bureaucratic regularity,
spending every evening in Montmartre (this meant that, after he had
religiously missed the last bus, he had to go for miles on foot), and

*Alfred Jarry's satirical force *Ubu Roi* appeared in 1896 and attracted a cult following.
†Emma, in Gustave Flaubert's novel *Madame Bovary*, published in 1857.

actually sleeping on a plank at the time he was suggesting to Willy he ought to take up asceticism. It was an epic battle, fought with a man in whom he denounced the incarnation of a triple ignominy (Willy, whose name was Gauthier-Villars, also signed himself l'Ouvreuse). Satie *possessed* his adversary with a sangfroid which Willy's insults and jibes were powerless to destroy. 'I am the Boiling Sword! I am the Closure!' Satie would ceremoniously proclaim. The well-sharpened, indeed poisoned, arrows that Willy let fly – he was losing face and was, in fact, taken in by his enemy's mock solemnity – found themselves blunted by Satie's impassivity. With an imperturbable seriousness, Satie replied to Willy's entertaining shafts with the simple words: 'I excommunicate you.'

He liked to affect the unctuous manners of a priest. They suited him so well, he played his role so accurately – being careful not to overdo things – that the question arose as to whether a slightly false air was not innate in him. From behind his monocle, his mischievous eyes looked into those of whomever he was talking to, to try and discover the limits of their naivety. The idea never occurred to him that he might, in his turn, have been taken in.

He was a dandy, of the sort who, as you might imagine, notices the dictates of fashion only so that he can violate them. One evening I asked him to go with me to the dress rehearsal of a very amusing melodrama adapted from *The Fatal Card*. He was wearing a hat, coat and shoes of velvet corduroy, and he asked me to let him go back home and change. He returned wearing a suit and an overcoat identical to those he had taken off, only with the velvet in very slightly better condition. As we left the theatre, I asked him to escort the lady I was with back to her house – she, like him, lived on the Butte of Montmartre, while I had to go back to my parents' house. I gathered subsequently that he fulfilled the mission with excessive enthusiasm. Already, the previous summer, it had been with some alarm that I received at Talloires a letter from the object of my affections, written from Satie's apartment.

The notepaper of this tender missive bore the heading 'Église Métropolitaine d'Art de Jésus Conducteur des Peuples'.* This temple was Satie's den in the rue Cortot, his *cupboard*, as his friends called it – 'Notre Abbatiale', as he himself described it in the 'cartulaires' which a tiny inheritance allowed him to publish in three or four monthly volumes.

*These last two words were never used by Satie, as far as is known.

The *Sonnerie de l'Ordre de la Rose-Croix* was written, at the request of the extraordinary Sâr Péladan, in the church of which he was the leader and the only member. It was on the window of this 'Abbey' that he stuck, as revenge for some ancient quarrel or for some more recent falling-out, posters sharply challenging the virtue of his neighbour, Suzanne Valadon.

I often used to meet Satie at Chez Paulus, a little restaurant in the rue d'Orsel run by the friendly wife of a cornet player and patronised especially by orchestral players who were colleagues of her husband. I remember the courteous obstinacy with which Satie one day tried to convince his table companion what a happy, peaceful life the Parisians had enjoyed during the siege of 1871. He knew, he was absolutely certain of it. The old clarinettist, who had lived through the whole episode, protested and slowly began to lose patience. Satie politely insisted. In a rage, the old man finally asked him where he had found this scandalous version of the facts: 'I've just read a remarkable book on the subject . . . The Parisians have never been so well off as they were during the siege. The documents are irrefutable,' Satie gently assured him. And when pressed for further details, added that the precious book in question had been published – he was quite sure of the date – in 1865 . . .!

Satie was very fond of the artist Dépaquit, who also had a reputation as a wit . . . Together they wrote a play,* the vestiges of which it would be better not to search for except in the halls of memory. The curtain went up to reveal the protagonist filing his nails; then he sorted out some papers, closed a drawer and counted up to 100,000. Enter a second character: 'Monsieur,' he said without preamble, 'you have just filed your nails, sorted out some papers and, after closing that drawer, you counted up to 100,000.'

'But, monsieur, how . . . could you possibly . . . have guessed?'

'Monsieur, I was behind that door and I was looking through the keyhole.'

Throughout the five acts a strange, mysterious character walked to and fro at the back of the stage, his arms full of clocks. Why? The answer was vouchsafed only at the end of the last scene: the man was carrying clocks because he was a clockmaker. I'm not sure whether that's very funny. In private, Satie's wit was of considerably higher quality.

If, when I think of him, I also think of Alfred Jarry – whom he didn't

---

*And also a pantomime entitled *Jack-in-the-Box* in June–July 1899.

know, or only slightly – it's because, being condemned to perpetual irony, both of them coped with the pain of living without ever asking any favours, or appearing tempted to escape. Am I wrong in suspecting that Satie never knew togetherness, or abandon, or innocent chatter, or the banality of love, or friendship? My memories of him are too good for me not to hope that I am mistaken. Was he, as I fear, a victim of that indifference which keeps one man apart from another? I wish I could be sure that, at one time or another, someone found warmth in Satie's company, because the fate of the prisoner of solitude, whether he is gloomy or cheerful, seems to me an unenviable one.

Francis Jourdain
Né en 76 (Paris, Éditions du Pavillon, 1951), pp. 244–8

REYNALDO HAHN
(1875–1947)

Reynaldo Hahn was born in Venezuela, but like Satie he was brought permanently to Paris in 1878 where he also became a piano pupil of Émile Descombes at the Paris Conservatoire. He studied composition with Massenet, whose influence is best seen in the charming salon songs that established his reputation and in his light and well-crafted music for the stage. He was a bourgeois socialite whose idol was Mozart, so it is not surprising that he viewed Satie with curiosity and disdain.

Many years ago now, I was one of a whole crowd of young men who used to meet at Édouard Risler's to gossip, laugh, swap ideas and make music. We often had as one of our number a blond boy, a sort of faded Christ-figure in a yellowish velvet suit who, blinking and lisping the while, would say: 'You like that, do you, my dear sir? Personally, I don't find M. Wagner's music very attractive, it's less attractive than M. Reyer's, yes, my dear sir!'

He put on childish airs to express opinions which, ingenuously, he thought would make us jump. His name was Erik Satie. He was the accompanist for the performances of the Rose-Croix directed by Sâr Péladan and used to compose incidental music for those occasions, which he jotted down in tiny notebooks; we were often treated to the first performances of these. We attached no importance whatever to these colourless and more or less formless lucubrations, regarding them as jokes of no significance and finding them extremely boring, with the possible exception of two or three dances called *Gymnopédies*, and a waltz in Db in the style of Benjamin Godard, which I can remember the beginning of and which appeared in a weekly journal.*

One day he announced that he was opening a subscription in order to publish one of his principal works, called *Uspud ou Le fils de l'étoile*.† We knew this dreary piece, which was all of ten or twelve pages long, but to please dear Satie we hastened to subscribe. Some time later, I had a letter from him in which he asked me to find more subscribers for him. I politely refused, not wanting to put pressure on my friends. As a result, he sent me a postcard on which were inscribed in red ink a collection of flaming hearts, swords and other symbolical figures, and in the middle these simple words: 'In the name of the Rose-Croix, be damned!'

Reynaldo Hahn
'Chronique musicale', *Le Figaro*, 9 December 1937

RENÉ PETER

He was a simpleton. He called himself a seer, no doubt thinking that was a euphemism. He used to emerge, wearing his long yellowish beard, from an endless garment made of corduroy, of the same colour, whose upper part reached up to his chin.

'Ah! There you are, Satie! How do you do!'

'My respects, good lady,' he would reply in a priestly tone, bowing to Gaby [Dupont], who was with Debussy at the time. Then he would say to Claude:

'My dear sir, may the Lord keep you under his high and holy protection!'

He was a rather extraordinary person, living more or less in a cupboard in Arcueil [Montmartre] on the 40 francs a month given him by his mother or some other anonymous benefactor. On Sundays he'd pour his

---

*The *Fantaisie-valse* of 1885 which appeared as a musical supplement in *La musique des familles* on 28 July 1887.

†Hahn is combining two works together here, through ignorance, as well as getting the title of *Le fils des étoiles* wrong.

soup, thickened with potatoes when he could get them, on to his bread and that lasted him for a week. For clothes he had his one suit, with a high collar hiding the absence of a shirt and the thick velvet defending him a little against the assaults of the weather. For entertainment, he came twice a week to drink coffee with Debussy, smoked his tobacco, talked about music and was totally happy; then he used to return, if the weather was sharp, 'to warm himself by the corner of his cold', according to his wonderful expression, which in fact he had got from Claude – the only thing anyone ever saw him borrow. In short, he was a model of simple and serene philosophy.

I realised quite well that in this respect he had Claude's admiration; but was he not also to some small extent, if not exactly Claude's parasite, at least under obligation to him?

If Satie was a seer, he was also a composer. He possessed enough technical knowledge of music to note down the ideas that came to him – tunes or motifs, let's say – but I'm sure his supernatural powers stopped there. As to harmonising them, I don't know. When it came to writing them down in full, he had to resort to the less celestial but less fallible talents of Debussy.

Claude gave himself to this heavy task with unceasing care and gentleness. I can see him now spending whole afternoons bent over those sketches from which, as a kind of protest against outmoded routines, the composer had excluded everything useless, including the division of the music into bars. The bar was an abstraction, he assured us, a purely analytical resultant of the main feeling of the idea, from which it should flow quite naturally without any need to plant these ugly black lines, like aggressive fence posts, on the field of inspiration with its myriad flowers.

He was at that time following his theories in writing a work 'of eminent originality' called the *Gymnopédies*, a title which, coming as it does from 'gymnos', naked, and 'pais', child, suggests a rather strange meaning. But Satie was a pure person and so there can be no doubt of the honesty of his intentions. When the work was performed at a concert shortly afterwards, it was not received with the utter seriousness with which the composer wrote it (see, for example, Willy's *Lettres de l'Ouvreuse*). But the critics' sarcasm was mixed with astonishment at seeing this 'poor thing' decked out in fine orchestral colours, in rich, iridescent ornaments . . . I make no comment. But when I hear Satie being mentioned these days by any number of knowledgeable people as having been Debussy's precursor, as having influenced his music and the shaping of his inspiration, then I cannot refrain from outright astonishment.

When he got off the train from Arras at the end of his military service, he came to find me at the Chat Noir with a request from Armand Robert, a brewer and painter from Artois and a close friend of mine, that I should introduce him to the inhabitants and geography of Montmartre. Never have I felt so uninspired as when dealing with that particular individual! Under his pretence of being a good fellow he was a troublemaker. His masquerade was designed to fool his comrades, as when he would address them, lisping, as 'My dear sir!' and 'My good lady!' I remember that at that time he wasn't anything much, though he called himself a composer (perhaps because his father was a music publisher).

René Peter
Claude Debussy (Paris, Gallimard, 1931; 2/1944), pp. 69–72, 151–2

VICTOR-ÉMILE MICHELET
(1861–1938)

> Victor-Émile Michelet was a poet and playwright with a strong interest in esotericism and the occult. His poetic collection *La porte d'or* won the first Prix Sully-Prudhomme in 1902, and Debussy considered a theatrical collaboration with him in the following year. Michelet remained in contact with Joséphin Péladan long after Satie broke with him in 1892, and after Péladan's death in 1918 Michelet organised reunions of his former friends, to one of which Satie was invited in November 1924. Edmond Bailly's bookshop specialised in writings on the occult and had a celebrated clientele in the 1890s, including the Symbolist poets Mallarmé and Henri de Régnier; artists like Odilon Redon and Toulouse-Lautrec; and composers like Debussy, Satie and Chausson. It opened its doors at 11 rue de la Chaussée d'Antin in October 1889.

Claude-Achille Debussy (as he then signed himself) was the most regular of the visitors to L'Art Indépendant. He arrived almost every day, either alone or with his faithful friend Erik Satie. Satie, a real liberal, whom Péladan had discovered so as to make him the appointed musician of his 'Rose-Croix catholique', arrived *chez* Bailly in a velvet corduroy suit.

The lenses of his pince-nez couldn't dim the fire of his laughing eyes.

He jestingly related the story of his visits to members of the Académie des Beaux-Arts. For, at each vacancy, he submitted himself for a place at the Institut. His aim, he said, was to preach the cult of real and living art to these upholders of academic formulae. 'I only met one man who understood,' he added, 'and that was Gustave Moreau.'* However, he always received one vote, that of [Ernest] Reyer.†

Victor-Émile Michelet
Les compagnons de la hiérophanie. Souvenirs du mouvement hermétiste à la fin du 19e siècle (Paris, Dorbon-Aîné, 1937), pp. 73, 75–6

JEAN COCTEAU
(1889–1963)

Jean Cocteau, the celebrated poet, author, film-maker and entrepreneur, needs no introduction. His presence was ubiquitous in avant-garde circles during and after the Great War and it was thanks to *Parade* that Satie achieved notoriety in 1917 and embarked on his later theatrical career. Although Cocteau did not meet Satie until 1915, his retrospective account of Satie's career was undoubtedly prepared with the composer's assistance.

It was in 1891 that Satie was composing the music of a 'Wagnérie' by Péladan‡ and that he opened, beyond all doubt, the door through which Debussy was to walk towards fame.

In those days Debussy used to frequent the Auberge du Clou. He was viewed askance by the artists of the left because he'd won the Prix de Rome. People avoided him. One evening Debussy and Satie found themselves at the same table. They got on well together. Satie asked Debussy what he was working on. Debussy, like everyone else, was writing a 'Wagnérie', on a text by Catulle Mendès.§ Satie grimaced.

*Gustave Moreau (1826–98) was a painter who specialised in elaborate biblical and mythological fantasies. His work was much admired by the Symbolists and his Paris studio has been preserved intact as a museum.
†Ernest Reyer (1823–1909) was a composer and critic with an independent frame of mind and strong literary interests. He set Flaubert's *Salammbô* (a favourite novel of Satie's) as an opera in 1890.
‡*Le fils des étoiles*.
§His unfinished opera *Rodrigue et Chimène* (1890–92).

'Take my word for it,' he murmured, 'that's enough of Wagner. It's fine stuff, but it's not ours. What's needed . . .'

. . . and here I quote a sentence of Satie's which was repeated to me by Debussy and which was decisive in settling the aesthetic outlook of *Pelléas* . . .

'What's needed,' he said, 'is for the orchestra not to pull a face when an actor comes on stage. Think about it. Do the trees in the scenery pull faces? The thing is to make musical scenery, to create a musical climate in which the characters move and talk. No couplets, no leitmotifs – *we should adopt a certain Puvis de Chavannes atmosphere*.'

Remember, at the period I'm speaking of Puvis de Chavannes was a dangerous artist, mocked by the right.

'And you, Satie, what are you working on?' asked Debussy.

'I'm thinking of *La Princesse Maleine*, but I don't know how to get Maeterlinck's permission.'

A few days later, Debussy got Maeterlinck's permission and started on *Pelléas et Mélisande*.

Don't think I'm blaming Debussy or complaining on Satie's behalf. It was for the best. Masterpieces belong to whoever discovers them.

Masterpieces don't introduce or announce anything. They close a period. They're a full stop. One must go on to the next line. A masterpiece is the place where a thousand confused experiments, plasmas, sketches and fumblings are crystallised. Satie's stroke of genius was to realise immediately, in 1896, that *Pelléas* was a masterpiece and to be generous and astute enough to recognise that his friend Claude had hit the jackpot.

'Nothing more one can do in that area,' he wrote after the first performances in 1902. 'I've got to find something else or I've had it.'

He knew perfectly well that masterpieces give birth to a succession of minor masters who refine the discovery, but that the true creator must contradict, and that the next masterpiece must necessarily be the violent contradiction of the masterpiece that has gone before.

Jean Cocteau
'Fragments d'une conférence sur Erik Satie', *ReM*, 5, March 1924, pp. 220–21

GUSTAVE DORET
(1866–1943)

Gustave Doret was born at Aigle, near Lausanne, and although he began his career as a composer (and a pupil of Massenet and Dubois), he established his reputation as a conductor who specialised in propagating modern French music throughout Europe. His first concert as chief conductor of the Société Nationale, on 22 December 1894, included Debussy's *Prélude à l'après-midi d'un faune*, which met with such great enthusiasm that it had to be repeated. Thereafter, Doret became one of Debussy's staunchest supporters, though his jealousy of Debussy's close friendship with Satie was sometimes allowed to influence his views.

At the time of *L'après-midi d'un faune*, Debussy would arrive at my home every Monday evening with Erik Satie. The memory of the wild gaiety of those evenings has remained with everyone who came to them. Ah! What a wonderful time that was!

Gustave Doret
Letter to Robert Godet of 31 March 1918, cited in *Cahiers Debussy*, no. 16, 1992, p. 60

It was in these surroundings that there were born, sometimes on the spot, the ironical, witty productions of our friend Erik Satie, which were later taken very seriously by an élite public of snobs and clever publishers!

I remember a short ballet called *Sainte-Uspude* [sic], and Satie telling the story as he played the score on the piano. In the final scene, the saint spat out her teeth and expired!

One Monday evening Satie brought me his *Gymnopédies* for piano, in a de luxe edition. Pince-nez to the fore, he seated himself at the piano. But his playing was a good deal less than perfect and didn't do the pieces justice. 'Come on,' said Debussy, 'I'll show you what your music sounds like.' And under his miraculous fingers the heart of the *Gymnopédies*, with all their colours and nuances, was laid bare in an astonishing manner.

'The next thing,' I said, 'is to orchestrate them *like that*.'

'I absolutely agree,' replied Debussy. 'If Satie doesn't object, I'll get down to it tomorrow.' You can imagine Satie's joyful surprise.

Some months later I conducted Satie's *Gymnopédies*, orchestrated by Debussy, at a Société Nationale concert.* If I insist on that precise titling, it's because, after Debussy and Satie were dead, some kind souls began to insinuate that Debussy had completely transformed these pieces. Nothing of the sort; not a single detail of the original piano score was changed.

Gustave Doret
Temps et contretemps (Fribourg, 1942), pp. 98–9

OLGA SATIE-LAFOSSE
(1868–1948)

Satie's younger sister Olga was brought up after the death of her mother in 1872 by her great-uncle, Nicolas Fortin, in Le Havre. She may have spent some time in Paris in the 1880s, for Erik dedicated his song *Sylvie* to her in 1887 and her father wrote a waltz in her honour in 1888. On her great-uncle's wishes, she married a doctor, Pierre-Sperator Joseph-Lafosse, in April 1891, but he died unexpectedly that November, before the birth of their child in January 1892. She seems to have fared badly at the hands of her grand-mother's relatives, and she finally fled to Argentina to escape their oppressive clutches after she was refused custody of her child in 1902. She spent the rest of her life in Buenos Aires, giving piano lessons and even a course on her brother's music. She never saw him again.

My brother was always difficult to understand. It doesn't seem that he was ever perfectly normal. And he was a spiritist rather than a true mystic.

Cited in Alfred Cortot
'Le cas Erik Satie', *ReM*, 19/183, April–May 1938, p. 248

CONRAD SATIE
(1869–1938)

Conrad trained as a chemical engineer who specialised in perfumes and, apart from a few periods when Erik broke off

*On 20 February 1897, at the Salle Érard in Paris.

relations with his brother, they were extremely close. In childhood, Erik nicknamed him 'Tiby' or 'Pouillot', and their relationship has aptly been compared by Ornella Volta with that of Vincent and Theo Van Gogh, for Conrad both supported Erik financially and acted as his closest artistic confidant.

The following article was the first to appear on Satie's music and aesthetic. Although it was designed to appeal to the readership of the Catholic esoteric journal *Le coeur*, it contains some perceptive observations on Satie's attitudes in 1895 and first-hand information about his *Messe des pauvres* that is not found elsewhere.

Erik Satie is a man of transcendent idealism, and he has nothing but disdain for the realism which has clouded the intelligence of his contemporaries. Idealism is not understood by the masses. How many people cultivate the arts only so as to get their hands on worldly goods and satisfy their vanity? Satie, on the other hand, prefers to follow his thoughts in poverty rather than live without them in a state of material satisfaction; his works are made singlemindedly for the sake of art. As John Stuart Mill has said, 'Writings one lives by will not live.'

It is easy to understand that a Christian idealist like Satie could not find fulfilment at the Conservatoire, and that his lofty soul underwent peculiar suffering at finding itself enclosed in sterile academic formulae. He was quick to escape from that refuge of adolescents with artistic pretensions; for what has such a place to offer those who were born to invent new forms? Shortly after leaving, he published the *Gymnopédies*, and the *Sarabandes* which are works of a mystic pagan, and which give a foretaste of the Catholic who was to write the *Danses gothiques*.

At this period, he used to like spending whole hours in the gloomy light of Notre-Dame, and his thoughts used to follow the curves of the vaulting and rise towards the Creator; from these hours of ecstasy were born the *Ogives*, published nearly ten [6] years ago. Then his thoughts blossomed; he pondered only the imponderable, and the Christian mystic was revealed. His works began to follow hard upon one another. There were the preludes for Henri Mazel's *Nazaréen*, and *Le fils des étoiles* for Sâr Péladan's Chaldean/Wagnerian concoction. He has just finished the score of *La porte héroïque du ciel*; but his treatment of this drama, by the eminent esoteric writer Jules Bois, is above all Christian in attitude. I should like to mention also *L'hymne au drapeau*, from Sâr Péladan's *Le Prince de Byzance*: it is the hymn of a group of chosen ones saluting the immaculate flag of the absolute.

His *Neuvaines pour le plus grand calme et la forte tranquillité de mon âme, mises sous l'invocation de saint Benoit*,* are the work of a mystic who has been visited by the Holy Spirit, as St Benoit was during the years when he was unknown to everyone except a holy Roman monk. It is also important to point out that all his works are decorative and Catholic. As for the *Gnossiennes*, one has appeared in this journal and two others have been published in the *Figaro musical*.

At the moment Satie is working on a mass called the *Messe des pauvres*. It begins with a very characteristic prelude which forms the basis of the mass, namely motets which return regularly during the office and which are repeated by the main organ, by the choir organ and by the choir. Between the Kyrie and the Gloria a prayer is inserted called 'Prière des Orgues'. Through the children's and men's voices the faithful have just asked for pity; the task of the organ is to condense all these cries of distress and to carry the prayer of the whole congregation up to the Creator. For this mass is essentially a Catholic work, and it will be an actualisation of that unconscious mysticism which exists in all mankind and which is now universally manifested in art and philosophy.

This mass is music for the divine sacrifice, and there will be no part for the orchestras which, I'm sorry to say, find their way into most masses. It is not an entertainment laid on for the faithful; its aim is to increase the intensity of their prayers by acting directly on their souls, already bowed as they are before the Redeemer. These chants, these sounds go to make up a prayer that subsumes the prayer of the whole congregation as they kneel and beg for divine mercy. After hearing this mass, we may recall what Sainte-Beuve said about Pascal: 'We may remain unbelievers, but it is no longer permissible to mock nor to blaspheme.'

> *Beati mundi corde: quoniam ipsi Deum videbunt*
> (Blessed are the pure in heart: for they shall see God.)

Conrad Satie
'Erik Satie', *Le coeur*, 2e année, June 1895, pp. 2–3

*The *Danses gothiques* of 1893.

VINCENT HYSPA
(1865–1938)

Vincent Hyspa was a popular Montmartre cabaret singer and songwriter who began his career, like Satie, in the Chat Noir. He first collaborated with him in December 1891 on a shadow theatre piece (*Noël*) for the Auberge du Clou, which has since been lost. He engaged Satie as his pianist late in 1898, when Satie both arranged his songs and set some of his topical verses to music (like *Un dîner à l'Élysée* and *Le veuf* (1899)). They performed together at venues like the Boîte a Fursy and the Quat'z Arts until at least 1907, and in October 1909 Hyspa, Paulette Darty and Jules Dépaquit performed an assemblage of songs by Satie entitled *La chemise* at the annual Matinée Artistique in Satie's home suburb of Arcueil-Cachan.

At the Auberge du Clou I came across my old friend Eric Satie. 'A small inheritance', as he called it, had brought him several 1000-franc notes and he rushed immediately to the store called La Belle Jardinière to order half a dozen (perhaps even a dozen) chestnut-coloured suits in velvet corduroy, which would last him some time. He also had the same number of hats made out of the same material.

When, some years later, he got on to the last suit, he confessed to me that they were beginning to give him indigestion and that he could not bear to look at velvet any more, even in paintings. So one fine morning (had he perhaps received a further inheritance?) he appeared in a black suit and what our friend, the Spanish painter Miguel Utrillo, used to refer to as a 'roond hat that people call a booler' ['chapeau ronn' qu'appé- lonn' démi-mélonn'].

This was the period of my first collaboration with Satie. I gave him a *Noël*, which he set to music, and for which Utrillo did the décor and the shadow puppets. This *Noël* was performed in the shadow theatre in the basement of the Auberge du Clou.

Vincent Hyspa
'Souvenirs de cabaret du Chat Noir au Chien Noir', in *L'esprit montmartrois* (ed. Léon Ulmann) (Joinville-le-Pont, Laboratoires Carlier, 1938), pp. 226–7

III
At home

In the rue Cortot

After leaving his family's home in December 1887, Satie
spent all his life in dingy bed-sitters. He first rented a large
room at 50 rue Condorcet, below the Butte Montmartre and
very near the Chat Noir cabaret in the rue Victor Massé. He
certainly had a piano in the rue Condorcet, for on 20 July
1889 he advertised as a 'past pupil at the Conservatoire' for
pupils to participate in 'piano classes at his home'. In the
spring of 1890 he moved to a smaller second-floor room on
the summit of La Butte 'to escape his creditors'. Here, at 6
rue Cortot, he occasionally received close friends and composed his Rose-Croix music, as well as establishing the so-
called Abbatial residence of his Église Métropolitaine d'Art.
It is unlikely that he had room for a piano, and Santiago
Rusiñol's famous portrait shows him sitting despondently by
an empty grate, 'au coin de son froid' as Satie put it, with
only his gilded mirror remaining from his former luxury
items.

In July 1896 acute poverty forced Satie into an even smaller, ground-floor room at 6 rue Cortot, for which he paid his
landlord (M. Bibet) 20 francs a quarter instead of the previous 35 francs 10 centimes. But Satie still took his portraits
by Zuloaga, La Rochefoucauld, Desboutin, De Feure and
Valadon with him. The uncongenial nature of his new room
explains why he spent so much time with friends and composed relatively little besides the aptly named *Pièces froides*
during 1896–8.

FLORENT SCHMITT

(1870–1958)

Florent Schmitt was a French composer who entered the Paris
Conservatoire in 1889, studied composition with Massenet
and Fauré, and finally won the Prix de Rome (at his fifth
attempt) in 1900. His friendship with Satie lasted from the
1890s till at least 1907, the year in which he wrote his

celebrated ballet *La tragédie de Salome*. After the war, Satie
became antagonistic towards Schmitt, criticising the heaviness
of his orchestration and the Germanic complexity of his scores.

At the time I got to know Satie he had just received the belt of Parcener,
the highest office conferred by the Église Métropolitaine d'Art, corre-
sponding more or less, from the point of view of the financial and other
prerogatives it brought with it, to the Pope among the Protestants or the
Chief Rabbi at the court of Spain.

He was living then in the rue Cortot in Montmartre, in a tiny room
kindly put at his disposal by his landlord, a good man who feared both
God and expelled lodgers. In this pure and peaceful retreat, where no
other mortal ever set foot, Satie, being an indoors kind of person, had
arranged himself in tasteful comfort: one of the shelves served as a work
table as well as an altar, while a special kind of lock gave him air and
light and at the same time protected him from the curiosity of people on
the landing. As his furniture didn't include a piano, when he came to the
end of his long hours of study in his room he would visit friends to have
the pleasure of hearing his music other than in his head. This was how I
came to hear the *Gymnopédies* and the *Gnossiennes*, and the first sketches
for *Le fils des étoiles*. I can still recall the harmonies of the prelude, which
upset the traditional minds of the time and which are now quoted by
pedagogues in their manuals as examples of chords that are daring but
perfectly 'acceptable and logical'.

Florent Schmitt
'Erik Satie', *Montjoie*, November–December 1913, p. 11

AUGUSTIN GRASS-MICK

(1873–1953)

Augustin Grass-Mick (originally Grasmick) was an artist who
met Satie around 1896. Together with the writer Henry
Pacory, they formed a familiar trio in the bars and haunts of
Montmartre, especially over the next two years. Grass-Mick
left an invaluable archive of sketches and portraits of Satie
around the turn of the century, showing him in the company
of Toulouse-Lautrec, Jane Avril and other celebrities.

Satie's biographers talk of a gap of two years in his life. It's true, nothing is known of the years from 1896 to 1898. What was he doing? Nothing, absolutely nothing. He wandered round Paris, thought his thoughts and lived a free and easy life away from his musical contemporaries. It was at this time that I got to know him, as the family friend of a man I met in my regiment, called Henry Pacory, later to be the author of the words of the waltz *Je te veux*, first performed by Paulette Darty in 1903, with music by Satie.

We know that around 1891 he was playing the piano at the Chat Noir, then at the Auberge du Clou, where he got to know the young Prix de Rome winner Debussy; and that he was a friend of the humorous writer Jules Dépaquit, who was a neighbour of his on the Butte of Montmartre, as well as of Alphonse Allais, Vincent Hyspa and other dry wits of the time, from whom he took some of his ideas and whose way of looking at things he was to keep all his life. His friend Pacory followed him on this route to the point of exuberance – I was a little calmer about things, despite being a comic artist. We spent most of our time together, and had lunch and dinner with Pacory's family. In the afternoons we'd go out for a stroll, all of us, and especially Satie, being great walkers. We went to cafés, to the 'apéritifs-concerts' at the Petit Casino, and to the Café des Princes. Never, in the years between 1896 and 1898, when he left the Butte for a change of scenery, did I see him either working or writing or making notes. At the Pacorys he just might sit down at the piano. But not often; and if he did sit on the stool, it was usually with his back to the instrument.

At that time I was still living with my parents on the boulevard Garibaldi, in the south-west of Paris. Satie said to me: 'Why not come to Montmartre? We'd see more of each other!' I'd already had this idea. So I started to look for a place to live and was soon able to tell my friends that I'd found a bedroom-cum-studio on the fifth floor of No. 67 rue Lepic, with a balcony from which I could look out over the whole city.

They were delighted and decided to help me move. This was in 1897. An odd-job man with a handcart waited for my removal men outside my parents' house. They arrived on foot at 7 in the morning, and within ten minutes it was done: mattress, sofa, easel, frames, paintbox, a table, a chair . . . all put on to the cart with extreme care. The procession moved off, with the odd-job man between the handles. Pacory and Satie pushed from behind, and I from in front of the left wheel. And so we crossed the whole of Paris, like soldiers on a forced march. The passers-by looked on with considerable amusement at this picturesque scene, like something out of Murger's *Scènes de la vie de bohème*. Pacory looked like a bourgeois, I like an art student, and Satie, dressed entirely in beige velvet, including his hat, with a double-knotted black cravat and soldier's hobnailed boots, like a special kind of almoner.

When we reached the rue Lepic, the going got hard, even when we zigzagged, and we ground to a halt. Two or three kindly souls, seeing our predicament, helped us push the cart to my lodgings. Satie was marvellous; without any apparent exhaustion, he climbed the stairs like a professional removal man, carrying several things at once and without dropping anything. I must say, he really threw himself into it. Within twenty minutes, I was installed in my 'pad', a free man. It was nearly midday so, without sorting anything out, we went off to have a well-earned apéritif in a café on the place Clichy, and from there to the Pacorys at 22 rue de la Boétie where lunch was awaiting us. After that, Satie and I went back to my lodgings on our own to straighten things out. He had taste, and a mania for arranging things which I shared. He used to say: 'I like things in order, but dust doesn't bother me.'

One morning my caretaker gave me an envelope containing Satie's visiting card, asking me to go and see him in his hideaway in the rue Cortot – a rare occurrence, because he never invited people. As he used to say, 'I'm afraid of unwholesome visits.'

The original, which I have in front of me, is a clear indicator of Satie's mentality in everything he did: on the envelope, my name is written in red ink, my address in black. On the visiting card are the words: Erik Satie, choirmaster of the Église Métropolitaine d'Art de Jésus Conducteur, 6 rue Cortot. Then, in calligraphic writing, in red ink: 'Would you be good enough, my dear Grass-Mick, to put off until Saturday, 10 o'clock, the honourable visitation which you were to have made me tomorrow,' and then in black ink: 'Your servant: Erik Satie'. My servant! Good old Satie . . . It's true that he'd been very willing to help me move. He seemed to be even happier than I was, that day. He regarded the occasion as an entertaining treat.

After the family dinners, he and I would go back up to Montmartre, talking about art. Satie was very good on painting. When we reached the rue d'Orsel, we'd have a beer at Paulus's, then we'd link arms and walk slowly up towards the Butte along the rue des Saules, which used to remind him of the rue Berton at Passy, where Balzac used to live.

Satie used to tell us: 'Artists have a right to beg. In the café, I'm not a composer, you're not a painter, we're customers.' He used to say: 'Good morning, my good lady, my good sir,' and to the waiter: 'My kind man, thank you, my dear fellow.'

Augustin Grass-Mick
'Le souvenir d'Erik Satie,' *Les Arts*, 4 August 1950

In Arcueil

By 1898 Satie had had enough of his cupboard in Montmartre and realised that its temptations were impeding his compositional career. His new room was taken over from an alcoholic Montmartre celebrity known as 'Bibi-la-Purée' (André Salis), who was a relative of Rodolphe Salis, the 'bonimenteur' of the Chat Noir. He seems to have had some pretty disgusting habits, for Satie was forced into domesticity for the only known time in his life to make his new abode at the Maison des Quatres Cheminées habitable. He told Conrad in November about scrubbing the floor with washing soda before waxing it, and he had to cover the window up to prevent inquisitive neighbours watching his activities with binoculars. Later that month, his 'pictures, mattress, chest and bench' arrived by handcart from Montmartre, with the 'precious' items following on in December – including two grand pianos which he apparently placed one on top of the other (using the upper one as a post-box for unsolicited letters and parcels). A narrow passage with a wash-basin led into the room, though Satie had to fetch any water he needed from a 'fountain in the place des Écoles' nearby. By early 1899 he had moved in permanently.

AUGUSTIN GRASS-MICK

He was an excellent walker, going from Montmartre to Arcueil on foot, when he needed to. Indeed, one afternoon in October 1898, Pacory, Satie and I made that journey on foot to rent the room he was to live in until his death: 22 rue Cauchy, a house with four chimneys. It was quite a large room, with a window looking out on a cottage and some trees – it was usually shut, to stop curious neighbours looking in. He never had visitors here, any more than he did in his hideaway in the rue Cortot, where his furniture consisted of a camp bed, a chest, a trunk, a bench and two or three pictures on the walls, including the portrait of him by Larochefoucault [sic]. There was one tiny window opposite the door, which you had to shut in order to get between the bed and the trunk. This was how a great composer lived. The same furniture went on a handcart to Arcueil, with the addition of two pianos.

When he shut himself off in Arcueil, he said: 'I'm withdrawing, completely.' I knew what he meant, because he was coming back to the idea of working. I felt in him an uneasy, sometimes bizarre spirit, which seemed very distant from us. For all his pretending gaiety and wit, there was hidden within him a dissatisfaction which he wanted to disguise with humour. Pacory, who loved Satie like a brother, never noticed it. But there was no doubt, Satie was trying to distance himself, to spend his time dawdling.

I never knew him look at a woman. Was he a misogynist, then? No, he was simply very shy and frightened of them. When he laid aside his almoner's outfit for the waistcoat and detachable collars, his character remained as mysterious as ever. He was Satie to the depths of his soul, in other words a capricious child in the body of a young old man. He preferred rain to full sunlight, smoked a red or white earthenware pipe, drank absinthe and had a huge appetite. He'd go out in the most terrible weather. He liked the open air and hated being indoors. He could be annoyed by little things and little things could also delight him. No one ever really knew what he felt about politics or religion. I never teased him and we never had a quarrel.

One afternoon, sitting outside the Auberge de Clou, he spotted a pushy individual he didn't want to see, and sank his head behind the screen of his newspaper. But his clothes gave him away and the man came up to him: 'Good afternoon, Satie, how are you?' Satie, without looking up, replied: 'Monsieur, kindly leave me alone.' The man stood there dumbfounded, and then slunk off with his tail between his legs. When he'd gone, Satie looked at me with a satisfied smile. That was all. No confidences from him, no questions from me. With Satie, that was how you had to behave – to avoid a quarrel.

Augustin Grass-Mick
'Le souvenir d'Erik Satie', *Les Arts*, 4 August 1950

In ten minutes the rental was arranged. Satie had a new home. If three or four friends, including his brother Conrad, entered his room after his death, no one ever set foot in it during his lifetime. Consequently, if

Pacory is still alive, he and I are the only people ever to have seen this room, the first and the last, for, once Satie had moved in, it was to close the door on the world outside. Who would have thought it, seeing this man who in himself was so correct? Here was a dwelling which he occupied for twenty-seven years and which wasn't to be known to even ten people. Pacory and I saw it bare, the others rummaged through it. That was all.

From the unpublished memoirs of Augustin Grass-Mick
Cited in Ornella Volta, *Satie Seen Through his Letters* (trans. Michael Bullock) (London, Marion Boyars, 1989), p. 70

JEAN WIÉNER
(1896–1982)

Jean Wiéner was a pianist, composer and concert promoter who was one of the first devotees of jazz in France. He was frequently to be found with Cocteau and his circle in the 1920s at cabarets like Le Boeuf sur le Toit. Satie often visited his home or met him socially, and Wiéner later teamed up with Clément Doucet in a piano duo specialising in jazz improvisations which achieved great popularity between the wars. Wiéner was also largely responsible for introducing the music of the Second Viennese School to Paris, and it was at one of his concerts in January 1922 that Milhaud conducted the first French performance of Schoenberg's *Pierrot Lunaire*.

He used to sleep there on a pillow as hard as metal, without a mattress or sheets. At night he used to go to sleep rolled up in an army blanket. For years on end he never opened his window and there were objects on the two grands that were so thickly covered with dust it was impossible to identify them straight away. I discovered a box containing an incredible collection of writing paper, cards and envelopes engraved with his name and the name of an imaginary order that he'd invented from nowhere.

Jean Wiéner
'Aimer Erik Satie', *L'Humanité*, 43/645, 4 September 1946, p. 3

ROBERT CABY

(1905–92)

Robert Caby was a French composer who shared Satie's communist sympathies and remained a lifelong admirer of his music. They first met in 1924 and Caby looked after Satie during his difficult final illness with admirable devotion. In the 1960s he made colourful orchestrations of some of Satie's piano pieces and edited many of his unpublished sketches and drafts for the publisher Salabert. His own music was influenced by Satie and includes some particularly sensitive song-settings of the poetry of Apollinaire.

It has to be said that the problem of evil haunted him all his life. Allusions to the devil are frequent, both in his music and in his writings and drawings. He dreamt sometimes of the devil being a generous philanthropist. On the wall of the building opposite his window in Arcueil was an old *graffito* including the word 'devil'.

Early on in my friendship with him I made the mistake of going out to see him in Arcueil one Sunday afternoon. He was out, but I was naive enough to tell him about my visit. He was duly astonished, but did not break off our relationship. Later, he even sent me to the rue Cauchy to collect some laundry from the concierge.

No one, in his lifetime, set foot inside his room, not even that large and splendid concierge, against whom his only complaint was that she tried to force the door one day when she was worried, knowing he was ill and hadn't been seen for a very long time!

It was an extraordinary room, and the life he lived in it smacked of magic.

It's enough for me to say that when Milhaud, Roger Désormière and I, with his brother Conrad, got into the room to try and sort out the layers of papers and objects covering the floor, we couldn't begin until we'd sent two cartloads of rubbish to the public tip in Arcueil! So long after the event, I can say now that I discovered, all along one skirting board, numerous lumps of excrement, hardened and blackened with age, which I hastily stuffed into newspapers so that Satie's brother shouldn't see them.

The man who emerged every morning from this unbelievable slum was the same man we saw strolling round Paris, looking stylish, full of energy, cheerful, spruce and clean, except when one of his long walks had left a light covering of dust on him. It was in this extraordinary hovel that Satie wrote his music. He wrote *Relâche* there, on the piano at night, and the other tenants in the block put up with it. 'Monsieur Satie' was an important person in the big world of Paris! As for that piano, when we got into the room it was almost unreachable: the only way you could play it was balancing on piles of paper.

Robert Caby
'Il y a vingt-cinq ans mourait Erik Satie "musicien médiéval" aux prises avec les hommes, les rêves et le démon', *Le Figaro littéraire*, 24 June 1950, p. 6

IV

On foot in all weathers

Like Wordsworth, Rimbaud, Mayakovsky and others, Satie was a great walker, and this was his main means of keeping fit. On most mornings after he moved to Arcueil, he would return to Paris on foot, a distance of about ten kilometres, stopping frequently at his favourite cafés *en route*. According to Templier (1969, 56), 'he walked slowly, taking small steps, his umbrella held tight under his arm. When talking he would stop, bend one knee a little, adjust his pince-nez and place his fist on his hip. Then he would take off once more, with small, deliberate steps.'

When he eventually reached Paris, he visited friends or arranged to meet them in other cafés by sending *pneumatiques* (the postal service then being fast and efficient). Often, the walking from place to place continued, focussing on Montmartre before the war, and subsequently on Montparnasse. From here, Satie would catch the last train back to Arcueil at about 1 a.m. or, if he was still engaged in serious drinking, he would miss it and begin the long walk home during the early hours of the morning. Then the daily round would begin again, although Satie rarely reached his first stop (Chez Tulard in Arcueil) before 11 a.m.

Roger Shattuck, in conversation with John Cage in 1982*, put forward the interesting theory that 'the source of Satie's sense of musical beat – the possibility of variation within repetition, the effect of boredom on the organism – may be this endless walking back and forth across the same landscape day after day . . . the total observation of a very limited and narrow environment'. This becomes the more relevant when we consider that most of Satie's pre-Arcueil music has a very slow pulse, while the faster, more mechanical regularity all belongs to the latter half of his career. *Parade*, with its constant pulse of 76 beats per minute, may thus reflect his slow walking speed as much as the human heart-beat. During

*In *Contact*, 25, 1982, p. 25.

69

his walks, Satie was also observed stopping to jot down ideas by the light of the street-lamps he passed. During the war, when these lights were often extinguished, a wicked myth circulated that Satie's productivity had dropped as a result. So although he invariably walked alone, he must have been a most familiar figure.

GEORGE AURIOL

(1863–1938)

George Auriol (born Jean Georges Huyot) was an artist, journalist and fellow Bohemian who knew Satie from his Montmartre days in the late 1880s through to the end of his life. He was a close friend of Contamine de Latour too, and seems to have been able to rival them both in eccentricity and whimsical humour (in the vein of Alphonse Allais). Both Latour and Allais contributed to Jehan Sarrazin's weekly journal *La lanterne japonaise* in 1888–9, and Satie also wrote for it under the pseudonym of Virginie Lebeau. Auriol shared Satie's fascination for calligraphy and published three volumes of collected monograms, trademarks, seals and bookmarks between 1901 and 1924. The walk described immediately below probably took place in the summer of 1899 when Satie had just moved to Arcueil but returned frequently to Montmartre to collaborate with Jules Dépaquit on the bizarre theatre piece called *Jack-in-the-Box*.

Twenty-four pairs of sturdy boots would not be an exaggeration for what such a champion of 'footing' needed. His intrepidity as a walker was so great that he made it into a pastime – and a daily one at that – to cover the distance that separates Montmartre from Arcachon . . . or rather Arcueil-Cachan. But all the same it was a 'long, long way' from Sacré-Coeur to the Aqueduct [near Satie's home].

This 'marche bourgeoise' often took place around 2 in the morning, across the wild and barbarous quarters of la Glacière and la Santé where prowling 'apaches' were not unknown. This was why our musician carried a hammer in his pocket, by way of a tomahawk.

Under the insidious pretext of keeping him 'under control', Satie was sometimes accompanied by his friend [Jules] Dépaquit. They would gulp down a cup of hot chocolate beneath an overhanging porch and, the sun having risen when they reached their destination, the two pilgrims, regardless of any need for rest, rubbed themselves down rapidly with a sponge and set out once again for the mountain [Sacré-Coeur]. They arrived there towards midday and one could predict that they would do justice to the tasty nosh in Mme Spielmann's café, as well as to her table wine.

I still have tender memories of the merry *Club de la Clay-Pipe*. There were no members, not even honorary ones, but three presidents: the delightful artist George Delaw, Erik Satie and myself. I rejoiced, what's more, in the somewhat extravagant title of 'armourer', because I was the supplier of this group which met at the cabaret in the place du Tertre, in the days when it was no longer run by a fellow from Alsace but by a Savoyard called Revenaz. It was only a few steps away from the friendly old church of St Peter, where Franc-Nohain was married to the daughter of a talented musician, Léopold Dauphin, who took a fatherly interest in Satie.

By hunting in mysterious shops in the suburbs, I used to unearth those long English pipes stamped with two slaves chained together, with red varnish on the ends. We'd puff away there peacefully, in the Flemish manner. Then, in the middle of the afternoon, Delaw and I would regretfully put our pipes back in the rack and lay aside our assumed personas of retired sea-captains.

But Erik would wrap his pipe in a copy of *Gil Blas* — I remember exactly — and put it in his pocket, so that it looked like a walking-stick with the stem coming practically up to his ear. Thus equipped, he'd walk across Paris to go and see Debussy — and in the evening he'd be back, with his pipe!

That went on for months and, thanks to the gods' protection, no damage was done to the fragile implement thus imprudently transported . . .

Did he have hatreds? No, but strong antipathies which served as targets for the arrows that whistled from his bow.

'There's that pig come to annoy us again,' you'd hear him grumble, when there was no pig to be seen — human or animal. It would turn out to be poor old Phoebus.

'You don't like the sun, then?'

'He's a brute!' Satie would reply. 'If only my legs were long enough to give him a good kick in the eye! A brute and a malefactor: not content with grilling our prison windows, he gets malicious enjoyment out of burning the peasants' crops. What a lout!' . . .

As nobody is perfect, I should like for the moment to take him to task with some vehemence on one point: 'My dear friend, you have covered yourself with shame by swapping your velvet cap for a businessman's bowler!'

In fact he was wearing this outdated hemisphere the other day, when I met him down by the Seine:

'Still out in Arcueil?'

'I'm afraid so, my dear fellow . . . I can't find anywhere in Paris. I need something huge, you realise . . . Thirty rooms, at least . . . I've got so many ideas to house!'

George Auriol
'Erik Satie, the Velvet Gentleman', *ReM*, 5, March 1924, pp. 210–11, 214–16

GEORGES AURIC

(1899–1983)

Georges Auric came to prominence as a member of Les Six, though he first met Satie after writing a perceptive article on his music at the age of only 14. He studied first at the Paris Conservatoire and then as a composition pupil of d'Indy at the Schola Cantorum (1914–16). Subsequently he became one of Satie's Nouveaux Jeunes and their works regularly appeared in the same concert programmes. Satie's enthusiasm for his young protégé reached its height in 1919 when he described Auric and Milhaud as 'two artists [who] are my consolation in the future and even in the present'. But cracks in their relationship soon began to appear when he suspected Auric of 'slandering' his 'musique d'ameublement'. He became increasingly suspicious of Auric's growing attachment to the homosexual circle of Cocteau and Radiguet in 1922–3 and the break came after Diaghilev's Monte Carlo opera season in January 1924.

He stayed at home as little as possible, going from Arcueil to Paris each day on foot. And (however he managed it) we would see him arrive in the same impeccable shirt and the same smart clothes. Frequently, as night fell, I saw him set out again, still on foot, often in the snow, during the worst weeks of winter, but always with the same smile. Those who didn't know him well (and there were many) had, I'm sure, no idea from looking at him that he was destitute, or even poor. I don't know whether I should give evidence on this point? I can still hear him muttering sometimes: 'My dear fellow, have you got a two-franc piece?' There were two-franc pieces in those days, and for someone penniless they represented a fair sum. At his death, Satie was still penniless, whereas for his heirs and publishers the royalties on his works today bring in a tidy sum.

Georges Auric
'Inoubliable apparition d'Erik Satie', in *Quand j'étais là* (Paris, Grasset, 1979), p. 24

PIERRE DE MASSOT

(1900–69)

Pierre de Massot was a writer and journalist and a faithful communist friend of Satie's in the 1920s. He was born Pierre de Massot de Lafond and seems to have acted as a go-between, keeping Satie in touch with the latest news in avant-garde literary and artistic circles. He had close links with Picabia, Cendrars and the Dada movement in Paris and contributed to the journal *391*. He and his wife Robbie often entertained Satie to dinner, though Satie seems to have regarded him as a willing 'dogsbody' who needed the prestige he brought him rather than vice versa.

He was the soul of impatience and couldn't bear to have his pleasures postponed. As an example, I remember one evening when we were walking towards the gare d'Austerlitz to have dinner (I loved these long walks, because Satie knew the history of old Paris down to the last detail and his colourful monologue was entrancing), I made apologies for having to go into a shoe shop as the soles of mine were giving up on me. Satie was furious at being interrupted and at the impending delay of that delightful moment when we would all three sit down outside Le Pied du Mouton. His only response was to grumble: 'Keep walking on them, no one will notice . . .' and I had to give in so as not to exacerbate his fury.

All the same, this sarcastic old man was more charitable than anyone towards those whom life had treated roughly or unjustly. I'll give just one example, but a significant one. One night, very late, we arrived at the gare de Sceaux in company with 'le bon maître', as we all called him. Once again, the last train had long gone: too much iced beer, too much calvados and too many stories, sitting outside the tabac Denfert-Rochereau! Satie seem unworried at having nearly two hours' walking ahead of him and, seeing we were anxious about him marching off alone into the darkness, stopped and said: 'You know, dear friends, when I leave you at this time of night and go home on foot, I get to Arcueil around dawn. As I go through the woods, with the birds chirruping all round, and see a large tree with its leaves rustling, I go up to it and throw my arms round it, and as I do so I think: what a good sort, he at least has never harmed anyone! . . .'

Pierre de Massot
'Quelques propos et souvenirs sur Erik Satie', *ReM*, 214, June 1952, pp. 127–8

FERNAND LÉGER
(1881–1955)

Fernand Léger met Picasso and Braque in 1910 and by 1917 he had developed a form of Cubism that was inspired by the dynamic shapes of machinery and their geometrical bases, as well as by Futurist ideas. These curvilinear Cubist forms also influenced the massive robot-like figures he painted, and intensified the effect produced by his strong, unbroken colours and stark industrial backgrounds. He designed sets for the Ballets Suédois and made the first abstract film in 1924 (*Le ballet mécanique*) using objects rather than animated drawings. Satie preferred discussing art to discussing music and seems to have found an ideal companion in Léger during at least one of his long walks home.

We were having lunch, Satie and some friends, in a restaurant. The music was so loud we simply couldn't stand it and left. But Satie said:

'Even so, there's room for a "musique d'ameublement", that's to say, music which would be part of the noises around it and would take account of them. I think of it as being tuneful, softening the noise of knives and forks without overpowering them or making itself obtrusive. It would fill in the silences which can sometimes weigh heavy between table companions. It would banish the need to make banal conversation. At the same time it would neutralise street noises, which can be tactless in their behaviour.' It would, he said, be responding to a need.

Another day, as we were walking along the road from Montparnasse to Arcueil: 'Tell me, Léger, don't you find there's a little too much of "doing what we want", whatever comes into our heads? I'm surrounded by a small band of friends and admirers who've lost all critical sense when it comes to talking about me. It's lovely, delightful, wonderful! You've heard them. They've no sense of moderation. Long live Freedom, of course; but even so: tell me now . . .

'Suppose there were someone, a hunter, say. He likes hunting, he hunts pheasants. He likes chasing wild animals, and he comes to you and asks you, as a painter in colour: "Monsieur Léger, I know your work. I should very much like to have in my dining-room a picture that's very free as to subject; we can agree on that, but I should like to have a pheasant in it, a fine male pheasant with multicoloured feathers. You've got those colours on your palette . . ." What would be your answer?'

And the conversation rambled on. He was indefatigable. Still, very late in the evening, or very early in the morning, we stopped in a bistro to have a coffee. Leaning on the bar were two solid, relaxed men. Outside, a huge lorry was waiting for them.

Satie looked at them with considerable interest:

'Have you come across types like that one? Or that one? During the war! It took a war for you to discover them! Why aren't we friends with them? They're magnificent, and we wouldn't be quite the same afterwards.'

Fernand Léger
'Satie inconnu', *ReM*, 214, June 1952, pp. 137–8

GABRIEL FOURNIER
(1893–19?)

Gabriel Fournier was one of the many painters Satie knew and he was also extremely interested in the advent of American jazz to wartime Paris, which gave them an additional common interest. Fournier was a cultivated and erudite man with forward-looking tastes and he first met Satie around 1916.

The walk described below occurred after Satie's trial for libel
brought by the critic Jean Poueigh after *Parade* in 1917.

I asked his permission to go with him on his return journey to Arcueil.
I was greatly honoured by his acceptance, and I could see, when he said
how pleased he was at my suggestion, that he realised what a strong
impression the events had made on me. He did his best to play down for
me the tragic and unpleasant side of the farce we'd just been through and
then, on foot naturally, we made our way through Montparnasse to the
Porte d'Orléans. I knew perfectly well that to go further than this would
be to infringe his liberty: throughout his life, his lodgings were forbidden
territory.

Satie's conversation all through this walk was a delight, talking about
life in all its aspects, imbuing the smallest detail with the originality of
his wit. He would stop with his hand on his hip, his left arm leaning on
his umbrella and his head thrown back to help emphasise some statement;
then, pointing his index finger at the sky, he'd bring his soliloquy to an
end. This exhibition of fireworks would be repeated and prolonged with
explosions, rockets and sparks until the final, crowning display. There
was certainly nothing of the 'literary' man about him, nor was he anybody's
pawn. He was the opposite of an aesthete, and that was what I liked so
much in him. He kept on thanking me for my kindness in refusing to
abandon him, and seemed almost proud of his adventure; it had, after
all, allowed him to see the judicial process at close quarters, and to take
part in it and draw his personal conclusions from it all. He talked about
what he was writing, about *Socrate* which was occupying his thoughts; in
this pure masterpiece, he truly identified with his model and invested him
with the rarest essence of his genius.

Naturally, this walk included a number of stops at cafés, ending up
with a small glass of champagne at La Rotonde. After a series of polite
effusions Satie, hat in hand, bowed, said his last 'thank you' – and we
went our separate ways.

Gabriel Fournier
'Erik Satie et son époque', *ReM*, 214, June 1952, p. 132

LÉON-LOUIS VEYSSIÈRE
(1875–1955)

Léon-Louis Veyssière was a friend and neighbour of Satie's in Arcueil (he lived at 11 rue Cauchy). He was a house-painter by profession and, like Satie, he was a committed socialist. But his efforts to prevent Satie moving further left towards communism in the 1920s were predictably unsuccessful.

One day when we were strolling along in the streets of Arcueil, a friend came up to us and asked us a question: 'To where are your steps directed?' We were really at a loss in replying for we were just strolling anywhere without any definite goal, but this question, however banal it seemed, plunged Satie into deep reflection. Several days later, he was still thinking about it and racking his brains to know why this passing friend wanted to know the object of our walk. Our questioner was a Freemason, which explains a lot.

Léon-Louis Veyssière
Unpublished memoirs in the Archives de la Fondation Erik Satie, Paris. This extract was translated from *Les bulles du parcier* (ed. Ornella Volta) (Fontfroide, 1991), p. 91

BLAISE CENDRARS
(1887–1961)

Blaise Cendrars was the pseudonym of Frédéric Sauser-Hall, the Swiss-born novelist and poet. His life was one of constant travel in search of new experiences to fertilise his creative work, and he supported himself through a variety of occupations, from salesman and journalist to film director. He kept in close touch with avant-garde artists in all spheres, and his rather unlikely friendship with the travel-hating Satie developed in 1916. Each admired the other's unpredictability, artistic independence and lively conversation, and it was through Cendrars that Satie became involved with Rolf de Maré's Ballets Suédois in 1923–4.

One night during one of the last and most violent bombardments of 1918, I came across someone lying at the foot of the obelisk in the place de la Concorde. I leant over him, thinking he was dead. It was my old friend Satie.

'What are you doing down there?' I asked.

He answered: 'I realise it's silly and I'm not under shelter. But you know, that thing goes up into the sky and I have the feeling of being under shelter. Anyway, I'm composing a piece of music for the obelisk. A good idea, don't you think?'

'Very,' I said, 'as long as it's not a military march . . .'

'No danger of that,' he replied. 'It's for the pharoah's wife who's buried down there. No one ever gives her a thought. It's only because of those damned guns that I'm here now – for the first time. It's not a bad bit of work.' And he chortled, with his hand on his beard as usual, while he looked the monument up and down with a sardonic expression.

'Do you know who's buried down there?' I asked him. 'Cleopatra's mummy, apparently; at least, that's what I've been told . . .'

'Impossible,' retorted Satie. 'I was right to compose a bit of music for her. Listen:

> '*Ta, tarâ, ta, ta, ta, ta, ta*
> *Ta, tarâ, ta, ta, ta, ta,* . . .
>
> Fah, do-oh, soh, ray, lah, me, te – Fah, do-oh, soh, ray, lah, me.'*

Blaise Cendrars
Interview with Michel Manoll, in *Blaise Cendrars vous parle* (Paris, Denoël, 1952), pp. 209–10

---

*The musical equivalent of this can be found in Orledge, *Satie the Composer* (CUP, 1990) as Ex. 1 on p. 18.

V

In cafés and restaurants

We have already seen in the Pierre de Massot souvenir, in Section IV, how eagerly Satie anticipated the pleasure of his evening meal and how angry he got if it was delayed in any way. This was clearly the highlight of his day and, by all accounts, he had just as prodigious a capacity for food as he had for alcohol. Perhaps this came from the many hungry days during his early period in Montmartre, and there were certainly many more people who were willing to foot the bill after he became more celebrated in 1911. But when he had money, Satie was an equally generous host, and dining with him must have been quite an experience. He preferred simple dishes cooked well and was a gourmet rather than a gourmand, though he could consume an omelette made of thirty eggs at a single sitting!

While he composed in cafés, such as Le Lion in Montparnasse, he never did in restaurants, for dining was an altogether more serious matter. The list of cafés and restaurants that enjoyed his patronage is endless, though they varied from period to period and the artistic clientele each attracted was an important factor in Satie's choice. Thus, he was often to be found in La Rotonde around 1916, when it was a favourite meeting-place for Cubists, or in the 1920s *chez* Graff (rue Saint-Lazare), or in Le Boeuf sur le Toit (28 rue Boissy-d'Anglas) when this was a rendezvous for Cocteau and Les Six. The restaurants he favoured were mostly in Montparnasse and within close walking distance of the station which would take him back to Arcueil on the last train – such as Le Pied de Mouton (near the gare d'Austerlitz) or the Grill-Room Médicis and Le Nègre de Toulouse (near the gare de Sceaux).

JEAN COCTEAU

Eating bread in the approved manner means doing so at table, as you do a brioche. Satie, gourmet that he was, never left the table without taking with him a crust to nibble, claiming it was an old custom he'd picked up in his youth from the finest gastronomic experts in Honfleur.

Jean Cocteau
'Petite lettre à la dérive', *L'almanach de Cocagne pour l'an 1920*, p. 136 (*AFS*)

VALENTINE HUGO
(1887–1968)

Valentine Gross was the daughter of an Alsatian music professor who married the stage designer Jean Hugo in August 1919. She was primarily an artist and designer herself, but she was also a musician. Satie met her at the house of the young composer Roland-Manuel in early 1914 and seems to have been sufficiently attracted to her to call her his 'chère grande fille' and dedicate his *Menus propos enfantins* to her. She was also known as 'the swan' because of her long neck, and would have made an ideal subject for Modigliani. Above all she had Satie's confidence, and proved extremely useful as a go-between in the problematic collaboration of *Parade*, especially when Satie fell out with Misia Edwards (who was paying for Diaghilev's ballet). She also assisted Satie financially when she could, and was particularly helpful to him during the summer of 1918 when he was so destitute he nearly gave up composition.

Satie must often have done without meals, but he was very fond of good food, and of very good food, as well as good wine and good alcohol. He used to eat quietly. When it came to dessert, he used to keep back a piece of bread. He would carefully cut off the crust with a knife and discreetly take it with him when he left the table, to eat while he was drinking his coffee.

Personally, I never saw Satie out of control or drunk.

Valentine Hugo
'Notes pour un portrait de Satie', unpublished MS, dated 1958. Catalogue of Hôtel Drouot, Paris, 10 December 1986

GABRIEL FOURNIER

His unexpected arrivals at La Rotonde used to give me great pleasure. In general, they were simply stops on his way home after his walks through Paris, so we usually saw him covered with dust, but always affable and smiling his angelic smile. He was always dressed very correctly – like a lawyer – with bowler hat, high collar starched and pointed, grey cotton gloves and his umbrella on his arm, and he'd come and sit at our tables and have an amiable chat, putting his right hand in front of his mouth to muffle a laugh he didn't want to sound startling, or else to mask an over-violent expression on his face – for this gentle creature could get angry, I'm afraid, if he was pushed. His conversation was racy and enchanting. Certainly he could give a sharp bite, but never with any hint of spitefulness: he was easily upset as most people are who are used to suffering in silence and to employing jokes as camouflage for their heightened sensitivity. He stuck obstinately to his own opinions and some people found him hard to get on with.

Gabriel Fournier
'Erik Satie et son époque', *ReM*, 214, June 1952, pp. 129–30

RENÉ LANSER

René Lanser was a Belgian journalist who went in search of Satie whenever he came to Paris from Antwerp. They met by chance, but established an instant rapport, and their intermittent friendship seems to have been kept alive by Satie's sparkling conversation.

We saw a lot of him. Our friendship began when, one day, we'd gone to see Les Halles at dawn. We found ourselves opposite a man at the same wooden table in a snack bar, his eyes twinkling with mischief behind his pince-nez, and in front of him two steaming bowls of cheese soup. We soon got to know each other in that free and easy atmosphere in which general amiability lowered the barriers of convention in force elsewhere.

After a few minutes and some brief thoughts on the phonetic qualities of the cries, shouts and interjections which reached us from the street, we were the best of friends.

It was a sparkling conversation: brilliant *aperçus* about the arts, unknown facts about the leaders of contemporary thought, and flights of the most extraordinary fantasy. Among his aphorisms were: 'Being a sod isn't everything. You must be modest with it.' And again: 'Menelaus' fame really upsets me.' Satie was probably the first to make the joke which amused Edward VII so much: 'An Englishman is a Norman who's gone to the bad.' And he would guffaw. To see Satie guffawing was quite an experience. His whole face was just one big grin, from his large bald forehead to his goatee beard.

Later we saw him ever more rarely, on the few occasions when we came to Paris. But during the war we knew we could always find him in the bar on the rue d'Amsterdam where J.-K. Huysmans set des Esseintes's abortive journey – des Esseintes being determined to buy a ticket for England at the gare Saint-Lazare, but finding the atmosphere of this bar so British, and smelling of fish and strong beer, that he reckoned he'd achieved his aim and went back home. Satie was generally in the corner of the room where Alphonse Allais liked to sit. Satie's humour was every bit as sharp as his compatriot's, even in those fearful times filled with the sinister wailing of sirens and the noise of shells from the huge German guns.

Satie used to call Debussy 'my dear Claude', was immensely erudite, and had immersed himself in the works of Henri Cain, following the footsteps of that most evocative of writers in his walks through the historical treasure-trove that is Paris. Satie used to say: 'It's odd! The bars are full of people quite happy to offer you a drink. But none of them ever thinks of standing you a sandwich.'

René Lanser
'Notes et souvenirs – Erik Satie', *Matin d'Anvers*, 9 July 1925 (*AFS*)

GEORGE AURIOL

He was for years the friend and companion of Lord Cheminot. Everyone knows that for the English aristocracy the popular soup of the covered markets is a feast second to none. When His Lordship came to Paris, he took the precaution of adopting another name so as not to be pestered, calling himself Condamine de la Tour [sic].

One day our two friends were having a companionable lunch outside some café or other, when at the next table they saw some poor fellow and were struck by his air of depression. Condamine took the opportunity to set the hare running and enquired as to what had blighted and blackened the existence of this individual.

The stranger replied that he had no job, that all his efforts to find one had been in vain and that he was at the end of his tether.

'But,' said Erik, as though struck by divine inspiration, 'why don't you set yourself up as a doctor?'

'Doctor . . .' mumbled the stranger.

'Yes.'

'I don't think you can be a doctor just by willpower . . . You have to take exams, gain diplomas . . .'

'No, you don't. Diplomas aren't necessary. Indeed, they're a waste of time. The profession's open to everyone. It's the most liberal profession of all, and you make a damned good living!'

'You think so? . . .'

'I'm certain of it. And to prove it, as of now I hand my practice over to you.'

'Mine too,' added Condamine de la Tour.

'If that's true, I'll give it a go. Thank you for your good advice . . .'

And with a spring in his step the poor fellow went off, with Satie's 'bonjou! bonjou!' ringing in his ears.

In the cabarets around the same period (so long ago and yet so near) they used to serve, at the same time as the coffee, small graduated carafes containing a liquid generally known by the name 'cognac' – what we savages call firewater. These carafes were conical and had three compartments, each compartment representing a customer's normal portion. But Satie, with his hereditary cunning, had observed that the bottom compartment was a little larger than the others.

While his companion was sinking a beer, Satie had ordered a coffee and its complement. They were served; they weren't enough. He asked for an empty glass as well.

The bar owner, impressed by such refinement, brought them. Erik explained to him that he wanted to drink the bottom portion: he preferred it to the two others because it hadn't been contaminated by contact with the air.

'But, monsieur,' said the owner, 'you have to take it as it comes: if you want the bottom portion, drink the other two first!'

'Certainly not,' retorted Satie, accentuating the satanic acuity of his gaze with a slight shift of his pince-nez. 'Certainly not! I'm absolutely within my rights. The law even allows me, if I so wish, to drink the portion in the middle. If I don't do so, that's merely so as not to upset you.'

Then, having meticulously emptied the first two-thirds into the empty glass, he poured the rest into his coffee.

'And now', he concluded, 'let's smoke a nice pipe.'

The owner, beaten, took away the unwanted glass and went back behind his counter – without so much as a shrug of the shoulders.

George Auriol
'Erik Satie, the Velvet Gentleman', *ReM*, 5, March 1924, pp. 212–14

JEAN OBERLÉ

(1900–61)

Jean Oberlé was an artist, illustrator and caricaturist, born in Brest, who was well acquainted with Cocteau and his circle in the early 1920s. His wittily observed drawing, *Cocteau présente les Six à Erik Satie*, appeared originally in *Le crapouillot* and has been much reproduced since.

One evening, at the Boeuf sur le Toit, I left at the same time as Satie. I was going to the place de la Sorbonne and he to the boulevard Saint-Michel, to wait for the tram to Arcueil. It was a fine night, so we walked. When we reached the boulevard Saint-Michel, I suggested we have a beer outside the Café de Cluny.

'I accept, young man,' he said, 'but as I shall have to leave you abruptly when I see my tram, perhaps with no time to say goodnight, we'll say our goodbyes now, then it'll be done.'

He raised his bowler hat:

'Goodnight, my dear sir, it's been a great pleasure to get to know you.'

'Goodnight, *maître*,' I replied, somewhat disconcerted.

'And now,' said Satie, 'let's have that beer.'

We clinked our glasses and he told me any number of stories, each funnier than the last, when suddenly he saw, on its way from the place Saint-Michel, his tram for Arcueil. He leapt from his chair, jumped on board the tram and, from the platform, offered me a discreet gesture of farewell. I never saw him again, but I cannot hear that refined music of his without imagining him sitting outside the Café de Cluny, and our premature goodbyes.

Jean Oberlé
La vie d'artiste (Paris, Denoël, 1956), pp. 114–15 (*AFS*)

E. L. T. MESENS

(1903–71)

Édouard-Léon-Théodore Mesens was primarily an artist and a leading member (with Magritte and Witters) of the Belgian Surrealist movement. But he also studied music and wrote some songs around the time he first met Satie, which was in Brussels in 1921. When Mesens came to Paris shortly afterwards, Satie introduced him to Man Ray, Brancusi and others, and briefly gave him composition lessons. The lunch he treated him to must have been particularly welcome as Mesens at this time was even poorer than Satie. Mesens encountered problems with the Parisian Surrealists; André Breton was jealous of his collages and he was generally regarded with suspicion because of his passion for music. Needless to say, his association with Satie (who was pro-Dada and anti-Surrealist) did not help.

He was known to be poor and some people made out that he was stingy, but in fact he was extremely generous. One morning he arranged to meet me, as usual, outside a café and asked me to come with him to the Société des Auteurs. One of his works had been performed abroad and he had several hundred francs to collect. As we came out of the building, he said perkily: 'Now, I'm inviting you to have lunch in one of the best places in Paris, and it's something you'll remember!' It was indeed an unforgettable meal, and his boyish pleasure at doing me a good turn was plain to see.

E. L. T. Mesens
'Le souvenir d'Erik Satie', *ReM*, 214, June 1952, p. 150

JACQUES GUÉRIN
(b. 1902)

Jacques Guérin is one of the few people still alive who knew Satie well. Between 1922 and 1924 the Guérin family (including his artist brother Jean) dined regularly on Sundays with Édouard Dreyfus and his wife (formerly the singer Paulette Darty) at Luzarches. As Satie had known Paulette since the turn of the century, he was a frequent visitor there too. Jacques Guérin, being wealthy, has long been a bibliophile and patron of young artists, being the first to recognise the talents of the writer Jean Genet. He still lives in Luzarches, to the north of Paris.

My brother often saw Satie at lunch. They used to eat at Couteau's, which was a little restaurant in the rue d'Orléans. I was studying in Toulouse, so I wasn't very often in Paris, but each time I came back there for three or four days in the holidays I regularly had lunch with Satie in this little bistro, side by side – which was a great honour for me, to be next to this great man who was so modest, so friendly with a young whippersnapper who had no interest for him, since I couldn't even talk to him about music. But I used to listen to him, and he liked talking to young people – whether it was that he was more at ease talking to the young than dealing with society people who were impressed by him, or that he found pupils among them who were easier to persuade.

He didn't like rich food. I think he liked simple dishes. That's why for dessert he used to refuse things that were too rich – I don't think it was a question of being on a diet, that wouldn't fit in really with his love

1 Satie's birthplace in Honfleur. No. 88 rue Haute is the house with the plaque

2 The first *Prélude du Nazaréen*, 1892 (BN MS 10037(1),1)

3 Satie upsetting the Holy Grail and being haunted by the swan in *Lohengrin*, ?1891

4 The rue Cortot, Montmartre, *c*1900. No. 6 has a street lamp

5 The Alcazar d'été, *c*1903, with an advert for Paulette Darty

6 Satie's home in Arcueil (facing, at end of rue Cauchy). His room was the third window from the left on the second storey

7 The place de la Concorde, *c*1920

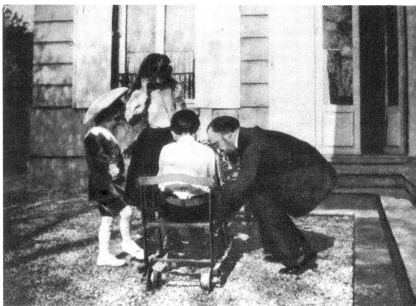

8 Satie in a suburban tavern, in his 'Velvet gentleman' outfit, 1895

9 Satie with his clay-pipe, 3 March 1898, by Augustin Grass-Mick. The inscription refers to Grass-Mick's moving house in 1897, assisted by Satie and Henri Pacory

10 Satie entertaining Sheridan Russell, Dolly Bardac and Tosti Russell (seated) in the garden of Debussy's house, 1906

LUDIONS

SPLEEN

11 Debussy and Satie, 1910, in Debussy's salon at 80 avenue du Bois de Boulogne

12 Calligraphic letter to Jean Lemoine, 1920, showing Satie using the twelve-
and twenty-four-hour clocks

13 Manuscript of 'Spleen', the second of the *Ludions* songs, 1923

14 Satie and Valentine Gross, photographed by Jean Cocteau at his home in 1916

15 Satie in his first smoking-jacket, a gift from M. Henriquet, 1922

16 Satie photographed by Brancusi in his studio, 1922

17 Satie on the balcony of Mme Guérin's house at 8 avenue du Parc Monceau, *c*1923. This is the only known photograph of Satie at work

18 Satie outside the Théâtre de la Cigale, in front of a poster advertising Comte Etienne de Beaumont's 'Soirée de Paris' season in June 1924 (including the première of *Mercure* on the 15th)

19 René Clair, Satie and Picabia on the roof of the Théâtre des Champs-Elysées during the filming of *Entr'acte*, June 1924

20 Satie on his death bed, by Robert Caby, July 1925

of apéritifs! – no, he would regularly ask for his 'apple-in-the-air'.* It was one of his little ways, his little idiosyncrasies.

Jacques Guérin
In conversation with Robert Orledge, Luzarches, 17 September 1993

PIERRE DE MASSOT

Over a period of some years, I saw Satie every evening. He used to come and collect us, Robbie and me, around 7 o'clock from the rue des Petits-Champs where we then lived, and we used to go and have dinner together. Sometimes it was in the Grill-Room Médicis, sometimes at the Nègre de Toulouse on the boulevard du Montparnasse, at Le Pied du Mouton over near the gare d'Austerlitz, or at Le Stryx in the rue Huyghens. The meal would go on late into the evening, because he was a gourmet of meticulous tastes, and afterwards we'd find our way to the café-tabac on the place Denfert-Rochereau (now a site of historic interest for music historians, as this was where he composed *Parade*). Here [at Le Lion] we'd go on with a discussion which had never really been interrupted, sitting behind glasses of beer and calvados which we'd got into the habit of drinking alternately.

When it was nearly time for the last train to Arcueil, we'd go with him as far as the gare de Sceaux. But as often as not he'd miss this last train and set off on foot, his umbrella under his arm, his bowler hat pulled down over his eyes and his hands in their grey cotton gloves crossed over his stomach.

Any reminiscence of Satie has to say something about his often incisive humour. He was a sceptic *par excellence* and he turned on the world a clear, blue, pitiless eye. No failing, no absurdity, no folly escaped him. And he had an absolutely individual way of making fun of people and things, a mixture of benevolence and cruelty. This comes out most clearly in the articles he published from time to time in avant-garde journals; *Mémoires d'un amnésique* and *Cahiers d'un mammifère* which many of us enjoyed enormously. André Suarès once said: 'Not to be taken in: that's the cardinal rule for wit.' Satie was never taken in by anything or anybody, and still less by himself.

*'Pomme-en-l'air', as opposed to 'pomme de terre' (potato).

I remember the day we were guests of the painter Francis Picabia in the little village of Tremblay-sur-Mauldre, near Montfort-l'Amaury. Satie was writing the score of *Relâche*, the Picabia ballet which was to provoke such a scandal at its première at the Théâtre des Champs-Élysées. Before lunch, Satie took my wife and myself off to have the ritual pernod at a bistro, and after that we strolled through the village and came to the monument dedicated to the fallen in the First World War. Satie leant down, read the names engraved on the stone, and then said, in an inimitably serious voice: 'What! Are those all the dead they can muster? . . .'

Pierre de Massot
'Quelques propos et souvenirs sur Erik Satie', *ReM*, 214, June 1952, pp. 125–7

HENRI-PIERRE ROCHÉ
(1879–1959)

Henri-Pierre Roché was a novelist whose best-known work is *Jules et Jim* (subsequently immortalised in François Truffaut's film of 1961). From his recently published diaries for 1920–21, he seems to have been something of a sexual athlete, and he certainly knew everyone who mattered in artistic Paris in the early 1920s, from Brancusi to the rich American patroness Sybil Harris. His diaries include references to private dinners as well as to those in restaurants, and all the interesting entries relating to Satie in 1920–22 are included together here.

1920

Saturday 30 October: Colonne Concert – performance of Milhaud's *Protée*. – Satie, Auric, Cocteau, the whole group, very serious, except Satie, on sparkling form, who shouts: 'Down with the drunks!' – Protests, uproar.

I leave with Satie – long talk at a nearby café. He takes me to dinner in the place de l'Observatoire. – Talk about Socrates till midnight.

Monday – All Saints' Day – 1 November: Satie midday on the boulevard

Arago* – splendid lunch at the 1000 Colonnes. – He takes me to the dancer Caryathis's studio to see the dance rehearsals for January† with Cocteau – an interesting and attractive spectacle – Cocteau a great talent, a genius as producer and rehearser – Auric and Milhaud arrive – tea on the ground floor – the carpet, the ices – the dances – Cocteau's white visor with a single eye, invented by him on the spot. Caryathis working flat out.

Tuesday 21 December: Picasso evening at the Ballets Russes – *Pulcinella* – *The Three-Cornered Hat* – *Parade* – superb – the curtain for *Parade* – Satie on the organ to play the two [pedal] notes – his triumph – Cocteau too – bravo! The scenery – the horse – etc.

1921

Friday 7 January: At 7 in the evening Satie comes to collect me and we go to dinner with Mme Harris – just the three of us – a fine American dinner, Louise, the cook, surpassed herself: lobster Newburg, chicken Maryland, ice cream with hot hazelnut sauce, which Satie partakes of after considerable hesitation – long conversation in the dining-room in front of the fire – Satie looks happy, he tells good stories, about his life, about himself, about Franck (César) – the other two have a good chat – I gaze at the fire. – Very handsome and successful brick surround. – They discuss music.
    Erik and I on foot as far as Irène Lagut's,‡ not there.
    Home at midnight.

Friday 1 July: Lunch with Bigey§ and Satie at Prunier's. She too restless, too enthusiastic or critical about superficial things. She and Satie: two parallel monologues. – But the three of us get on well together: crayfish, clams. – We take her to the gare du Nord. – Then beers with Satie.

Monday 18 July: Midday – Louise Norton on boulevard Arago describes to me her idea for the scenario of a ballet on *Alice in Wonderland* by Satie – a bit complicated.

---

*Roché lived in an apartment at 99 boulevard Arago, with his mother.
†Of Satie's 'fantaisie sérieuse', *La belle excentrique*, first performed *chez* Pierre Bertin on 8 January 1921.
‡The stage designer and one-time mistress of Picasso, born in 1893.
§Alias Sybil Harris, also referred to as Big Eyes, Sylla etc.

12.30 the floor below Derain's studio – business talk with Quinn – we go up, the portrait's finished, good, awkward.

Lunch for all with Satie in the Grill-Room of the place Médicis – my plans for lectures in America on our modern painting begin to take shape – outside Le Balzar with Satie we read and rework the idea for an *Alice in Wonderland* ballet. – Home, quiet evening, work.

Tuesday 9 August: I work on *Alice in Wonderland* for Satie. It bores me, I give up on it: decidedly not for me.

Saturday 19 November: Dinner at Mme Harris's: Yvonne, Brancusi, Satie, Auric, Serge [Ferat] – it's gay and friendly – a certain rivalry between Brancusi and Satie – all the hats and theatrical wigs Mrs Harris bought at the Hôtel Drouot yesterday. – She tries them on: Russian, Spanish, bishops' mitres, etc.

1922

Wednesday 18 January: Dinner at Bigey's: Satie, Auric, Cocteau, Booth. Good talk. Later arrivals Marcelle Meyer, [Pierre] Bertin, [Léopold] Survage, Germaine [Everling], Serge [Ferat]. We dance. Even Satie, who provides an innocent, brilliant caricature of modern dances. Marcelle plays, everything well.

Saturday 28 January: Dinner at Brancusi's, splendid. His famous purée of cold beans with vinegar and garlic. His grilled steak. He's everywhere, cooking, serving, doing everything. There – Syb, Booth, Satie, Serge. There are two violins. Brancusi, Satie and Booth take turns to play duets and tease each other. Our jaws are aching with laughter. A galop for the larger members. Brancusi's agility. Nice people and great men: he and Satie.

Henri-Pierre Roché
Carnets 1920–21 (Marseille, André Dimanche, 1990). 1922 entries supplied by *AFS*

VI

With friends and other artists

One of Satie's many virtues was that he showed no trace of snobbery or condescension in a strictly stratified social world where both were very much in evidence. Consequently, he got on equally well with people in all walks of life. He was fastidiously polite to those socially above him, although he delighted in flaunting his shocking (and genuine) Bolshevist sympathies in Parisian high society. In fact, his world revolved entirely around Paris. He was really much more interested in talking about the other arts than he was about music and he had a broad knowledge of painting and sculpture in particular. His range of artistic friends was extremely wide, though only a few bothered to recall their impressions of the man who understood Cubism better than the Cubists themselves, and who owed his 'return to classical simplicity with a modern sensibility to his "Cubist" friends'. In overall terms, Cocteau and Picasso had the greatest influence on the direction of Satie's career, but his closest friends among the 'greats' were Brancusi, Derain and Milhaud.

PAULETTE DARTY
(1869–1939)

Paulette Darty, the 'Queen of the Slow Waltz', was a music-hall star for whom Satie wrote several songs around the turn of the century, including *Je te veux* and *La diva de l'"Empire'*. She married the wealthy lace manufacturer Édouard Dreyfus in 1910, living a life of bourgeois luxury at his country estate called Thimécourt (near Luzarches) until the mid-1920s. Satie often visited her there, though the souvenir below describes their first meeting. It probably dates from 1902, shortly before *Je te veux* was published by Bellon Ponscarme in Paris.

95

Usually I received composers in the morning when they came to present their new tunes to me. That morning, my secretary admitted Erik Satie, whose name was then completely unknown to me. He was accompanied by M. [Jean] Bellon, a music publisher, who had an attractive voice. That morning I was in my bath. I heard the now-famous tune of *Je te veux* that M. Bellon was singing, which had such a special charm and such an attractive quality about it. I quickly got out of my bath to express my enchantment personally. He sat down again at the piano and I sang *Je te veux* for the first time.

Since then I have sung these waltz-songs (*Je te veux*, *Tendrement*, and the delightful *La diva de l'"Empire'*) everywhere with the greatest success, and Satie has never deserted me. No one could be bored when Satie came to the house for a family meal. What an unforgettable man! He always turned up trumps!

Paulette Darty
'Souvenirs sur Erik Satie', in the collection of the late Robert Caby

BLAISE CENDRARS

Q: When and how did you get to know Erik Satie?
BC: I met Satie in 1916 at the house of the widow of a friend who had just been killed at Verdun, on the first day of the battle. Every Friday morning this young lady used to be sent a basket of fish from Marseilles, her home town, and on the Friday evening she used to eat bouillabaisse with Satie, who presided over the meal, and a young musician called Georges Auric, whom I took at the time to be just a young pianist. He turned out later to be a composer. This excellent young man, who read a lot, always brought a knapsack stuffed full of rabbits, and we all used to spend Friday evenings talking of this and that.
Q: Satie was a curious character, wasn't he?
BC: Yes, but he was above all good company, at table. He *adored* bouillabaisse, and used to tell lots of silly stories in his own inimitable vein. He talked a bit like a parrot, with his hand always over his mouth, stroking his nose and fiddling with his pince-nez, and the tales he told were often, well, pretty far-fetched.
Q: Satie wrote some waltzes to be sung by the turn-of-the-century diva Paulette Darty. Did you know her?

BC: Yes, I saw her fairly often, but not at the young lady's where we had the bouillabaisse. It was at the house of a great lady, extremely rich, who was a great friend of Paulette Darty's and one day invited Satie just to please her. They hadn't seen each other for some twenty years, they'd lost touch. Satie was quite overcome with emotion. He sat down at the piano and played the two waltzes – as well as the *valse chaloupée* and a song whose name I've forgotten – which he'd written twenty or thirty years before, for Paulette Darty. She was a very nice woman, a little on the heavy side by the time I knew her, decidedly mature and given to the bottle, but she had a wonderful laugh, extraordinarily young-sounding. She sang and then Satie took her on his knee and they played a piano duet which, I suppose, they must have improvised.

Interview with Blaise Cendrars
Broadcast on French Radio on 3 July 1950; published in *Cahiers Blaise Cendrars*, No. 3 (Neuchâtel, Éditions de la Baconnière, 1989), pp. 101–2 (*AFS*)

HÉLÈNE JOURDAN-MORHANGE
(1892–1961)

> Hélène Jourdan-Morhange was a professional violinist who specialised in quartet-playing as well as solo work. Satie started writing a piece called *L'embarquement pour Cythère* for her in March 1917, possibly as a companion piece to his *Choses vues à droite et à gauche* of 1914, but never completed it. She was married to the artist Luc-Albert Moreau, and was also a close friend of Ravel.

It was at the first performance of Debussy's *La mer*.* One of the movements is entitled 'From dawn to midday on the sea', and Satie went one better than the rest of Debussy's admirers, with their ardent adjectives, exclaiming: 'Ah, my dear friend, there's one particular moment between half past ten and a quarter to eleven that I found stunning!'

Hélène Jourdan-Morhange
Ravel et nous (Geneva, Éditions du Milieu du Monde, 1945), pp. 95–6

*At the Concerts Lamoureux on 15 October 1905, when the conductor was Camille Chevillard.

LOUIS LALOY

(1874–1944)

Louis Laloy was a French musicologist, critic and scholar. With Jean Marnold, he founded the *Mercure musical* in 1905 and he became secretary-general of the Paris Opéra in 1914. Laloy was an immensely erudite man: a staunch defender of French contemporary music and a close friend of both Debussy and Ravel. Because Satie hated all music critics (and perhaps because he was jealous of Laloy's close friendship with Debussy), he often attacked Laloy in the press after Debussy's death in 1918. His enmity reached a head early in 1924 when Laloy, who was in charge of producing the programme for Diaghilev's Monte Carlo season of operas and ballets, failed to mention Satie's name once, even as the author of the new linking recitatives for Gounod's opera *Le médecin malgré lui*.

Just before the war Debussy had introduced me to Satie, and we sometimes met at his table, where we exchanged ambiguous compliments and oblique looks which, I think, Debussy found amusing. Between Satie and himself there existed a turbulent but indissoluble friendship. Or rather, it was one of those family hatreds which are exacerbated by the repeated shock of incompatible faults, but without destroying the sympathy the two sides feel for each other, which is due to a community of origin. It was like seeing two brothers, placed by the events of their lives in very different conditions, one rich and the other poor; the first welcoming, but proud of his superiority and ready to make it felt, the other unhappy beneath his jester's mask, paying his share by means of jokes to entertain his host, hiding his humiliation; each continually on watch against the other, without being able to stop themselves loving the other dearly. A musical brotherhood, yet a rivalry of musicians.

Debussy was not a Christian, any more than Satie was. The only difference was that he never hid his pride. What is more, during the war years when Satie saw the first glimmerings of fame, Debussy was depressed at the state of the world, consumed by a disease that nothing could arrest, absorbed in bitter thoughts and less capable than he had ever been of any kindly gesture or word of flattery. When concerts were organised consisting entirely of works by Satie, Debussy was unable to go; confined to his room, he found it hard to believe the news of their success, and thought it must be the work of a cabal, or perhaps a practical joke. Satie got to know of his opinion and was infuriated, to the point of writing a letter that was little short of insulting.* Debussy read it lying in bed, where he had been for some weeks, and where he was shortly to die. His trembling hands crumpled the letter on the sheet, then tore it up. 'Forgive me!' he murmured, like a child who's going to be scolded, with tears in his eyes. I was angry with Satie for behaving so cruelly – more cruelly, no doubt, than he realised. It was only after his death, seven years later, that I forgave him, when I learnt from his friends how much he too had suffered, praised by others but refused the approbation he valued the most in the whole world. And that, through the fault of both of them, was the pitiful end of their friendship.

Louis Laloy
La musique retrouvée (Paris, Librairie Plon, 1928), pp. 258–9, 261–2

VLADIMIR GOLSCHMANN

(1893–1972)

Vladimir Golschmann was born in Paris of Russian descent and, like Satie, studied counterpoint at the Schola Cantorum (as well as composition). From the age of 10 he had wanted to be a conductor and it was only with Satie's help, and that of his rich pupil Albert Verley, that he achieved his goal. He conducted for Diaghilev's Ballets Russes and made his American début with the Ballets Suédois in 1923. Later, in 1931, he moved permanently to the States as conductor of

---

*Satie actually fell out with Debussy over his derogatory opinions of the ballet *Parade* in 1917, when Satie sent the following curt note via Emma Debussy on 8 March: 'Decidedly, it will be preferable if henceforth the "Precursor" [Satie] stays at home, far away. P.S. Painful teasing – and again and again too! Quite unbearable, anyhow.' This is hardly insulting and neither does it date from 1918, as Laloy imagined. In fact, Debussy did attend the première of *Parade* on 18 May and went again on 25 May, though he never reviewed it in the press and did not modify his opinion of it (as far as we know). Furthermore, Satie did write to Debussy to try to heal the rift between them shortly before his death, as we know from a letter to Henry Prunières of 3 April 1918. It was this letter of reconciliation that must have caused Debussy to murmur, 'Forgive me!'

the St Louis Symphony Orchestra, becoming an American
citizen in 1947.

We [Auric and I] both had met Erik Satie, whose music we knew well,
and I was more than happy when the great man came to our home where
he and Auric enjoyed the traditional *thé à la Russe* – it was great fun to
discuss music around the shiny samovar, drinking tea, eating a choice of
Russian delicacies.

Auric and I played all that Satie had written for the piano; one of us
would play with him what he composed for four hands. Once, after we
had played *Morceaux en forme de poire*, I asked our hero, whom we called
mon bon Maître, why he gave such a title, *Pieces in the shape of pear*, to
this ravishing music. He answered with a twinkle in his eyes: 'You do
know that I visit Debussy quite often; I admire him immensely and he
seems to think much of whatever talent I may have. Nevertheless, one
day when I showed him a piece I had just composed, he remarked, "Satie,
you never had two greater admirers than Ravel and myself; many of your
early works had a great influence on our writing. Your *Preludes* [sic] *de
La porte héroïque du ciel* were to us a revelation, so original, so different
from that Wagnerian atmosphere which has surrounded us in late years;
I liked so much your *Gymnopédies* that I orchestrated two of them. You
have some kind of genius, or you have genius, period. Now, as a true
friend may I warn you that from time to time there is in your art a certain
lack of form." All I did,' added Satie, 'was to write *Morceaux en forme
de poire*. I brought them to Debussy who asked, "Why such a title?"
Why? simply, *mon cher ami*, because you cannot criticize my *Pieces* in the
shape of a pear. If they are *en forme de poire* they cannot be shapeless.'

Vladimir Golschmann
'Golschmann Remembers Erik Satie', *High Fidelity/Musical America*, 22, August
1972, p. 11

GASTON PICARD

(1892–1965)

Gaston Picard was a prolific novelist and literary critic. In
his youth, he was also the visionary co-editor (with Roland-
Manuel) of the short-lived monthly revue *L'oeil de veau* which

appeared in 1912. Besides publishing Satie's first piece of
ironical journalism, his 'Observations d'un imbécile (moi)',
the revue also brought him into contact with Le Groupe
Fantaisiste, young poets who admired the work of Toulet and
Laforgue. They met at the Oasis café, near the Odéon, and
included Francis Carco and Tristan Klingsor; their light,
sceptical poetry had some influence on Apollinaire and his
circle.

The press has, in reporting the premature death of Erik Satie, quite
rightly made mention of the École d'Arcueil and the Groupe des Six. In
a more modest vein, I should like to recall the collection of young people
who gathered round Satie before the war. As for a name to give them, I
can't make up my mind between the Oasis and the Oeil de Veau. The
story begins in 1912.

The Oasis was, at that time, the inner salon of a café near the Odéon,
and the *Oeil de veau* was the review founded by that excellent composer
and critic M. Roland-Manuel and myself. The review grew from the
friendships made in the café, where music and poetry were enthusiastically
espoused, and you could find the same names on the tables, where simple
pots of tea were served alongside sweet-smelling cigarettes, and in the list
of contributors to the *Oeil de veau*. It was advertised as an 'encyclopedic
review for people of intelligence'.

The same names could be found adorning M. Roland-Manuel's charming dining-room one summer evening, when he had invited, as well as
Satie and some others of our own age, another of our seniors, Canudo,
though he was younger than Satie. The menu combined the desire to
provide a good meal with some strange literary and musical allusions. In
Satie's honour we had insisted, in the naughty but affectionate way of the
young, on including, for dessert, the inevitable 'morceaux en forme de
poire'.

Even though Satie was getting on for 60 [in fact, 46], and sported an
old man's beard, his smile and his laugh belonged to a young man. You
only had to hear him, as he left the dinner, recounting his set-tos with
Willy and his meetings with Péladan, and inventing any number of
outrageous tales, although in the *Oeil de veau* Satie specifically said that
he didn't like jokes 'nor anything approaching them'.

Gaston Picard
'L'écrivain chez Erik Satie', *Le Figaro*, 11 July 1925, p. 2

RICARDO VIÑES

(1875–1943)

Ricardo Viñes was a Catalan pianist who entered the Paris Conservatoire in 1889 as a pupil of Bériot. His technique and mastery of pedalling were exceptional, and in the first three decades of the present century he became the foremost champion of modern French piano music, giving countless first performances of the works of his friends Debussy, Ravel and Satie. In 1913–14, for instance, he premièred Satie's *Véritables préludes flasques (pour un chien)*, his *Descriptions automatiques*, his *Croquis et agaceries d'un gros bonhomme en bois* and his *Chapitres tournés en tous sens*, and in thanks Satie dedicated several pieces to him and his family.

In contrast with Ravel, who looked like a jockey, the silhouette of Erik Satie appeared to offer a hymn to the goddess Longitude, with his elongated arms and legs, his monstrous hands and feet, his giant body and his pointed head, like a meditating kid-goat, which was extended down on to his chest by a robust, pointed beard and emphasised at the top by an anachronistic, monumental and overpowering top hat which seemed to ascend to the stars, as though dissociating itself from the things of this vile world. And when, some time later, Satie decided to democratise his dress, to repudiate the frock-coat in favour of a simple jacket and to substitute for the top hat a derby [sic] of less vaulting ambition, this did not affect in the slightest his ironical gaze and sly solemnity, aided by the thick lenses that hid the malicious twinkle in his screwed-up eyes.

The combination of these disconcerting and paradoxical features explains why those who did not know him or only ran into him briefly took him, on seeing his imposing appearance, either for a schoolmaster, or for a priest of some new sect, or for a funeral director, or, finally, for a bailiff charged with impounding the furniture of some recalcitrant tenant and extracting from him the past quarter's rent.

Ricardo Viñes
Tres aristocratas del sonido (Buenos Aires, 1934), pp. 5–6

PIERRE BERTIN

(1895–1984)

Pierre Bertin was a well-known actor, singer, playwright and theatre director, who also wrote books on travel and theatrical history. He was a close friend of Satie's from the time his career began to take off in 1912. They met through the young composer Roland-Manuel, and Bertin later directed the Max Jacob play *Ruffian toujours, truand jamais* that was interspersed with Satie's 'musique d'ameublement' in 1920, as well as the first public performance of Satie's Surrealist play *Le piège de Méduse* at the Théâtre Michel in May 1921. Bertin married the brilliant pianist Marcelle Meyer, a pupil of Ricardo Viñes. Satie regarded her as one of the best interpreters of his music.

I got to know him in 1912, in the large apartment which Roland then shared with his parents on the rue de Chazelles, although his mother had thoughtfully let him have a little room of his own in it as well, which he decorated according to his own tastes. His mother used to invite all his friends to eat with them, and was delighted when we emerged from the darkness of his own quarters into the drawing-room where there was a grand piano and enough space to indulge in some crazy play-acting. So it was that one day I found myself in the middle of rehearsals for an oriental ballet (in imitation of *Shéhérazade*, which had just made a hit) in which our friends shared roles in a farce made up by Roland to the music of the Maître's *Morceaux en forme de poire*.

That was the first time I saw Satie, looking the same as he did thereafter, and forever: like an old piano teacher, smiling behind a quivering beard, wearing pince-nez through which his eyes sparkled with supreme intelligence. That day the smile was slightly cool, because there was no pianist to join him in playing his piano duets; I offered (or rather, Roland forced me to) and I was playing a number of wrong notes. Has any composer ever been forgiving about that? But in fact the goings-on in the drawing-room didn't interest Satie in the least. It was always like that. Whether it was *Parade*, or *Mercure*, or any other stagey activity invented to go with his music, Satie never paid the slightest attention to the work taking place in the theatre. Only sounds interested him – his own sounds. I can't count the number of times I've seen him at a concert, when it happened they were playing one of his works, leave the hall as soon as his piece was over, or walk up and down the corridors outside until it was his turn. I think he may have made an exception for Chabrier.

To come back to the Roland-Manuel ballet, I finished sight-reading the *Morceaux* and Satie was kind enough to smile at me and stammer: 'There were just one or two things . . .', and then he gave a guffaw. He was in a good mood. At that time he was not the Satie of *Parade*, of Cocteau. He was still a humble 'troubadour', the talented composer of the *Sarabande* [*s*] of 1887 and the *Gymnopédies*, the friend of Debussy (who had just orchestrated one of his pieces), the friend of Ricardo Viñes, who at that time was the only person in Paris to play his music, the newly minted student of the Schola Cantorum where he'd decided to go to polish his technique (and where he'd met Roland), and the mysterious denizen of Arcueil. What was he living on? We shall never know.

He and I became friends. Questions of age didn't figure with him and when, some years later, I married Marcelle Meyer, he became a frequent guest of ours. We were living then on the boulevard de Montparnasse, and this stopping-off point was handy for him when he missed the Arcueil train at the Lion de Belfort station. He would dine and have lunch with us frequently, and he would also enjoy some good cooking, because he was a gourmet (he taught us how to cook cutlets, showing us how to make a crust to keep the blood inside the meat, which he relished). He also found a good piano and a splendid pianist who played his works as he liked them to be played, with that feeling of sonorous weight you get from a well-struck note, giving off harmonics which seem to be emanations from the musical thought – an art which Marcelle had learnt from Viñes. But Viñes played only some of Satie's pieces. Marcelle used to play them all, and was equally good at sight-reading them. Satie christened her 'Dadame', a grand title of honour which stayed with her.

Pierre Bertin
'Comment j'ai connu Erik Satie', *ReM*, 214, June 1952, pp.73–5

IGOR STRAVINSKY
(1882–1971)

Satie regarded Stravinsky with a mixture of admiration and awe and first met him at a luncheon *chez* Debussy in June 1911, shortly after the première of *Petrushka*. Stravinsky added the 'ice-cream wagon Valse' to his Three Easy Pieces for piano duet in 1915 'in homage to Erik Satie', trying to 'portray something of his *esprit*' in it. In return, Satie dedicated his song *Le chapelier* to Stravinsky in 1916. The first variation in the central movement of Stravinsky's Sonata for two pianos (1943–4) is pure Satie too. Satie wrote two adulatory articles on Stravinsky in 1922 and followed all his premières with consuming interest, but he was never disconcerted by his ascendant star, as Debussy was in his final years. Stravinsky, too, placed Satie in the forefront of modern music, exclaiming after a performance of *Socrate* in 1919: 'There is Bizet, Chabrier, and Satie'.

He was certainly the oddest person I have ever known, but the most rare and consistently witty person, too. I had a great liking for him and he appreciated my friendliness, I think, and liked me in return. With his pince-nez, umbrella and galoshes [sic] he looked like a perfect schoolmaster, but he looked just as much like one without these accoutrements. He spoke very softly, hardly opening his mouth, but he delivered each word in an inimitable, precise way. His handwriting recalls his speech to me: it is exact, drawn. His manuscripts were like him also, which is to say as the French say *'fin'*. No one ever saw him wash – he had a horror of soap. Instead he was forever rubbing his fingers with pumice. He was always very poor, poor by conviction, I think. He lived in a poor section and his neighbours seemed to appreciate his coming among them: he was greatly respected by them. His apartment was also very poor. It did not have a bed but only a hammock [sic]. In winter Satie would fill bottles with hot water and put them flat in a row underneath his hammock. It looked like some strange kind of marimba. I remember once when someone had promised him some money he replied: 'Monsieur, what you have said did not fall on a deaf ear.'

His sarcasm depended on classic French usages. The first time I heard

Socrate, at a séance where he played it for a few of us,* he turned round at the end and said in perfect bourgeoisie: 'Voilà, messieurs, dames.'

I met him in 1913, I believe, at any rate I photographed him with Debussy in that year. Debussy introduced him to me and Debussy 'protected' and remained a good friend to him. In those early years he played many of his compositions for me at the piano . . . The music of Socrates' death is touching and dignifying in a unique way. Satie's own sudden and mysterious death – shortly after *Socrate* – touched me too. He had been turned towards religion near the end of his life and he started going to Communion. I saw him after church one morning and he said in that extraordinary manner of his: 'Alors, j'ai un peu communiqué ce matin.'

Igor Stravinsky and Robert Craft
Conversations with Igor Stravinsky (London, Faber & Faber, 1959/ repr. 1979), pp. 67–8

SYLVIA BEACH
(1887–1962)

Sylvia Beach was born in Baltimore and her family moved to Paris when she was 14. In 1919 she opened her American bookshop, *Shakespeare and Company*, at 8 rue Dupuytren (near the Odéon), and among her first customers were the composer George Antheil and the poet Ezra Pound. Gertrude Stein and Alice B. Toklas were among the first subscribers to her lending library, which soon gained a reputation in avant-garde literary circles. In 1922 she made literary history by publishing James Joyce's *Ulysses*, which was then banned in every English-speaking country in the world. Satie, who loved bookshops, often visited *Shakespeare and Company*, as well as the nearby bookshop of her friend Adrienne Monnier. Here, performances of his works often occurred after the war and Léon-Paul Fargue's group of 'Potassons' frequently met ('Potasson' being the name of Fargue's fat cat).

A great friend of mine was Satie. Satie, perhaps because of English blood on one side of his family, seemed to like *Shakespeare and Company*. He

---

*Probably at Adrienne Monnier's bookshop, *La Maison des Amis des Livres* (7 rue de l'Odéon), on 21 March 1919, when Satie accompanied the soprano Suzanne Balguerie.

called me 'Mees', the only English word he knew, I imagine, and turned up regularly, always carrying an umbrella, rain or shine; no one had ever seen him without one. It was probably a wise precaution for somebody who came on a trolley-bus from distant suburbs of Paris intending to stay in town all day.

Seeing me writing something, Satie asked me if I wrote. I said yes, business letters. He said that was the best kind of writing: good business writing had a definite meaning; you had something to say and you said it. That was the way I wrote, I told him.

Satie and Adrienne were good friends. His *Socrate* was heard for the first time in her bookshop. Fargue and Satie were cronies, then had a terrible falling out, I believe over an unfortunate incident in society circles where the composer and the poet shared popularity. At a certain salon [that of the Princesse de Polignac], the master of ceremonies announced songs by Erik Satie but quite forgot to mention that the poems he had set to music were by Fargue [the *Ludions*]. It was no doubt unintentional, and certainly it was not the fault of Satie, but Fargue was furious. As usual, in Fargue's feuds, he spent a good deal of time and took a lot of trouble to write the most dreadfully insulting things he could think of in daily letters to Satie. Not satisfied with mailing them in Paris, he would go all the way to Arcueil-Cachan, where Satie lived, to slip another insulting note under his door. Even the final one, too outrageous to repeat, failed to get anything but a laugh from Satie, a mild, philosophical-minded man, the composer, after all, of *Socrate*; and I think that was the last shot fired.

Sylvia Beach
Shakespeare and Company (London, Faber & Faber, 1960), pp. 159–60

VALENTINE HUGO

Satie was generally cheerful, very amusing. His jokes weren't forced, sometimes kind, sometimes extremely sharp. Even when he was in the depths of poverty, he couldn't resist making fun of his problems and of the tiresome stupidity of material difficulties.

He was very sensitive. If there was anything he judged to be an insult, or a want of affection, or an unfair piece of gossip, he'd protest in the strongest, most violent language. When he was angry, he either closed up, looking offended, or else burst out into brutal sarcasm. When he was happy, pleased by some stroke of good luck or moved by some act of kindness (which he used to appreciate at double strength – sometimes more than was called for), then he became really touching, almost overwhelming in his happiness.

Certain wounds inflicted on him made him very miserable; especially when they came from people he loved or admired in his own way. Despite his bouts of rage, you could see quite clearly how much he was hurt.

There was an Alfred Jarry side to Satie's nature, but less bland, less hail-fellow-well-met, less expansive than with Jarry – drier, more incisive, angrier. More explosive and aggressive.

Satie was ageless, neither old nor young. When people call him 'an old man', that's wrong, he didn't look like an old man any more than he did like a young one. When I saw Satie, I never asked myself what he looked like. He was Satie, and unlike anybody else. Now we're told: 'He looked like this, or like that.' Sometimes I don't understand, or don't agree with the portrait that's drawn of him.

You could say, I suppose, he had the serious, ponderous look of a provincial schoolmaster: serious, because of the pince-nez fixed firmly on his nose and the bowler hat tilted slightly forwards; ponderous, because his movements were rather slow. He took small steps, with his rolled-up umbrella on his arm. He didn't gesticulate except when he was cheerful or angry.

There was nothing remarkable about his voice. It was well-pitched, rather gentle and slow in serious conversations. When he told jokes, it became lower, more theatrical and singing; and when he wasn't happy, it was high and acerbic.

He used to laugh either secretly or noisily, depending on what provoked it. It was his eyes that laughed – his eyes which were hard to see through the reflection in his glasses. One day I wanted to take a photograph of him with Georges Auric and Jean Hugo, on the balcony of the Palais Royal where we were living, and I asked him to remove his pince-nez. He took them off without any protest, which astonished me mightily, although I didn't say anything. You never had to decipher any of Satie's spontaneous words or gestures. The look in his eyes was clear and tender at the same time. The absence of his pince-nez made him look gentle.

Satie's face was regular, with not much colour in it. His slim, intelligent hands were always clean and, if he thought they weren't, he'd go and wash them as soon as he arrived. He'd wipe a wet flannel over his face and brush his hands vigorously with water, without soap. He hated soap.

His clothes were often 'sorry-looking', as he called them, but clean and proper, and that overcoat which has been described as 'squalid' was not elegant – it was more of a poor greatcoat – but it wasn't 'squalid', either visually or odoriferously. And I don't imagine he had a special one just to come and see us.

Satie was extremely good friends with the sculptor Brancusi, who told me that Satie called him 'Socrates' brother'. In fact, I feel they were both characters out of Plato's *Symposium*. Jarry, Satie and Brancusi died, like Socrates, calm, well-ordered deaths.

Valentine Hugo
'Notes pour un portrait de Satie', unpublished MS, 1958. Catalogue of Hôtel Drouot, 10 December 1986

MAN RAY
(1890–1976)

Man Ray (real name Emmanuel Radenski) was born in America and first came to Paris in July 1921, shortly after his friend, the avant-garde artist Marcel Duchamp. He soon became a leading participant in the Dada movement and, like Duchamp, he painted and produced 'ready-made' sculptures, though his main claim to fame lies in his superb photography. On 3 December 1921, Ray mounted his first Paris exhibition at the Galerie Six where, not knowing a word of French, he was rescued by Satie, who then proceeded to help him make his first 'ready-made'. The two subsequently became firm friends and Man Ray helped Brancusi with his own first efforts in photography as well as appearing in René Clair's film *Entr'acte*, for which Satie wrote his final revolutionary score in 1924.

A strange voluble little man in his fifties came over to me and led me to one of my paintings. Strange, because he seemed out of place in this gathering of younger men. With a little white beard, an old-fashioned pince-nez, black bowler hat, black overcoat and umbrella, he looked like an undertaker or an employee of some conservative bank. I was tired with the preparations of the opening, the gallery had no heat, I shivered and said in English that I was cold. He replied in English, took my arm, and led me out of the gallery to a corner café, where he ordered hot grogs. Introducing himself as Erik Satie, he relapsed into French, which I informed him I did not understand. With a twinkle in his eye he said it did not matter. We had a couple of additional grogs; I began to feel warm and lightheaded. Leaving the café, we passed a shop where various household utensils were spread out in front. I picked up a flat-iron, the kind used on coal stoves, asked Satie to come inside with me, where, with his help, I acquired a box of tacks and a tube of glue. Back at the gallery I glued a row of tacks to the smooth surface of the iron, titled it 'The Gift,' and added it to the exhibition. This was my first Dada object in France.

Man Ray
Self Portrait (London, André Deutsch, 1963), p. 115

JACQUES GUÉRIN

It's Sunday and, as always when it's fine, we're going with my parents to spend the day at Luzarches, with the Dreyfuses.

Their charming house is called, impressively, 'Château de Thimécourt'. Built in eighteenth-century style, with a well laid-out park, raked paths and a stream winding its way between the lawns, it houses birds, ducks and a large Pyrenean dog.

Everything about it calls to mind gracious images of yesteryear, and a beautiful, rather opulent lady reigns over it with grace and good humour – Mme Dreyfus, a well-known singer who, under the name Paulette Darty, was the first to perform many a waltz of the *belle époque*. Her lovely voice and the finesse of her diction used to enchant Erik Satie and he wrote numerous delectable songs for her, including *Tendrement* and *La diva de l'"Empire'*.

He has remained a loyal friend, the only one, I dare say, since she left the stage and, following the custom of the beauties of the time, cast her lot in with a rich admirer, Édouard Dreyfus. Like us, Satie too has arrived for this Sunday get-together. It's midday exactly. He's absolutely on the dot, neither early nor late. He's had to get to Paris from Arcueil and cross it, either by tram or bus, or on foot, in order to reach the station at Luzarches. Then he only has to soldier on for three kilometres.

He rings the bell, discreetly raises his bowler hat and, a slim, almost elegant figure in his unpretentious dark suit, with his cotton gloves and his stick, pronounces the following greeting: 'Good day, my dear lady, good day, my dear Monsieur Dreyfus.' He's welcomed with open arms. He feels at ease, they're almost like family. He has spoken those words all his life, and will go on doing so. In every way, he's loyal.

Before lunch, a brief tour of the garden is in order. Paulette, in her light-hearted, playful fashion, leads off by throwing bits of bread to her *ménage*. Satie follows right behind and we all take part in this obligatory rite. Sometimes Paulette takes a folding chair, sits down on the bank of the stream and fishes. Satie stands behind her and congratulates her when she catches something. He's at peace, he really admires her.

Was he once in love with her? In the days when, as an unknown, he played the piano in the Chat Noir, or when he launched into the world of the music-hall and found in her his finest interpreter?

He doesn't say anything of importance. No doubt he thinks of any number of things which he'll keep to himself. Sometimes he stops, adjusts his pince-nez, takes a little notebook out of his pocket and with his propelling pencil takes notes . . . musical ones, maybe . . . Suddenly, he starts walking again. Gazing at the ground, with eyes twinkling and a smile playing about his lips, he timidly offers a mild little joke, invariably the same, out of a polite desire to do his bit. 'He's made a mistake,' he says, 'and mistakes are fatal,' or, 'What's new, new on the dish?' or else, 'I'm rolling in money like a calf.' Everyone laughs and he's happy; they like to think his remarks are very nearly brilliant, or childlike. I listen and look at him without smiling. I'm sorry for him. That's where modesty gets you!

The day passes pleasantly. This pastoral scene is one we shall none of us see again. But the self-effacing *maître* is there, and his slim presence is palpable. We know that his silence and loneliness conceal a genius which has revolutionised music, which has created a totally new world of feeling, a poetry beyond compare, and which has given us great works such as *Parade* and *Socrate*. The candour and purity of his soul are his weapons; his inflexibly upright character and his profound sadness alienate him from the world. He accepts this, because he knows his own worth, and that his destiny lies elsewhere. Today we know that, passing over our uncomprehending heads, he has been recognised and fêted in every country as one of the truly great.

Who would think it, to look at him? If people try and push him out into the world, then he shuns applause and, after the triumph of *Parade*, refuses to go out on stage (as I saw with my own eyes). He makes fun of himself and replies: 'This morning, I looked at myself in the mirror in the presence of my manservant. I'm learning to pontificate.'

Dear Satie, that was what made you so lovable! Are you not the sage, the philosopher, the unsullied, the Socrates of music?

The daylight is fading and it'll soon be time to get back. It's always sad when Sundays come to an end! Paulette has thought of everything and gaily tells us: 'Don't go, we can finish the leftovers.' Which are tasty in the extreme. Too much so for Satie who, when it comes to dessert, asks timidly: 'Could I have an apple, an apple-in-the-air, naturally?' It's time to go, and to avoid answering my mother yet again when she offers him a lift in our car, he goes on ahead declaring: 'I'm leaving on foot, I have my way of doing things.' Three kilometres to the station at Luzarches. Then he has to cross Paris to the Lion terminus at Belfort. It's midnight. He sits down outside the café opposite the station, has a calvados and looks at the clock. He still has a few minutes. He calls the waiter: 'Another calvados.' These short stops in bistros would punctuate his long walks. When he gets to Arcueil, he has to reach his miserable apartment block on the corner of two deserted streets, and then climb a sordid staircase up to the fourth [second] storey. A bedroom, a wretched bed, a piano, always open and covered with mounds of unopened letters and dirty detachable collars: Satie was incorruptible.

That all took place between 1922 and 1925. Our friendship didn't last long, but it was firm. The last time I saw him was two days before his death in the Hôpital St-Joseph. A skeletal body under a sheet, from which his head protruded: a 'shadow' of what he had been, like a piece of dead wood. That evening I left for my regiment. My mother was one of the few people who followed his body to the cemetery.

Paulette Darty died in a modest boarding-house in December 1939. Shortly before her death she handed me a packet of letters tied with a ribbon, saying: 'Keep that rubbish.' They were her letters from Satie.

Jacques Guérin
'Erik Satie: "Un dimanche à Luzarches" ', *L'optimiste*, 2, June–July 1992, pp. 8–9

GEORGES AURIC

Shortly after Léon Vallas and I met again, he agreed to read and then to publish in his journal an enthusiastic article of mine on the great discovery of my Montpellier days: Erik Satie.

When it appeared in October or November 1913,* I naturally got hold of Satie's address and sent it to him. He replied at once and, although I've lost the letter, like so many others, I remember very precisely what it said. He couldn't have guessed that he was writing to a child or how astonishing it would seem to me.

'Dear Sir,' he wrote, 'I have read your article which is far too complimentary and is a veritable study. I should like to meet you in order to thank you for it. Suggest a date when you would be free to see me and I shall come straight away . . .'

As well as being somewhat overcome by surprise I was, at the same time, thrilled and delighted, and I hurriedly fixed a meeting for a few days hence. He was to arrive around 5 o'clock in the afternoon and from 4 o'clock onwards I was waiting impatiently. On the dot of 5 o'clock, there was a ring at my parents' door (I was still living with them), I rushed to open it and there I saw Satie; bowler hat in hand, pince-nez, little beard, impeccably white detachable collar, likewise impeccable shirt, overcoat, umbrella – looking rather like an ultra-respectable provincial solicitor with, at the same time, something of mockery in his eyes and in his smile which I have never encountered elsewhere.

Only a few months earlier I had changed from short to long trousers. He asked me: 'Could I see M. Auric?' and I replied: 'That's me, yes, that's me!' I cannot describe his immediate delight. His mind was always thinking of the young, he pinned all his hopes on the fact that one day they would understand him and would make up that little universe which was so important, not only to him, Satie, but to the as yet unimagined music he felt was going to appear.

---

*Actually on 10 December 1913, as 'Erik Satie, musicien humoriste' in *Revue française de musique*, 12, pp. 138–42.

He sat down in an armchair and we talked. I was so overcome, I let him speak on. Then, later, I couldn't resist hazarding heaven knows what curious and fantastic notions. Even so, everything was going splendidly when suddenly my mother appeared. He proceeded to treat her with extreme politeness and this arrival of Satie passed off in the happiest manner.

My parents found him charming. He was thrilled at finding a 14-year-old disciple and soon came back; and before long he took to coming to lunch with us once a week. So we went on seeing each other and talking, to my great benefit, for years, until the sad day when, much later, he and I quarrelled.

But for the moment we're still at the beginning of our friendship and I must say that Satie occupied a very important place in my youth and in my development as a composer. This may be difficult to understand for someone comparing Satie's music with that of obviously greater composers like Stravinsky, for example. But really no comparison is possible in this field, and we should straight away acknowledge the fact.

Later on, and much to my chagrin, our relationship gradually deteriorated. I must tell the curious story of the umbrella, crazy as it is; crazy, but interesting and highly revealing of this most unusual character. It happened during the First World War, when I'd just been called up. One of my female acquaintances had had the idea of organising a little party on the night before I departed. I left it quite early, as time was getting on and I began to think rather gloomily of the following day. Perhaps it was raining, I can't remember. But Satie left immediately after me and, when he got out into the street, he found there was a hole in his umbrella. Instantly, he became convinced that it was I who, driven by some devilish urge or other, had accomplished this dastardly act some minutes before! It was, then, a species of criminal who was to don military uniform on the morrow, and from that (to me) fatal day my poor *maître* began to have strange misgivings about Auric the soldier. His friends succeeded in calming him down, even so, and finally he seemed to forget about the 'wrecked umbrella' – but did he ever really forgive me?

Several years later we met at a birthday dinner given by our friends Pierre Bertin and Marcelle Meyer. An American lady* had brought a delectable cake and Satie, looking at it, seemed to be in an excellent mood. Cocteau was there too and, as he often did, began right from the start of

*Sybil Harris.

the meal to improvise a brilliant monologue. I'd grown so used to these exploits that I was listening with only half an ear, so I can't remember exactly what he said. But what I do recall is that at a particular moment he ventured to speak at rather too great a length about music. Satie suddenly went white with anger, got up and went over to Cocteau's chair. We were terrified, seeing him with his pince-nez, and his serviette in his hand, looming over Cocteau who had stopped talking or even moving, ready to receive a serviette and a plate on top of his head. Satie lifted his arms as though about to brain him, then delivered a single word: 'Imbecile!' His face suddenly took on an appearance of extraordinary cruelty, and Cocteau's was rigid with terror. We were all petrified, and waited for the worst. But the 'bon maître' almost immediately moved away and slowly and calmly went back to his place. He gave us a relaxed, happy smile and said, in amazingly tranquil tones: 'Ah! That's better. We can breathe again.' It was without doubt one of the strangest, most awkward and disconcerting spectacles I've ever seen in my life.

As in all 'opéras-comiques' of the period, Gounod's unfortunately contain, in between the arias, duets and ensembles, passages of spoken dialogue, some of them short, some rather long. It has to be said that these passages did no favours to their interpreters, who were often excellent singers but nearly always appalling actors. Diaghilev had the idea of setting these spoken passages to music, so that each act could be sung without interruption.

Three Gounod operas were chosen: *Le médecin malgré lui*, *La colombe* (which had been forgotten from its earliest days, thanks to an extraordinarily vapid libretto), and *Philémon et Baucis*. To these was added Chabrier's *L'éducation manquée* [sic], which pleased us enormously because we were full of youthful enthusiasm for this then underrated master – as he is now, I'm sorry to say. The considerable task of setting the spoken passages was given to Satie (*Le médecin*), Poulenc (*La colombe*), Milhaud (*L'éducation manquée*) and myself (*Philémon*).

When we'd finished the work, our versions had to be submitted to Gounod's heirs who, to my great shame, refused 'my' *Philémon*! On the other hand, *La colombe*, in which Poulenc had been very successful in producing a ravishing pastiche, and even Satie's *Le médecin* (which surprised me rather) were accepted. As for Chabrier, he had no heirs: and I was sorry that Milhaud could not be given such a seal of approval in his turn. His additions were remarkable and highly effective in the way they filled out Chabrier's masterly score . . . And so these three operas were given by Diaghilev at Monte Carlo.

If Brussels had been three thousand kilometres from Paris, Satie could not have been more amazed and stupefied, and he set about discovering its cigars, its beer and its restaurants with an engaging enthusiasm [in 1921]. The trouble was that, before he got to make the journey back to Paris, this enthusiasm led him to find the time and the means to have three lunches a day. He sat in a corner of our apartment crimson-faced and ill as a result of his inordinate admiration for Belgian cuisine . . . Which is why, reaching Paris in a dreadful state, he had only unpleasant memories of those three or four days. Ever after, he was to hate travelling and Arcueil-Cachan was the finest city in the world. Despite that, Diaghilev the magician managed to get him to come to Monte Carlo [in 1924]. Monaco and Satie: this new (and final) journey away from home soon took on extraordinary proportions! Monte Carlo after Brussels, it was Satie on the Himalayas, like Herzog on Annapurna.

He arrived in a terrible mood, he loathed the country, its ostentatious wealth, the overcomfortable Hôtel de Paris, everything seemed detestable to him. Furthermore, he was furious with Poulenc and myself. On the corner of a street he'd spotted Louis Laloy, one of the people he most hated, perhaps because he'd seen too much of him at Debussy's. As it happened, Laloy had written some extremely nice things about Poulenc and myself, so we couldn't simply spit in his face or turn our backs on him. The day after the rather dull production of *Le médecin malgré lui*, Satie left abruptly. Poulenc and I each received shortly afterwards the same postcard from Paris: 'Don't trust that swine Laloy! He's a traitor . . .'

From that time on, I became ever more suspect in Satie's eyes. He kept making the rudest and most absurd allusions to my 'friendships', demonstrating his bad character as well as a definite persecution complex.

Our relationship grew worse month by month, until finally it broke up altogether. This happened over a new ballet he'd composed for Francis Picabia. The dances in *Relâche* are not masterpieces from the musical point of view (come to that, the whole ballet wasn't up to much). But the occasion did contain one episode which was truly an event.

It was a film by René Clair, joining the two halves of the ballet, which was called *Entr'acte* and which, of course, had music by Satie. I fell in love with the film immediately, even if I didn't at once understand what a strange score it was and, for a variety of reasons, both bold and interesting. It was, quite rightly, to be a date in the history of film music.

We should remember that *Entr'acte* was written at a time when the cinema was still 'silent'. A number of awkward problems presented themselves to a composer who intended to write a musical accompaniment to a film which was itself silent (in fact, the showings were almost always accompanied by a single pianist, or by tiny instrumental groups in the better-off cinemas, or by real orchestras in one or two of the largest auditoria. A number of pieces were thrown together at random and, as the film programmes changed each week, the choice was made at the last moment.) The problem became severe when it was no longer enough to match the pictures with a few bars distributed more or less accurately. In the case of the film by René Clair, the composer's perilous task was to write a real score.

With *Entr'acte* Satie found the best way of solving the problem. He broke up his score into a series of fragments, each of them cleverly proportioned to go with successive episodes in the film, and each of them capable of being repeated as many times as was necessary; and they followed on from each other amazingly naturally and easily right up to the final frame.

I was lucky enough to see not only the ballet *Relâche*, which I still find uninteresting, but a revelation which can now be seen to be of importance. I didn't realise this importance that first evening – and I'm not proud to admit it.

The ultimate hatred of my old 'maître' was visited on me as the result of a thoroughly unpleasant article which I published in haste. I in my turn became a 'traitor', a frightful boy, an appalling scoundrel. Our friendship was over for ever, and I regret it profoundly.

Georges Auric
'Inoubliable apparition d'Erik Satie,' in *Quand j'étais là* (Paris, Grasset, 1979), pp. 21–32

MAXIME JACOB
(1906–77)

Maxime-Benjamin Jacob was born in Bordeaux, but studied
composition in Paris with Koechlin and Gedalge. His music
came to public attention in 1923 when he became one of the
four members of the École d'Arcueil, a group launched by
Satie as successors to Les Six. The other three members (all
pupils of Koechlin) were Henri Sauguet, Henri Cliquet-
Pleyel and Roger Désormière and the group was assembled
around Sauguet by Milhaud, who knew from past experience
that strength lay in unity. In 1929, the year of this souvenir,
Jacob was converted to Catholicism and took holy orders.
As a Benedictine novice, he made extensive researches into
Gregorian chant and assumed the name of Dom Clément
Jacob. He should not be confused with the Jewish-born poet
Max Jacob (1876–1944), who was also a close friend of
Satie's and who was also converted to Catholicism, but in
1914.

Auteuil, where I live, is not very far from Arcueil, so our 'bon maître'
often used to come to the house for a rest, when I was not joining him at
Graff's. I remember especially a dinner at which, apart from my family
(respectfully silent), the guests were a collaborator of mine, Robert Aron,
Darius Milhaud (majestic and at the same time delightfully simple), and
Désormière, who had brought a symphonic poem called *Monluçon*, which
he analysed for us over dessert. Because space in my parents' modest
dining-room was limited, Sauguet turned up only after the meal. I was
the first to regret his absence, but Milhaud too was upset by it and told
me so. Since then Sauguet has often dined with me, Milhaud never.

In the hall, while I was relieving him of his bowler hat, overcoat and
umbrella, Satie handed me an envelope with that air of mystery familiar
to us all. The envelope contained best wishes from Cocteau for the
budding school of Arcueil which was to consist of Cliquet, Sauguet,
Désormière, Benoist-Méchin and myself. Cocteau hadn't wasted any time,
as you can see, and over dinner his friendly gesture provoked any number
of responses, which I shall spare you.

Even if Satie dived headlong into the tortuous byways of musical politics, that didn't affect the purity of his intentions, because the politics remained on the level of words. After Robert Aron had made a nervous, hasty departure and Sauguet a discreet arrival, the party consisted entirely of musicians.

I won't describe Satie's extreme goodness to you, since you've experienced it yourself. It beamed continually at Désormière's learned dissections, at Milhaud's vigorous thrusts, at Sauguet's insinuations and at my puerile tales. He was totally at his ease in that *petit bourgeois* salon, always cheerful, always friendly and above all always loving.

That's what strikes me when I look back to that evening, and when I remember the numerous occasions which I had the pleasure of spending with him. Whatever you may think, a revolutionary would not have spoken and behaved as Satie did. The red flag has different effects on people who are really in love with it: it makes them either exalted or bitter. With Satie, nothing of the sort. That was principally due to his Christian sentiments, which were always with him, even if unseen – as I hope to show in a moment – and also to his innate attraction towards the traditional virtues. It is, indeed, rather remarkable that the majority of artists in France are profoundly bourgeois; I know composers who flirt to some extent with Moscow, but who are even so not exempt from class feeling. Happily this sentiment did not exist with Satie but, I repeat, his character was based on a solid foundation of traditionalism, allied with a fantasy that sprang from the Celtic mists.

This fine spiritual equilibrium blossomed quite naturally in his demonstrations of love and understanding. His famous rages were short, though violent, and if his grudges sometimes lasted a good while, he had an inimitably charming way of putting an end to them. Those were the qualities I loved at each of our meetings, and particularly at the dinner I've just described.

I could go on to recall our evening walks through Paris to the station where Satie used to take the train for Arcueil; suppers at Graff's, evenings in his box at the Théâtre des Champs-Élysées, or at Rolf de Maré's. For me each of these episodes is full of entertaining images and memorable quips. But I strongly believe that it would be a betrayal of Satie to try and fix his character by means of conversations and anecdotes. None of us can boast that we knew him. He vouchsafed us, discreetly, the secret of his pure, mischievous spirit in his music. That is the only mirror in which we can see again the face that is dear to us, relieved of its peripheral attributes. We can see, in a few chords, the true nature of his soul: its extraordinary humility and sincerity. It is the better part of himself that he has left us, and this authentic voice is expressed with a surprising unity: while ours is raised in communal admiration.

It's one further proof that Satie is many miles above squabbles about parties, doctrines and schools, and it's a demonstration of the overwhelming power of love. Myself, I wish with all my heart that the example of our 'bon maître' may soon be understood in its entirety, because his music is an expression not only of genius, but above all of faith, hope and charity.

Maxime Jacob
Letter to Robert Caby, October 1929

VII
Vexations and vicissitudes

Satie was well-known for his erratic behaviour and lost friends as easily as he gained them, usually with apparent unconcern. Only a few close ones (like Milhaud and Diaghilev) remained wholly unaffected by this, and perhaps this was because Satie needed them more than they needed him, and because they never doubted his importance as an artist. He must have relied on the fact that ordinary, wholly affable people are seldom the ones that others talk about, and being talked about mattered a great deal to Satie. He had plenty of real 'vexations' in his life, which he rarely discussed, and friends had to know him really well to be able even to begin to understand the strange logic that governed his uncompromising actions.

PIERRE BERTIN

Satie loathed *arrivistes*. He used to say: 'I find newcomers far from being antipathetic. They have a sense of movement which is in no way unpleasant. It's just the goal they're aiming at which leads me to anxious reflection (though not much of it, I have to say). I simply question myself politely, saying: "Where do they want to arrive at? Arrive at what? At what time? In what place? I feel uncertainty and fear on their behalf." I've seen some *arrivistes* over a period of forty years, and the ones in my day were as cunning as those nowadays. All of them – all, you understand – "arrived" at nothing, and less than nothing. Even though some of them "arrived" in various academies and other places . . . of ill repute.'

As to personal appearance, Satie was always correctly dressed: a black overcoat with the collar turned up, an umbrella and a bowler hat. That was how he looked when I first met him at Roland-Manuel's in 1912, and that's how he remained until he died. You'd have said he was a good schoolmaster. He had a dignified, almost ceremonious bearing.

One day, at the Comte de Beaumont's, there was a ceremony in honour of the Queen of Rumania and Satie was introduced to the Queen after a performance of some of his works.* I saw him slowly cross the drawing-room with two fingers to his mouth, as often. He bowed like a chamberlain, kissed the Queen's hand and leant down to listen to her and to reply with extreme formality. This went on for a long time and we were asking ourselves what on earth they could be talking about. Then he came back across the room, steeped in politeness and wearing an utterly serious expression.

'What did she say?' I asked.

Unsmiling, he murmured in my ear: 'She told me I had a fine old man's head!'

He would place his hand on his mouth and beard and from behind it, in a rather leisurely voice, he would let out mysterious confidences, or else he'd start to laugh, a huge, stifled, inextinguishable laugh. And you had to laugh with him, even if you didn't know why, otherwise he'd get angry. He'd lose his temper suddenly, for no reason – because in the cloakroom someone had slipped another umbrella into his, as happened to Auric at Hélène Jourdan-Morhange's on one famous occasion, and because of that he wouldn't speak to you for months.

In Satie's work *Le piège de Méduse*, a certain Baron Méduse laid a trap for a young man who had designs on his daughter. Playing the part of the old baron, I made up my face to look like Satie's and talked like him. He broke off relations for nearly a year after that, thinking I'd intended to make fun of him. But the baron was so like him in so many ways, I couldn't help copying the composer's mannerisms and appearance.

This piece of nonsense contained some delightful music 'by the same gentleman', written for a mechanical monkey which, from time to time, and for no reason anyone could see, started to jump around. The music was exquisite.

Pierre Bertin
'Erik Satie et le groupe des Six', *Les annales*, February 1951, pp. 52–3, 57–8

*On 2 April 1919.

ÉLISE JOUHANDEAU (CARYATHIS)

(1889–1971)

Élise Jouhandeau was an eccentric and outspoken dancer for whose stage debut as 'Caryathis' in 1920 Satie composed a suite of dances recalling his music-hall years. This was appropriately entitled *La belle excentrique*, and Satie eventually chose a single costume, designed by Cocteau, for all three dances, which, according to Caryathis, made her look like 'a mad American woman from the Salvation Army who was out for revenge'!

Caryathis was born Élisabeth Toulemon and she married the writer Marcel Jouhandeau in 1927, with whom she maintained a tempestuous and frenetically jealous existence. Before their marriage, the couple gave extravagant, orgiastic parties which Satie attended with a certain degree of voyeuristic delight in the early 1920s.

The score was in three parts: *La marche franco-lunaire*, *Le mystérieux baiser dans l'oeil* and *Le can-can grand mondain*. Satie and I made the rounds of painters and dressmakers.

Van Dongen upset him considerably by his mercenary attitude. At Poiret's, hardly had we seen three dresses when he turned to me. Out of the side of his mouth he muttered four words: 'Down with the harem!' Faced with Marie Laurencin's model of the set, he grew fidgety. 'No, no! To hell with gracefulness!' Then Jean Hugo's model was received with favour. 'But,' he said, 'my music calls for something outrageous; a woman more like a zebra than a doe.'

So that was my rôle!

Simple and open as he was, Satie was not much bothered by practical questions. When I was in a bad mood, he used to scold me:

'Belle Dame (that's what the musicians used to call me), to prefer oneself to one's art is an error. You must serve it with self-denial. Put yourself in order; that way you will bring your sensibilities to be at one with magnificent privations. You know, inconveniences are part of the fate of every living thing.'

Satie appeared not to care about others, but he had a kind heart, even if it was, certainly, intolerant of stupidity, which he dealt with by irony.

His existence was governed by music and his whole life sacrificed to the toil of inspiration and to the pursuit of true knowledge.

Élise Jouhandeau
Joies et douleurs d'une belle excentrique (Paris, Flammarion, 1960), pp. 141, 143
(*AFS*)

RENÉ CHALUPT

(1885–1957)

René Chalupt was a young poet with a sense of fantasy who shared Satie's forward-looking views on the arts. They met at the family home of the composer Roland-Manuel in 1913, and remained close friends into the 1920s. Satie set Chalupt's poem 'Le chapelier', based on the Mad Hatter's Tea Party from *Alice in Wonderland*, as a parody of Gounod in 1916. He also chose him to write the preface to *Socrate* in 1919. Chalupt's perceptive 1922 article on 'Gabriel Fauré et les poètes' shows how right Satie was to trust in his critical abilities.

I don't know whether it was a benign form of persecution mania, but Satie's character was so constituted that at one time or another he had to quarrel with his best friends, almost always without the slightest justification. Debussy, Cocteau, Auric, Roland-Manuel – they were all subject to this law, and so was I. One afternoon in 1922 I went to the Trianon Lyrique, then directed by that excellent musician Louis Masson, to attend the dress rehearsal of Fred Barlow's *Sylvie* and Roland-Manuel's *Isabelle et Pantalon*. Satie was in the auditorium, but he pretended not to know me and didn't speak a word to me. Knowing how moody he was, I thought nothing of it. Time passed and we continued to avoid each other deliberately, to the extent that we never saw each other except in gatherings large enough for us not to have to meet.

But then, one evening at the Koussevitsky Concerts at the Opéra, I realised, just as I was about to take my seat, that Satie was in the one next to it! I had no idea how he would react, so I asked a mutual friend to sound him out and ask him what exactly he had against me. It turned out to be nothing: just that one day I'd walked past without seeing him. I passed back the assurance, which was true, that if I had indeed failed to greet him on such an occasion, it was absolutely unintentional. He accepted my explanation and we listened to the whole concert sitting next to each other as though nothing had happened.

Did I ever break through to the real Satie? I don't think so, and make no claims in this direction. No one really knows another person, certainly not one like him, a complex, secret, mysterious man, full of obscure and inaccessible crannies. But a few bars of his music are enough to recall to my mind the silhouette of a bearded Frenchman of middling height, a correct-looking official, a faun wearing pince-nez, and as he leaves I seem to hear him say: 'Farewell, my goodly friend. I give you my old hand to kiss.'

René Chalupt
'Quelques souvenirs sur Erik Satie', *ReM*, 214, June 1952, pp. 45–6

CONSTANTIN BRANCUSI
(1876–1957)

Constantin Brancusi was a Rumanian sculptor who settled in Paris in 1904. His early work was influenced by Rodin, but in 1907 he became more interested in abstract forms, and it was through his simple, highly polished works that he became the foremost name in modern sculpture. Satie was a regular visitor at his Paris studio in the impasse Ronsin in the 1920s, where everything was white (Satie's favourite colour), and where he enjoyed Brancusi's excellent cooking and stimulating company. They both shared an interest in the occult and photography, and Satie's music has often been justifiably compared with Brancusi's sculptures in its quest for perfection in simplicity. Brancusi created several works under the inspiration of Satie's *Socrate*, and Satie in turn claimed that he found the key to writing his opera *Paul & Virginie* in one of Brancusi's sculptures.

Brancusi told a wonderful story of Satie. Brancusi liked him, because he was the only man who made him laugh. After lunch, one day, they were walking past the Ministère de la Marine. There was a sailor standing guard in uniform. About thirty feet away from him Satie stopped, lowered his glasses and said: 'Quoi, mon grand, vous jouez encore à ça?' [What, big boy, are you still playing at sailors?] Another time Brancusi made an *éloge* on Satie for his versatility. He wrote as a critic, played politics, saw people, and yet worked on his music. Brancusi never could [occupy himself with sculpture and politics simultaneously] and said: 'Since I cannot, I will stay out of politics.' He told this to Satie, and Satie said: 'Why, even that is politics.'

Jacqueline Matisse Monnier
Notes on an interview with Brancusi on 14 November 1950, in Friedrich Teja Bach, *Constantin Brancusi* (Cologne, Dumont, 1987), p. 230 (*AFS*)

ANDRÉ BEUCLER
(1898–19 ?)

> André Beucler was a historical and romantic novelist who came to Paris from St Petersburg as a young man in the early 1920s. He moved in the circle of the poet Léon-Paul Fargue, and in this account Ravel, Fargue and Beucler are walking home together across Montmartre at dawn and remembering Satie.

The spring air was light and keen, as though Paris had in a few hours been lifted a few thousand feet above sea-level. It was stimulating and we were in no hurry to separate. We sauntered off together and hadn't gone far when we came upon an old man huddled under a vault playing the violin. He played the same tune over and over again, a hardly recognisable fragment of a waltz of Satie's. Fargue sang a verse of it:

> *J'ai compris ta détresse,*
> *Bel amoureux;*
> *Et je comble tes voeux,*
> *Fais de moi ta maîtresse.*

The two men stopped. The words had stirred emotions. Ravel told us that Satie had come to hate the tune and even the name of the waltz [*Je te veux*] on account of the evil memories it brought back to him.

'This was his favourite quarter,' he went on, 'and most of all the Chat Noir. He wouldn't hear of anything being better. I've played some Satie in my day! And it was in a place not far from here that I played the first piece.* If it wasn't so late – or so early – I could take you there with my eyes shut. I was playing Satie before Debussy ever heard of him. And the things he'd put to music! Small advertisements, for instance! He would gravely consult us on the subject, Ricardo Viñes and me, suggesting some miniature orchestration to indicate: *Respectable family wishes to exchange butler for wardrobe with mirror doors.* And the way he'd laugh at it! Do you remember his laugh?'

'Indeed I do. And I can see him as clearly as if he was standing before us. He had stepped straight out of a Toulouse-Lautrec picture – as though alighting from a tram. He came from Arcueil, which he'd turned into a little town with only one inhabitant – himself. I can remember, too, the time when he staggered a meeting, chiefly of painters, by announcing that he had discovered twenty-seven entirely new colours. The audience was perplexed, and for a long time he kept them guessing, till finally someone asked him point-blank how he'd done such an extraordinary thing – for, after all, to discover twenty-seven new colours that had no relation to the old ones was nothing less than earth-shaking.

' "Like this . . .," he [Satie] explained to the old bearded painter. "By suddenly and remorselessly obliterating the colours of the spectrum with an india-rubber."

'The audience breathed again.'

André Beucler
Poet of Paris: Twenty Years with Léon-Paul Fargue (trans. Geoffrey Sainsbury) (London, Chatto & Windus, 1955), pp. 56–7

HENRI SAUGUET

(1901–89)

Henri Sauguet (real name Jean-Pierre Poupard) was born in Bordeaux, and as a budding composer he founded a local group there in 1921 called Les Trois, in imitation of Les Six in Paris. He wrote to Milhaud, who asked to see some of his compositions. After playing his *Trois françaises* for piano in 1923, Milhaud invited Sauguet to come to Paris, where he introduced him to Koechlin (who gave him lessons) and Satie

*Ravel is probably referring to the Café de la Nouvelle Athènes, where he first met Satie in 1893.

(who presented him to the public as a member of the École
d'Arcueil). He was most successful as a ballet composer,
writing *La chatte* for Diaghilev (1927), *David* for Ida Rubinstein (1930) and *Les forains* for Roland Petit (1945), for
he had a natural attraction to the theatre and was also a talented
actor and artist. In Sauguet's case, the music reflected the
man: civilised, refined, charming and intelligent; radiating
the lyricism and spontaneous good humour of Chabrier rather
than Satie's irreverent wit.

Despite what has been said and written, it was easy to get to know Satie
and to make friends with him. His approach wasn't as familar as that of
Max Jacob, who gave you the impression the very first time you met him
that you had become his closest friend (which never failed to cause
considerable irritation to his oldest acquaintances), but he was amiable to
meet, extremely well-mannered, courteous, prepossessing and very tactful.
He listened to you, allowed you to speak, never said anything which
might upset you, and was a fluent talker on every subject. It was only
when you got to know him better that he let himself go with enthusiasms,
changes of mood, gloomy susceptibilities and sarcasms, and showed himself to be aggressive and uneasy in his mind.

I don't think any of his friends escaped one or more quarrels with him
– except perhaps Milhaud (but that was an exception, and because he was
angelic in his treatment of Satie). As for me, poor little shadow as I was
of the *maître*, I put him in such a rage one evening that for a time he
expunged me from the list of his friends and from his life, going to the
extreme of appearing not to recognise me when we met (which in those
days was often, our hosts imagining that the place of a young disciple was
by his master's side). This was the reason: he was supposed to accompany
Suzanne Balguerie in *Socrate* at the Salle Gaveau. The same evening [20
June 1923], at the Théâtre Sarah-Bernhardt, Diaghilev was reviving
Parade. Satie, who wanted to go to this revival and thought he could
manage it if the concert didn't end too late, was in a frightful state of
nerves, made worse by a sort of panic which used to overtake him when
he had to accompany his pieces in public. I was sitting on stage beside
him to turn the pages (he'd sent me a *pneumatique* asking me to do this
favour), and saw him, pale, with glinting eyes, apparently glued to the
piano. Hardly had he begun when I heard him asking me to turn the
page. He was right at the top of it. I hesitated; but he ordered me, with

ever-increasing grumbles, to 'turn'. Just as I was about to obey: 'But not just yet, wait.' I lowered my arm, 'turn, are you going to turn?' . . . And this game went on right through *Socrate*. And if you know the score, you know how many pages there are, thanks, among other things, to the overlarge type used by the engraver, chosen originally by Blaise Cendrars for the Éditions de La Sirène (but that's another story). When we left the stage for the wings, Satie was beside himself and began to abuse me roundly . . . Suzanne Balguerie looked on in total amazement, as the whole charade had taken place behind her back. I'd been supposed to go on with Satie to *Parade*, but there could be no question of that now. I was left alone 'with my despair'. Because I was truly in despair at having annoyed 'le bon maître' and lost his friendship, even if only temporarily. I wrote, asking his pardon. He sent a *pneumatique* back: 'Don't let's mention it again; but seeing what you were up to "terrorised" me.' But not mentioning it meant not seeing each other any more. And that went on for nearly three long months. Then, one morning, my concierge handed me a *pneumatique* (Satie liked this rapid means of correspondence; he hated the telephone, never used it and used to take it off the hook when he went to visit friends who had one), it was from Satie. With beating heart, I opened it: was it a message of peace or a formal ban on ever seeing him again? As though nothing had happened, Satie was asking me to have lunch with him and 'his dear friend Diaghilev, to whom he had spoken about me and who wanted to meet me'.

This story sheds considerable light on Satie's character and emotions. He was not a blind slave to his changes of mood and abandoned himself to them as much out of liveliness as out of any intention to tease. Finding himself in a difficult situation, he made it impossible, not, this time, by playing the joker, but by going too far, and then the only way out he could think of was through a dramatic gesture.

Henri Sauguet
'Souvenirs et réflexions autour d'Erik Satie', *ReM*, 214, June 1952, pp. 95–6

BLAISE CENDRARS

Q: People have often talked about Satie's humour . . .

BC: Satie's sense of humour was often cruel. M. Contamine de Latour, who started out in life with Satie, told me how they shared a bedroom in Montmartre. They had only one pair of trousers between them. M. Contamine wore them to go to work in the daytime and then Satie would have them in the evening to play the piano at the Chat Noir. One morning, as a joke, Satie didn't come back. M. de la Contamine waited till 9 o'clock, 10, 11 o'clock, midday. He missed going to his office and was sacked, which caused innumerable problems and was not designed to make anyone's life easier.

Q: Were you at that scandalous first performance of his ballet *Parade*, with scenario by Cocteau and designs by Picasso?

BC: I certainly was. I went to almost all the rehearsals, and that included the dress rehearsal and the première. The scandal was largely confined to the owners of the boxes, but the most scandalised person of all was Satie himself. He couldn't get over hearing the tapping of a typewriter which he'd not included among the instruments of his orchestra. He'd had a running battle about this all through the rehearsals with Cocteau, who insisted on having, not just one typewriter, but a whole battery of typewriters. Right at the last minute, Diaghilev found him an instrument which had nothing to do with typewriters except that it made them louder, so every now and then Satie's marvellous music was somewhat drowned . . .

Q: What did you find so attractive about Satie?

BC: The thing I found attractive was his suburban side. He lived in the suburbs. He was a communist at a time when nobody else was. He was the conductor of the local choir in Arcueil-Cachan. He wrote music for the schoolchildren of Arcueil-Cachan. He was extremely shy.

Around 1925,* I'd arranged a commission for Satie from the Ballets Suédois. They were off on a tour of the United States and their director, Rolf de Maré, didn't have time to sign a cheque straight away. They came to an agreement, he and Satie, in the entrance to the Théâtre des Champs-Élysées, and as Rolf was leaving he said to Erik: 'Now don't

*Actually in 1923.

worry, my dear chap, I'll send you a cheque from Le Havre. You'll get it tomorrow morning or the day after . . .'

For the next two or three days, Satie called on me three times a day (coming from Arcueil to the Batignolles, where I was living in those days) in order to complain that he still hadn't had the famous cheque, and that the Swedes were dunderheads (he was always very violent in the terms he used). One fine day, the fourth or fifth, he turned up at about 7 in the morning, brandishing Rolf de Maré's cheque, which had not been posted at Le Havre but somewhere else, and which was drawn on de Maré's bank, a Swedish bank at the top of the avenue George V, in a small private house in a large garden. Satie started to carry on, protesting, as only he knew how, that the Swedes were dolts and worrying that he wouldn't get paid. 'But look,' he said, 'it's not a bank. You don't put a bank in a large garden, you don't put a bank in a small private house . . . It takes a Swede to do a thing like that! They're completely crazy.'

I tried to calm him down, saying: 'Listen, my dear fellow, present your cheque, I'm sure you'll be paid.' Which is what happened. And once we got out into the street, I realised the responsibility I'd taken on in accompanying Satie to that Swedish bank: I had to get him back to Arcueil with all that cash in his pocket. I took him along the rue François I (where there were no bistros in those days) and he arrived safe and sound at the tabac on the corner behind the Grand Palais, in the avenue Emmanuel III – where, of course, he bought two or three packets of those dreadful cigars he liked, which he called 'crapoulos'. Then we sank two or three glasses and I took him next down the Champs-Élysées, but through the gardens on the left, because there are no bistros in the gardens. I took him across the place de la Concorde (no bistros in the place de la Concorde), through the Tuileries gardens, the cour du Louvre and along the *quais* from the pont des Arts as far as the Châtelet.

At the Châtelet, unfortunately, there was the Brasserie du Châtelet where Satie, right from when he was little, had been in the habit of eating sauerkraut. There was no way out of it. So we sat down, ate our sauerkraut. It was a quarter past 11, or thereabouts. We sank a number of glasses, and smoked several of those appalling 'crapoulos' he was so fond of, and all the while I was saying to myself 'the hard bit's going to be getting up the boulevard Saint-Michel. How'll we manage? . . .' We got as far as the Cité without mishap, and into the place Saint-Michel without a single stop when, suddenly, before crossing the boulevard Saint-Germain, Satie made a leap, crossed the boul' Mich', and dived into a shirtmaker's opposite.

When I caught up with him, he said: 'You see, my dear boy, when for once I can afford to buy some detachable collars, I intend to buy some detachable collars! . . . It's the only shop in Paris which sells the collars I wear!' God knows, there was nothing extraordinary about those collars; they were slightly out of fashion, with bent ends, but apparently indistinguishable from thousands of other detachable collars with bent ends . . . and he bought twelve dozen of them. Twelve dozen detachable collars! A gross. We left the shop and then Satie was so thrilled with his purchase that he didn't even think of stopping at a bistro. We went all the way up the boul' Mich' as far as the gare du Luxembourg and I left him, having put him on the train which would take him back to Arcueil-Cachan.

Interview with Blaise Cendrars
Broadcast on French Radio, 3 July 1950; published in *Cahiers Blaise Cendrars*, No. 3 (Neuchâtel, Éditions de la Baconnière, 1989), pp. 102–4 (*AFS*)

JEAN HUGO
(1894–1984)

Jean Hugo was a costume and stage designer, and the grandson of Victor Hugo. He was involved in various of Satie's theatrical projects in the 1920s from *La belle excentrique* to the *Divertissement: La statue retrouvée* in 1923. He married Satie's close friend Valentine Gross in 1919.

Satie was a guest at my grandmother's house in the rue de la Faisanderie with Auric, Milhaud and Poulenc. There they heard Marie Olénine sing Mussorgsky's *Sunless* cycle, and they themselves sang *Cocardes*, the *Fête de Montmartre* and *Socrate*. M. Satie did his duty by the food and the cognac. As a member of the Communist Party of Arcueil, he reproached my grandmother for remaining a socialist.

'And your dear grandmother,' he would ask me, 'she's still thick with the priests?'

One day she invited him with some of the first Germans to visit Paris after the war. After dinner he crossed the drawing-room with a small glass in his hand, went up to one of them and asked him:

'Sir, you are German, are you not?'

'Yes, sir,' replied the other coolly, expecting some unpleasant rejoinder.

'Ah! Nice *boche!*' exclaimed Satie, shaking his hand vigorously and slapping him on the shoulder, 'good old *boche!*'

He also used to frequent the most elegant salons, without being in the least snobbish. Étienne de Beaumont introduced him to the Queen of Rumania: he made her a charmingly polite little bow. Elsewhere his reception was not so welcoming. At a musical evening where his works were being played, he was taking a drink to a lady who was thirsty when the hostess, the Princesse de Polignac, intervened saying, 'Monsieur Satie, the musicians' buffet is in the other room.'

Princesse Eugène Murat, on the other hand, welcomed him warmly.

'She swigs it down,' Satie used to say; 'she can allow herself to do that; she comes from Moscow!'

Jean Hugo
Avant d'oublier (Paris, Librairie Arthème Fayard, 1976), pp. 62–3 (*AFS*)

JEAN WIÉNER

His handwriting was an example of this [exterior sign of genius]. It is absolutely perfect, but *he took a full twenty minutes to write a pneumatique six lines long*; because he was so determined the formation of his letters should be perfect in every way – the joins, the down- and up-strokes – that he wrote like a painter on the outside of a shop he's decorating.

On one occasion at my house, after dinner, Satie asked for writing materials. I left him (with a bottle of good champagne nearby) to get on with his 'delicate work'. Over half an hour later, he was just beginning to sketch the address; and these letters were, more often than not, just a few lines to say he couldn't come to dinner.

Jean Wiéner
'Un grand musicien', *Arts*, 1/25, 20 July 1945, p. 4

GABRIEL GROVLEZ

(1879–1944)

Gabriel Grovlez was a French composer and conductor who was born in Lille. Like Satie he came to Paris in his youth and studied the piano at the Paris Conservatoire with Émile Descombes. He also studied composition there with Fauré and he was professor of piano at the Schola Cantorum during the first four years Satie studied there (1905–9). He was appointed a conductor of the Paris Opéra in 1914, a post he held for twenty years, and is now best known for his colourful piano pieces, like *L'almanach aux images*.

No question about it, in his everyday life Satie was a marvellous humorist. A conversation with him was beyond description and you could make a highly amusing book out of all his sallies. I can still hear him saying to me, in that confidential tone of voice peculiar to him: 'Polyphony? What rubbish! The music of the future is monophonic, a single sound, and always the same one!'

Gabriel Grovlez
'Ce qu'on a joué dans les *Lyriques* . . .', *Le Rideau de Paris*, 1937

'LUGÈRES'

He loved to mystify the uninitiated. One afternoon he was at the Pasdeloup Concerts, with Rhené-Baton conducting. He had the idea of striking up a conversation with the man in the seat next to him, a large, heavy-looking character:

    – Pretty, isn't it, this modern dance music? But I'm sure you'll agree that polytony and diaphony are simply nonsense.

The large man looked at him and then gave a slight shrug of the shoulders. Satie went on firmly:

    – Polyphony and euphony as well! Nonsense!

    – Yes, nonsense, agreed his neighbour casually.

    – There's only one true basis for music, Satie concluded dogmatically: that's monophony. One note, just one note!

    – One note? said his neighbour, looking fairly startled.

– Absolutely. Just one note, and always the same one!

The large gentleman then leant across to him and said, politely:

– I know what your note is, Monsieur Erik Satie: B, B and B, isn't it?

And as Satie, realising he was the mystified one, looked at his companion in astonishment, the latter with a smile introduced himself:

– I am Paul Souday, music critic of *Paris-Midi*.

'Lugères'
'Le 5ème anniversaire de la mort d'Erik Satie', Dossier Satie, Bibliothèque de l'Opéra, source unknown, (July 1930)

VIII

As composer and precursor

While Satie rarely discussed his music in any detail with others, he worked at his compositions with the utmost seriousness and made innumerable personal sacrifices so that he could remain wholly as an uncompromising professional composer. He pursued his isolated path with great moral courage and found a consistent road towards the future only after he left the Schola Cantorum in 1912. First and foremost, he was a man of ideas who questioned every aspect of inherited nineteenth-century tradition and rejected its concepts of Romantic expressiveness and thematic development. He was the first to challenge Wagner's pervasive influence on French music and he also bypassed Impressionism and the beguiling orchestral sonorities of Debussy and Ravel without regret. In many ways, his reinterpretation of the fundamental concepts underlying art derived more from writers, sculptors and painters than from any composer, though it was always important to him to remain in close contact with his roots in popular music.

It was Debussy who first christened Satie 'the precursor', and as his iconoclastic career progressed, he consciously forged a path that others would follow, foreshadowing organised total chromaticism (1893), Surrealism and the prepared piano (1913), neo-classicism, minimalism and even muzak (1917), and the concept of the synchronised (yet aleatoric) film score (1924). His overriding aims were simplicity, brevity and clarity of expression, and if it should be thought that he merely rejected elements that he was incapable of achieving technically, one has only to look at his completion of Gounod's opera *Le médecin malgré lui* (1923) to see how expert he was at nineteenth-century chromatic harmony, or to *Parade* to see an example of his distinctive, imaginative and accomplished orchestration. No one, least of all Satie himself, would deny that he found composition difficult. But then, so did Debussy and Ravel.

ROLAND-MANUEL
(1891–1966)

Roland-Manuel (Roland-Alexis Manuel Lévy) was a French composer and musicologist who is sometimes called the seventh member of Les Six, because of his close associations with the group. He spent much of his childhood in Belgium, but after his father's death he returned to Paris in 1905 to become a pupil of Roussel at the Schola Cantorum. He met Satie there in 1910, who recommended that he should study composition with Ravel. This proved to be extremely sound advice, for Roland-Manuel's impersonal, anti-Romantic approach fitted in perfectly with Ravel's aesthetic, and Roland-Manuel later wrote four valuable books on the mentor he so much admired. When Satie's own friendship with Ravel turned to antipathy after the war, it was perhaps inevitable that he should also have broken with Roland-Manuel, though this break was exacerbated by Roland-Manuel's dislike of *Socrate* in 1920, which Satie never forgave.

It was in 1910 that, flipping through the addenda of Hugo Riemann's dictionary, I came across the words, in the article on Debussy, 'He has orchestrated the *Gymnopédies* by Erik Satie (the Rose-Croix composer).'

The collection of syllables in this name suggested to my mind's eye a Scandinavian aesthete wearing a monocle and Oscar Wilde's green carnation. What could these *Gymnopédies* be, honoured with an orchestration by Debussy – and who was this composer, who was unknown either to my teachers or to any of my friends? When I asked a salesman in Durand's music shop, he replied: 'Hang on . . . Satie? That name means something to me: he's a fellow who's composed a cakewalk and some waltzes for Paulette Darty: *La diva de l''Empire'*, *Je te veux*, *Le Piccadilly*. I'm sorry,' he went on, 'but we don't have any of those in stock.' The prestige of my Scandinavian aesthete was crumbling. But as luck would have it, Paulette Darty, now Mme Édouard Dreyfus, was related to my family. I soon found out from the diva of the Empire and of the Casino de Paris that Erik Satie was alive and well, about 40 years old and living in Arcueil, and that she had a meal with him once a week.

Taking advantage of this, I found myself a few days later in the avenue de Villiers, in the presence of a man correctly dressed in a smart suit, with a twinkling, mischievous eye, a faun-like face and a tangled little beard, all of which made a curious contrast with the stiff collar and the bureaucratic pince-nez. At first sight, the whole man gave off an air of bourgeois kindliness. I felt at ease until the moment when the name of Debussy came up in the conversation. Although Debussy was only four years older than he was, Satie claimed to consider him a composer of the past, with Ravel illustrating the present and Albert Roussel being the hope of the future.

I quickly obtained the famous *Gymnopédies* from their composer and the extraordinary music for *Le fils des étoiles*, a 'Wagnérie Kaldéenne' by Sâr Péladan, and other pieces as well. But I was particularly fascinated by *Le fils des étoiles* with its chains of fourths. Satie, for his part, said he no longer had any interest in these old discoveries, made some twenty years earlier.

In 1908 he had finished his mature studies of counterpoint with Albert Roussel at the Schola Cantorum and, when I knew him, was following Vincent d'Indy's composition course.

His desire to undergo the punctilious, austere formalism of the Schola contrasted strangely with the jokes he made about his respected teacher, 'son vénéré maître d'Indouille'.* I learnt to understand and participate in this taste for mysterious jesting, in which Norman cunning combined with Scottish humour. This perpetual collusion between the Muse and the Angel of the bizarre led the composer of the *Morceaux en forme de poire*, a precursor of Jean Tardieu, meticulously to substitute one word for another. He urged us to admit the beauties of the *Symphonie sur un thème campagnard*[sic], talked about Alexandre Guilmant's organ and at the same time infuriated Debussy by telling him of the forthcoming publication of a piece called *Sous la futaille* [*The Bottom of the Barrel*].†

How can one explain this contradiction between the seriousness of a quest which was to lead to *Socrate*, and the absurd outer casing which covers the achievements and prophecies of the 'parcier de l'Église Métropolitaine d'Art de Jésus Conducteur'?

It appears there are two keys to Satie's secret domain. One of them

---

*A pun on 'andouille': a chitterling or, colloquially, a nit-wit, and Roussel's interest in Hindu culture.
†This was retitled 'Avec camaraderie' as the fourth of the *Préludes flasques (pour un chien)* in July 1912. But Satie changed very little of the music in the process and never published the collection in the end.

breaches the defences of a fierce, apprehensive modesty: that is the French key, because Satie was very like the honest man who always claimed his pearls were false. The other key – the English key – is more secret and reveals the essence of the man. It was forged in the workshop of the 'ironical conformism' so well described by Vladimir Jankélévitch. Ironical conformism denounces error, absurdity and scandal by flattering them with hypocritical collaboration. It encourages and cultivates the banal, the cliché, the full flowering of idiocy. It invests the practitioner's walk with a bourgeois solemnity. Once it is satisfied that confidence reigns in the kingdom of the golden mean, at the crucial moment it throws down the banana skin. Whoever has not heard Satie agreeing with an elderly person that times are hard and morals gone to the dogs, or suggesting to a patroness that she deserves to be placed between Bonaparte and St Joseph; whoever has not seen him asking the advice of a retired major, a fellow student at the Schola, about the development of the generative cell and vie in his commiseration over Schumann ('Poor Schumann didn't know how to develop his ideas; but you, my dear Commandant, you do, don't you?'); whoever has not been with Satie during his favourite exercises should go back, via Dickens, Shakespeare and Cervantes, to Plato's dialogues to find parallel delights, or, if he's a musician, look at some piece by Satie himself in which delicate, unbelievably graceful two-part inventions grapple with interminable cadential formulae.

This strange joker was filled with a spirit of luminous finesse and wisdom. We used to meet him in the Chope Latine, a tavern near the Schola Cantorum and the gare de Sceaux, the terminus for the train to Arcueil – where no one, ever, dared follow him.

A nice glass of wine and a beef salad would encourage him to hold forth. Listening to this prophet, at that time unrecognised, who had imagined, foreseen and prepared so many things in which he did not care to take part, we used to think of Alcibiades' speech, comparing Socrates with those statues of Silenus, which begins: 'His words at first seem completely grotesque. The expressions he uses to clothe his thought are as unappetising as the skin of an impudent satyr . . . But when you open his speeches, and examine what's inside, you suddenly find they're full of common sense.'

Satie's main preoccupation, during the time I knew him, was with decongesting music, with 'showing, in the words of Joubert, beauty absent', so that lyricism might be born of its opposite. He was already attracted by Plato's dialogues. I suggested the translation by Mario Meunier, but he preferred the one by Victor Cousin which was, he said, heavier, duller and for those reasons more to his taste. In the great days when the Ballets Russes were dazzling us with spectacle, he was beginning to preach poverty of material, art's ultimate resource in a world without love. This ancient faun was proposing a philosophy of asceticism.

Without abjuring the dignity of an admirable life of poverty, Satie, despising our idols, loaded us with benefits for which, because of his vocation, he would never see a reward. And we should lay less emphasis than Alcibiades did on the resemblance between Socrates and the satyr Marsyas: 'On the outside, Socrates, you will not disclaim the resemblance; as for the rest, hear what I have to say: are you not a shameless scoffer? If you deny it, I shall produce witnesses . . .'

As a witness to Satie's shameless scoffing, I should like to call attention to the divine image hidden inside the statue of Silenus.

Roland-Manuel
'Satie tel que je l'ai vu', *ReM*, 214, June 1952, pp. 9–11

RENÉ CHALUPT

During his belated studies at the Schola Cantorum, Satie had as one of his fellow pupils the young Roland-Manuel, and it was at Roland-Manuel's house that I first met him. We would often see each other too at Roland-Manuel's parents' house on the rue de Chazelles, and it was in those delightful surroundings that I saw the first private performance of *Le piège de Méduse*. Care had been taken on this occasion to put sheets of paper between the strings of the piano and the single female role was taken by Mlle Suzanne Roux, shortly to become Mme Roland-Manuel.

I would see him regularly, too, in the apartment of Cipa and Ida Godebski, whose famous Sunday salon on the rue d'Athènes was, for many years, the meeting place for the best artists in Paris, both foreign and Parisian. As for my parents, they warmly welcomed musicians, to some degree certainly out of conviction, but also to please their two children – both me and my younger sister, who was an excellent pianist and a passionate music-lover, but who was taken from us by the Spanish flu epidemic in 1918. Practically everyone who was anyone in the musical world came to us between 1910 and 1918 and Ricardo Viñes, my sister's teacher, was a close friend and always ready to take his turn at the piano. Satie was a regular visitor and his presence provided an opportunity for performing some of his most recent compositions. As a result, in 1914 he came to dedicate to Mlle Linette Chalupt the second of his *Trois valses distinguées du précieux dégoûté*, 'Son binocle', while to me he dedicated the third, 'Ses jambes'. Was he aware that I was crazy about dancing and spent every night on the dance-floor doing extended tangos and bostons, when he wrote the following words on these pages:

– They dance only the most refined dances.

– In the evening they dress in black.

– He wants to carry them under his arm.

– . . . often he embraces them and puts them on his neck.

– How good he is to them!

– Decisively he refuses to buy leggings. 'A prison!' he says, adding finally: 'Go on till you faint.'

He became popular with our boisterous little group of night-owls, centred on Valentine Gross, now Mme Jean Hugo, the painter Roger de la Fresnaye and the poet Jean Baguenier-Desormeaux. When we expressed surprise at seeing him set out calmly on foot for Arcueil at the most god-forsaken hours, which meant crossing deserted and decidedly unappealing suburbs, he would reply: 'There's no problem. If I spot some evil-looking type, I lie down in the gutter and pretend to be drunk.' That gives you some idea of what he was like.

I've kept a number of notes Satie sent either to me or to my sister. They're written in his calligraphic hand, with lots of decoration, the whole effect certainly unusual but totally unspontaneous. A headache for the graphologists! Sometimes he would illustrate these notes with a portrait of himself in the form of a bust, with his everlasting pince-nez on his nose. His signing-off phrases were unique to him: 'Amiably' or 'You are a fine, worthy man', and whenever he fixed the time of a meeting he would use both the new and the old designation: 'I'll be there at 1800 hrs (6 o'clock old style).'

After *Parade*, Satie devoted himself to what might be considered his masterpiece, the most important and lasting and the most human of his works, *Socrate*, a symphonic drama in three sections on dialogues of Plato, translated by Victor Cousin. To achieve the pure line, the limpid texture, the true accentuation and the moving simplicity of this work, he really burned the candle at both ends and imposed silence on his mystificatory humours. Well before the first public performance there were private hearings with the wonderful Suzanne Balguerie, first of all at the Godebskis in the rue d'Athènes and then in my apartment, given from the barely legible manuscript which Viñes refused to try and decipher because his eyes weren't up to the standard of his hands.

Socrate was published by Éditions de La Sirène in the rue de la Boétie, in the very same block I was living in. Satie wanted the edition to have a preface and he asked me to be responsible for it. I was flattered, but I suspected I'd been chosen because Satie didn't want to let himself be monopolised by Jean Cocteau, who would, I felt, have been the normal choice in the circumstances. Quite apart from my real admiration for his extraordinary talents, I was on excellent terms with this most delightful and courteous of men and continue to be so; but even if we saw each other regularly at this time, we were not in the habit of dropping in on each other without a reason. But the day Satie came to see me to talk about the *Socrate* preface, no sooner had he sat down than there was a ring at the door. It was Cocteau! Immediately, we changed the subject. I couldn't help thinking that this unexpected visit, which was without precedent or successor, was no accident. I wrote the preface with all the required concision and in the simplest, most homogeneous style. Passages from it have often been quoted and as a matter of course extracts (always the same ones) are reproduced in the programme whenever *Socrate* is given. Satie attached great importance to this preface. Right from the time I agreed to do it, he was urging me to make haste, saying: 'Is it coming on? Look alive, dear fellow.'

Or else he'd write me notes:

> Is your preface coming on? Short and precise . . . A clear exposé of what *Socrate* expresses . . . Its meaning in the musical context . . . . its *novelty*.
>
> My friendly request is for a text that's 'proud'. Speak with *authority*, without *arguing*.

René Chalupt
'Quelques souvenirs sur Erik Satie', *ReM*, 214, June 1952, pp. 41–2, 44–5

MICHEL-DIMITRI CALVOCORESSI
(1877–1944)

Michel-Dimitri Calvocoressi was a critic and musicologist of
Greek parentage who was born in Marseilles. He studied
harmony at the Paris Conservatoire and had a remarkable
facility for languages, specialising in translating opera libret-
tos and songs in addition to his other writings on music. His
main interest lay in contemporary music, particularly that of
Russia, and he acted as Diaghilev's main French adviser when
he first brought his Ballets Russes to Paris. In 1914 he moved
to England, as he was unable to serve in France because of
his Greek origins. Satie kept in touch with him, though
he had a low opinion of all music critics and did not find
Calvocoressi's opinions particularly perceptive. Despite a certain lack of depth, Calvocoressi was a fair-minded man and
he did not suddenly join the anti-Satie bandwagon after his
death in 1925, as so many others did.

It was through Ravel (in 1905 or thereabouts) that my attention was
drawn to Satie's music and that I got acquainted with him. Satie showed
me his published pieces (they were not easy to locate) and many things
still in manuscript, among which were the *Sarabandes*. I promptly saw
the truth of Ravel's assertion that Satie's music contained the germ of
many things in the modern developments in music, and I proceeded in
turn to call attention to it.

A uniform characteristic of his jokes, musical or not, is that they are
intended primarily for his own consumption. If you laugh with him, well
and good; if you laugh at him or betray irritation, there will be two jokes
for him to enjoy instead of one. The trouble is that in his music you
cannot always be sure where leg-pulling begins and ends. While his
Socrate, which represents his latest tendencies, was hailed by some as a
masterpiece, others have ventured the opinion that this very mild setting
of excerpts from Victor Cousin's insipid translation is one of the hugest –
and driest – jokes ever perpetrated by him. During a rehearsal of *Socrate*
in Paris he said to me: 'You see what I wanted to do. It's very simple:
originality through platitude.' Perhaps he meant it.

Michel-Dimitri Calvocoressi
'Erik Satie. A few recollections and remarks', *The Monthly Musical Record*, 55,
1 January 1925, pp. 6–7

FRANCIS POULENC
(1899–1963)

Francis Poulenc was, like Satie, a Parisian through and
through. As a precocious young composer in his teens, his
music was championed by Satie through his Nouveaux Jeunes
concerts and in 1920 he became a member of Les Six. Satie
admired the freshness and spontaneity of his music, and sometimes referred to him as a 'gamin' (urchin). He fell out with
Poulenc in 1924 because of the latter's close friendship with
his enemies Auric and Laloy, even though Poulenc was never
openly hostile towards him. In fact, Poulenc regarded Satie
as his mentor and, as a skilled pianist himself, was particularly
well equipped to give the following overview of Satie's keyboard skills.

Satie didn't often play the piano. I heard him do so at the most two or
three times, accompanying some of his songs, and then he would try and
get out of it right up to the last minute. More often than not, Ricardo
Viñes, Marcelle Meyer, Auric or I would do this favour for him.

The state his piano was found in after his death (the instrument was
later bought by Braque) proves that Satie never used it. I'm astonished
that such utterly pianistic music could have been conceived away from the
keyboard; unless Satie, mysterious as ever, tried out his precious pieces
on some unknown piano in Arcueil, which, I have to say, I don't really
believe.

In his youth he had studied the instrument, first of all in Honfleur,
with the organist of the Église Saint-Charles [Léonard], and then in
1885 at the Conservatoire with Georges Mathias, a pupil of Chopin and
Kalkbrenner!!! No doubt he preferred not to use it because it reminded
him of the time when he was a 'hired key-thumper' at the Auberge du
Clou. Even so, as I say, just as some mornings he used to borrow Jean
Cocteau's bathroom to trim his beard, it's quite possible that when he
found himself among friends, he asked to use the piano *just for five*

minutes, to test something, as he did several times with me. The basic fact is that Satie had an innate feeling for the instrument.

Whereas so many composers, even well-known ones, too often tend to think of the piano as a makeshift instrument which can cope with anything, Satie in his meticulous way knew exactly what suited it. The novel directness of his writing, a bold reaction against the other-worldly atmosphere of Debussy and Ravel, shows up as an influence as late as 1944, in Stravinsky's Sonata for two pianos.

Satie stated that it was forbidden under pain of major excommunication to read out the stories and funny remarks with which he decorated his music, either before or during performances.* (*They are the pianist's reward*, he sometimes used to say.) In the same way, when you start a piece like the second of the *Embryons desséchés*, you must not wink at the audience.

Francis Poulenc
'La musique de piano d'Erik Satie', *ReM*, 214, June 1952, pp. 23–5

LOUIS DUREY
(1888–1979)

Louis Durey was, like Satie, a pupil at the Schola Cantorum in Paris with strong left-wing views. He acted as secretary for the Nouveaux Jeunes during the war, and it was probably because of his developing friendship with Ravel in 1918 that Satie broke with him and the group on 1 November that year. Durey went on to become one of Les Six, though he never entered into its frivolous spirit and refused to collaborate with Cocteau and the others on *Les mariés de la Tour Eiffel*. In fact, he withdrew from the group in the year of its foundation (1921) and went to live in St Tropez, returning to Paris only in 1930.

It is impossible to classify with anything else the work of that inventor who was able to hold himself aloof from all schools and even to shun his own discoveries when he felt that they would become the prey of some colleague. He was one of those capricious plants which, feeling the

*In the score of his *Heures séculaires et instantanées*, published in 1917.

constraint of vegetating like its fellows, produces, one hardly knows how or why, a strange unique flower, attractive on account of its unexpectedness, in some solitary and inaccessible place. I would call Satie *un Caprice de la Nature*.

We should cherish an affectionate sympathy for Erik Satie, mystic or Bohemian, for what he brought that was new to music: a clear judgment, a horror of hackneyed ways, love of discovery and of risk, the relief of good humor and systematic rejection of all that was heavy and tiresome. It was a stone of small dimensions which was his contribution to the edifice, but one of very pure whiteness and brilliance.

Louis Durey
'Erik Satie', *Arts* [Brooklyn], 17, 1930, pp. 162–3, 164–5

CHARLES KOECHLIN

I dare say you know Rudyard Kipling's charming story, 'The Cat who Walked by Himself' . . . I can't think of Satie without calling to mind that free feline. His music has the same elegant suppleness, the economy of gesture, the precise paw movements in his witty inventions and the discreet sensitivity which the mob persist in misunderstanding; and finally, and especially, the same instinctive, absolute independence.

Socrate is, I believe, the most important work Satie has written so far. But I'm not surprised that many people still don't fully appreciate it, because it is absolutely new and *original*. Its undeniable Hellenism cloaks an individual form which was unknown until now. The nature of this is hard to define and, in order to understand it, one has to throw certain musical assumptions overboard.

Let's look back at the figure of that great philosopher and great ironist of antiquity. As he says himself (in part 1 of *Socrate*), 'You may think I'm joking, but I'm utterly serious.' Using humour to deal with profound questions is a very French tendency, which some foreigners might even feel to be a fault. Perhaps they would disapprove too of that reserve which Socrates maintained up to his final moments, and of his way of putting on a cheerful air when faced with the inevitable ('Let's sacrifice a cock to Aesculapius').

Maybe these various ancient Greek attitudes have their faults; but they also have their virtues, the main one being the propensity to know how *not to go beyond what you want to express*. You should not be surprised at finding similar characteristics in Satie, whose humour is often a withholding of expression, a retreat before imbeciles and fools.

Charles Koechlin
'Erik Satie', *ReM*, 5, March 1924, pp. 193, 203–4

Right up to his death, Satie remained *a child*. He had certainly seen life – a hard, unpleasant life – but there always remained in the depths of his heart the poetry of the happy dreams of his youth. It was a poetry he did his best to hide, because of the reserve I have already mentioned. But we should be grateful that it often manifested itself despite his efforts: you could see it sometimes in his eyes, and you can still find it, alive and well, in his music. It also existed silently in his passion for order and in the slightly puerile obsessions he had. He never outgrew the child who once upon a time had been filled with enthusiasm for the delightful, ironical, tender stories of Hans Christian Andersen. In his last years, Andersen's stories were his bedside reading.

Charles Koechlin
Unpublished MS of a lecture on Satie, December 1927

JEAN COCTEAU

I first had the idea of *Parade* during a period of 'leave' in April 1915 [1916] (I was then in the Army), on hearing Satie play his *Morceaux en forme de poire* for four hands, with Viñes.

A kind of telepathy inspired us simultaneously with a desire to collaborate. A week later I returned to the front, leaving Satie with a bundle of notes and sketches which were to provide him with the theme of the Chinaman, the little American girl and the acrobat (there was then only one acrobat). Gradually there came to birth a score in which Satie seems to have discovered an unknown dimension, thanks to which one can listen simultaneously both to the 'Parade' and the show going on inside.

Erik Satie's orchestra charms without the use of pedals. It is like an inspired village band.

It will open a door to those young composers who are a little weary of fine impressionist polyphonies.

Listen to it emerging from a fugue and rejoining it again with a classic freedom.

'I composed,' said Satie modestly, 'a background for certain noises which Cocteau considers indispensable in order to fix the atmosphere of his characters.'

Satie exaggerates, but the noises certainly played an important part in *Parade*.

Jean Cocteau
A Call to Order (trans. Rollo H. Myers) (London, Faber & Gwyer, 1926), pp. 50–51, 54

DARIUS MILHAUD

(1892–1974)

Darius Milhaud was a member of both the Nouveaux Jeunes and Les Six. Satie was first attracted to his music in 1915, but did not meet him till early 1919 when Milhaud returned from Brazil after a period as secretary to the writer and diplomat Paul Claudel. He was the only one of the young composers that Satie helped with whom Satie never quarrelled. This was mainly due to their mutual respect both as men and as composers, but Milhaud (who came from a wealthy Jewish family in Aix-en-Provence) often assisted Satie financially and was also instrumental in introducing him to new patrons and other useful social contacts. He and his wife Madeleine were particularly helpful to Satie during his final illness and it was Milhaud who was entrusted by Conrad Satie to act as Satie's artistic executor.

The event to which Milhaud refers below took place at the Galerie Barbazanges in the Faubourg St-Honoré on 8 March 1920, though all other accounts refer to the Max Jacob play as being *Ruffian toujours, truand jamais*.

Just as one's field of vision embraces objects and forms, such as the pattern on the wallpaper, the cornice of the ceiling, or the frame of the looking-glass, which the eye sees but to which it pays no attention, although they are undoubtedly there, Satie thought it would be amusing to have music that would not be listened to, 'musique d'ameublement', or background music that would vary like the furniture of the rooms in which it was played. Auric and Poulenc disapproved of this suggestion, but it tickled my fancy so much that I experimented with it, in co-operation with Satie, at a concert given in the Galerie Barbazanges. During the programme, Marcelle Meyer played music by Les Six, and Bertin presented a play by Max Jacob, called *Un Figurant au Théâtre de Nantes*, which required the services of a trombone. He also sang Stravinsky's *Berceuses du chat* to the accompaniment of three clarinets, so Satie and I scored our music for the instruments used in the course of these various items on the programme. In order that the music might seem to come from all sides at once, we posted the clarinets in three different corners of the theatre, the pianist[s] in the fourth, and the trombone in a box on the first floor. A programme note warned the audience that it was not to pay any more attention to the ritornelles that would be played during the intervals than to the candelabra, the seats, or the balcony.

Contrary to our expectations, however, as soon as the music started up the audience began to stream back to their seats. It was no use for Satie to shout: 'Go on talking! Walk about! Don't listen!' They listened without speaking. The whole effect was spoilt . . . Satie had not bargained for the charm of his own music. This was our one and only experiment with this sort of music. Nevertheless Satie wrote another 'ritournelle d'ameublement' for Mrs Eugene Meyer when she asked him, through me, to give her an autograph [in 1923]. But for this *Musique pour un cabinet préfectoral* to have its full meaning, she should have had it recorded and played over and over again, thus forming part of the furniture of her beautiful library in Crescent Place, adorning it for the ear in the same way as the still-life by Manet adorned it for the eye. In any case, the future was to prove that Satie was right: nowadays, children and housewives fill their homes with unheeded music, reading and working to the sound of the wireless. And in all public places, large stores and restaurants, the customers are drenched in an unending flood of music. Is this not 'musique d'ameublement', heard, but not listened to?

Darius Milhaud
Notes Without Music (trans. Donald Evans) (London, Calder & Boyars, 1952; 2/ 1967), pp. 105–6

MAX JACOB
(1876–1944)

Max Jacob came to Paris from Brittany, from a Jewish family, and soon established himself as an important poet. Like Satie, his existence was precarious and he moved freely in avant-garde literary and artistic circles, being closely associated with the Cubist movement. He converted to Catholicism in 1914, before he met Satie, and settled in 1921 at the Benedictine Abbey at Saint-Benoît-sur-Loire, though he often left its seclusion to travel back to Paris or abroad. His poetry is often racy and ironic and Satie seriously considered setting some of it in 1919. Jacob died in the German concentration camp at Drancy during the Second World War.

Satie's music is spiritual in being stripped bare, chiefly by a technique which is far from being indigent by nature, but which voluntarily espouses Poverty. Think of his disdain for effect. There is nothing more sincere in him than the spirit of renunciation. His bizarre life-style may have scandalised the Establishment, but did he not live it in such a way as to escape all compromise?

Dear Satie was moved by his natural goodness and by his instinctive thirst for justice, and if he belonged to any political party it was because he hoped to find in it that charity that lay within himself. He was not a man to be fooled. He was born a Christian and he died a Christian, in his final moments playing a last joke on his left-wing friends. It was the severing of a final link – not that he ever liked them much – and now, seated on the lap of Truth, he is laughing behind his beard.

But the most extraordinary thing is that he travelled directly, right from his earliest compositions, towards the technique that suited him, and from the *Ogives* to *Relâche* the spirit of that technique never varied.

Max Jacob
'L'exemple d'Erik Satie', *Vigile*, 2, 1930, pp. 127–8

IX

Success and the war years

Success came gradually for Satie and did not begin until 1911, when he was 45. On 16 January of that year, Ravel performed several of his early pieces at a Société Musicale Indépendante concert in the Salle Gaveau. Although Satie would have preferred these to have been more up-to-date works, he was delighted by the publicity the concert brought and subsequently by the increased demand for his piano music. Between 1912 and 1915, in an uncharacteristic burst of productivity, he composed over sixty piano pieces for publication by Demets, Rouart-Lerolle and Lucien Vogel. His second 'discovery' came by Jean Cocteau in 1916 and led to the commission for *Parade*, which enjoyed a *succès de scandale* when it was produced by Diaghilev the following year. This in turn paved the way for his later theatrical career (with Picasso in particular), though it also carried disaster in its wake after the critic Jean Poueigh brought a successful slander suit against Satie in the summer of 1917. Satie was profoundly depressed by the whole trial, fearing bankruptcy, a police record, and the destruction of his professional reputation. This and the very real state of poverty he reached during the summer of 1918 (when all his money-lending friends were away on holiday) worried him far more than the accusations of 'Bochism' had done after *Parade*. So, although the war years brought artistic success, and a host of young acolytes to Satie's feet, they did not bring Satie as much happiness as he might have expected. In fact, given the problems he experienced with Cocteau and Misia Edwards during the writing of *Parade*, one might say that he only briefly experienced a state of euphoria, in January 1917, after *Parade* had been composed and the Princesse de Polignac had sent him an advance for *Socrate*. Then, for a brief while, Satie was 'free as air, as water; as the wild sheep'.

CONRAD SATIE

July 1914

Cigar boxes with celluloid folders containing notes (one slips over another, as on a calendar) on precise, unreal subjects – the notes are in calligraphic writing, meant to be looked at and all making a similar impression. Among other things there he's got an island of his own, to escape to, more beautiful than the Mont St Michel, with a president dressed in green, whose portrait he's drawn.

(He doesn't want to show me his home, dreamer that he is, and I understand that. I'm the same in my own home. Friends' visits smash my imaginary toys and upset my thoughts where they're stacked in corners, in apparent disorder.)

He's planning some 'tedious' works about gas lighting and the training of horses, 'The horse is a horse-like animal'.

30 September 1914

One should have an antediluvian fortune.

Project for a newspaper: 'Musical defence. News sheet.'

The silver pince-nez with lenses of smoked gold.

Erik and Debussy – their friendship. How Debussy grumbles. Jupiter. Chouchou 9 years old, Debussy's daughter – and Kiki (Erik). Their bows and arrows – they walk on the grass and are grumbled at.

He has some esteem for Vaughan Williams and Cyril Scott. Slow development of his humorous, comic vocation. His new manner.

His way of talking quietly in certain places with only half his mouth. I can't hear him any more. Grill-Room Médicis and Spielmann.

His arrival at the Chat Noir – his role there, in a white suit. His friendship with Peladouille [Péladan] – he drinks three to five coffees, with small cigars, and can eat 150 oysters.

The lovely walk with him on the Butte. Changes. Places where he had a good time.

21 October 1914

– magnificent portrait attributed to an unknown artist

– the wing of the crayfish

– he doesn't like the sun, his personal enemy, brutal, says nasty things about him.

    CS: What are you doing the day after tomorrow?

    ES: Nothing wrong.

    CS: I mean, will you come for lunch?

Notes of conversations with Satie taken down by his brother Conrad in 1914 (*AFS*)

PRINCESSE EDMOND DE POLIGNAC
(1865–1943)

The Princesse Edmond de Polignac was born Winnaretta Singer in New York, the daughter of Isaac Singer, founder of the Singer sewing-machine empire. She achieved her elevated position in Parisian high society by marrying first Prince Louis de Scey-Montbéliard in 1887, and then the ageing homosexual aesthete, Prince Edmond de Polignac, in December 1893. A skilled musician herself, she devoted her fortune to promoting the arts, organising regular concerts at her opulent houses in Paris and Venice and commissioning works from composers such as Fauré, Stravinsky, Falla and Poulenc. In October 1916 she commissioned *Socrate* from Satie, and many claim this 'symphonic drama' (completed in 1918) to be his most important work.

I was very anxious to know Satie, and I intended to ask him to write music for the Death of Socrates in Plato's *Phaedo*. I asked Jeanne [sic] Bathori to bring him to dinner one evening. He was then a man of about 52 [50], neither tall nor short, very thin, with a short beard. He invariably wore pince-nez, through which one saw his kindly but rather mischievous pale blue eyes, always ready to twinkle as some humorous thought crossed his mind. I remember that the dinner included roast tongue, which he found particularly good, and when I asked him if he would have another slice, he at once answered, 'Yes, yes, with pleasure, but . . . not the head, I beg you, because I can't abide calf's head.'*

At the time when I met Satie I had been learning a little Greek and was

---

*Satie often referred to music critics as 'calves' heads' or 'muttonheads'.

becoming more and more enthusiastic as I managed to read the tragedies of Euripides or the Dialogues of Plato in the original text. Satie was equally enthusiastic, so he decided to write music for the *Death of Socrates*, and after much thought suggested that the scene should be set in a small salon in the Empire Style in which, in armchairs, Mme[s] de Wendel and Argyropoulo who knew Greek perfectly, and I myself, would read in turn the glorious words of Plato. At first this seemed an excellent idea, and we spent many evenings talking it over, but in the end Satie decided to give up the idea of the Empire Salon and to have no scenery at all, and he wrote an oratorio [sic] for a woman's voice and small orchestra. There is no doubt that this is his masterpiece, and nothing could be more moving than this music written for the beautiful words of Plato. When he had finished it he sent me the score, which is now in Paris in my collection of musical manuscripts. Jeanne Bathori sang *Socrates* for the first time in my music room accompanied by the ethereal music of Satie.*

Princesse Edmond de Polignac
'Memoirs', *Horizon*, 12/68, August 1945, pp. 137–8

VALENTINE HUGO

The first time I saw Satie, he was the Baron Méduse. At the beginning of 1914 I was taken by René Chalupt and Roger de la Fresnaye to Roland-Manuel's parents' flat. That evening saw the first performance, before an audience of family friends and friends of the composer, of *Le piège de Méduse, comédie lyrique en un acte de M. Erik Satie, avec musique de danse du même Monsieur*.

Satie, naturally, took the rôle of Baron Méduse. He was seriously funny in such an extraordinary and individual way that I've never forgotten that irresistible Méduse, which has remained for me the shadow of the Socrates I came to know so well later. We understood each other perfectly, and at once. I already knew most of his works. After the performance, I immediately hummed a few passages of his music and he was delighted with my memory.

Thanks to our shared tastes and having friends in common, a friendship

*On 3 April 1918 at 57 avenue Henri-Martin, Paris 16, with Satie at the piano and no invited audience.

began which was to last until his death. From that evening in the winter of 1913–14, Satie visited me at least once a week.

As soon as he'd jotted down some sketches in one of his tiny notebooks, he'd announce his arrival in advance to be quite certain of finding his *chère grande fille*, as he called me, ready to listen to him playing and singing his initial ideas.

And so, gradually, I became his child, his friend, his sister.

He confided in me with great simplicity, both by letter and face to face. He kept me abreast of his joys, which were few and far between, and of his severe problems and dissatisfactions, which were far too plentiful. Poor dear Satie! I did my best to calm his rages and resentments which, most of the time, were well justified. Sometimes I had to invent extraordinary methods of restoring social edifices that he'd demolished, and then I'd receive from him a little letter, more or less calligraphic in appearance, like the following, for example, written on manuscript paper: 'It's so nice when you say to me gently: "Satie, you mustn't get cross with them." '

Some time before he discovered Plato's Socrates, I'd been touched by what I couldn't help feeling was the 'Socratic' nature of our long dialogues. My part in these was extremely modest, but I knew how to listen to him. I'd just finished a long article, since lost, on Greek dancing, which was to be the sequel to the one I'd published on Egyptian dancing, and I was familiar with the rhythm and substance of conversation in the Ancient World. I often thought of Socrates' words, which I found rather difficult to obey: 'When people make long speeches at me, I lose sight of the subject under discussion . . . So compress your answers and make them shorter, if you want me to follow you.'

I'll pass over here the years 1915–16, when visits and letters followed each other at a variable pace dictated by the birth and growth of *Parade*.

In the postscript to a letter of 12 December 1916, Satie wrote: 'I've written the "Petit prélude du rideau rouge". It's a fugal exposition, very *meditative*, very *serious*, and even quite "crusty", but *short*. I like this slightly academic, pseudo-naive style of writing, absolutely "kono", as the "Japs" say.'

The music of *Parade* was completed, he finished his work with the prelude! On 26 December 1916, he asked me to organise a *purely friendly* read-through at the piano with a couple of friends. These readings continued at Ricardo Viñes's flat from 3 January 1917. A few days later came the discovery of the *Vie de Socrate*, which Satie told me about in a letter of 6 January 1917:

> Chère amie,
>
> Did you get my recent card? I hope so. you're much too good to me. Yes, much.
>
> How are you? What's wrong?
>
> I'm very sorry to know that you're ill.
>
> Poor Stern must be very upset.
>
> Are you seeing a doctor? Don't take any risks, whatever you do.
>
> I've got a terrible cold. I shan't be going to Mme Garrett's tomorrow. I've written to her asking to be excused. I'd have liked to go to that dinner but – truly – I'm too tired and too ill.
>
> I'm busy with the *Vie de Socrate*. I'm terrified of bungling this work, which I want to be as white and pure as Antiquity.
>
> I'm besotted with it and don't know where to put myself. There's a wonderful work waiting to be written on this subject, it's *extraoordinary*. Or, as the general public prefer to say, *extraordinary*.
>
> I've written to Diaghilev. I think he'll get my letter before he leaves for Rome. That way, he'll be nailed – well and truly nailed.
>
> All these 'tales' are very boring. I'm sorry, my dear, to have bothered you with them. Forgive me.
>
> If I'm 'awkward', Montparnasse has nothing to do with it. It's life – not that of Socrates – which is the reason behind it. My 'sister-in-law' – one-time aunt – Aubry,* Debussy and others think Montparnasse is giving me advice. They're the ones telling me what to do, they alone – and that's enough – too much, possibly.
>
> As for you, dear Valentine, you are an exquisite fairy, fit to be revered. Yes.
>
> Greetings from
>
> E. S.

We, Satie's friends, had just lived through a week of violent quarrels. This time, I'd had such a job dampening down his rages that I literally

---

*Georges Jean-Aubry, the music historian and critic.

became ill . . . I decided to leave Paris for a time with my friend Mimi
Godebska, and seek the sun in the Midi.

That winter of 1916–17 was the coldest and bitterest of the war. I
stayed at home, while all around me in the Île Saint Louis everything
froze.

Satie's letters delayed my departure. I couldn't go away and leave him
prey to all his violent fits, just when he was obsessed with pure fervour
for a new work. Then came the letter of 18 January 1917:

> Arcueil-Cachan, 18 January 1917
>
> Chère Amie,
>
>   . . . What am I doing? I'm working on the *Vie de Socrate*.
> I've found a fine translation: the one by Victor Cousin. Plato
> is a perfect collaborator, very easy-going and never a nuisance.
> Something one dreams about! I've written to the good Princess
> about it. I'm swimming in happiness. At last! I'm free, free
> as air, as water; as the wild sheep. Long live Plato! Long
> live Victor Cousin! I'm free! absolutely free! What joy! I
> embrace you with all my heart. You are my beloved *grande
> fille*.
>
> Your grandpa,
>
> E. S.

That letter allowed me to leave Paris. Satie was so happy and delighted
to be free at last to work without material worries and without being
harassed, that I felt quite reassured for some time.

In Cannes, where I was staying at the Hôtel de Californie with the
'petit poète' of the song *Daphénéo*,* I had a letter every week from my
grandpa and friend. Including this one, of 23 February:

> Chère grande fille,
>
>   All right? Mme Cocteau tells me that you're going from
> town to town, travelling on every side at once. That's splen-
> did. Have you got fine weather? Here the sun is as cold as
> the devil. The sun too must be short of coal. That doesn't
> surprise me. Some furnace!
>
>   And my dear *petit Poète*? Is she well? Give her warmest
> greetings from me, won't you?

*Mimi Godebska.

Goodbye, dear *grande fille*. See you soon.   E. S.

And a few days later:

You're coming back. Happy? In good health? As pretty as
ever? I'm as ugly! and as irritating: a pest! Jean is still in
Rome. He's a romer. Forgive the pun.
See you soon, dear *grande fille*.
Your grandpa,

E. S.

All of which showed Satie's 'medusan' side. His letters made us laugh
a lot. After we'd got back to Paris, and Cocteau and Diaghilev as well,
the orchestral rehearsals for *Parade* began. The interchanges between the
collaborators, sometimes harmonious, sometimes catastrophic, prevented
me from thinking of anything else. The first performance took place on
18 May 1917 at the Théâtre du Châtelet – an uproarious occasion, as we
all know, which I've described elsewhere.

The Princesse de Polignac's payment for the score of *Socrate* on 18
January had saved Satie financially for a time – 'saved him from skin and
bones', as he said – but by the following summer he was as poor as ever.

One concert followed another, from the rue Huyghens to the Théâtre
du Vieux Colombier, at Paul Guillaume's and at his friends' flats, at
which Jane Bathori, Marcelle Meyer and Pierre Bertin sang and played
Satie's works wonderfully.

But our poor friend was sad and disheartened.

Even so, he was working busily, going on with *Socrate* which he'd
started in 1917. I'd heard fragments of it, which he played for me as
usual; but it was at Jane Bathori's, that wonderful musician, that I first
heard *Socrate* complete.

On 24 June 1918, there were four or five of us to hear her singing
'Mort de Socrate', with Satie accompanying her on the piano. It was
unforgettable . . . the singer's marvellous, heart-rending voice, the overwhelming beauty of that unique work . . . We were all in tears.

The month of August 1918 was, I'm sure, one of the most tragic of
Satie's life. He was absolutely without a penny. I had no idea of this, as
I was away from Paris for a very short time and hadn't left a forwarding
address. On my return I found numerous letters from Satie waiting for
me. They were cries of distress.

Chère Valentine,

This is too much suffering. I feel I'm damned. This beggar's life disgusts me.

I'm really looking for a job – however small. I *shit* on art; it's brought me too many problems. An artist's is a bugger of a life, if I may so express myself.

Forgive me these true descriptions – but they *are* true.

I'm writing to everybody. No one replies, not even a friendly word. Heavens!

You, my dear Valentine, have always been good to your old friend. Please, I beg you, would it be possible try find a place for him where he could earn his living?

I don't mind where. The most menial tasks would not be below me, I promise you.

See what you can do as soon as possible; I'm at the end of my tether and can't wait any longer.

Art? It's a month now and more since I was able to write a note.

I no longer have any ideas, and don't *want* to have. So?

Your old friend,

Erik SATIE

I was unable to help him myself at that time, but I got in touch with a friend who I asked to come to the composer's aid.

He sent Satie 1000 francs anonymously. But now that this benefactor is dead, I can give him his due and say that he was called André Lebey.

Valentine Hugo
'Le Socrate que j'ai connu', *ReM*, 214, June 1952, pp. 139–44

MARCEL HERRAND

(1897–1953)

Marcel Herrand was an actor and theatre critic who took a close interest in the development of Satie's career both during and after the First World War. He made his début in Apollinaire's farce *Les mamelles de Tirésias* in 1917, to which Satie contributed some sound effects. He also appeared in Cocteau's *Les mariés de la Tour Eiffel* in 1921.

In the spring of 1917 we were rehearsing Apollinaire's *Les mamelles de*

Tirésias in a studio in Montmartre. During the rehearsals, we saw enter a man with a mischievous expression and a little pointed beard, dressed in black, wearing a bowler hat and clutching an umbrella under his arm. He was accompanied by a thin, very young man carrying a briefcase stuffed with music manuscripts. Immediately Apollinaire stopped the rehearsal and introduced us to Erik Satie and Georges Auric.

I had an enormous admiration and respect for Satie. He was an extraordinary innovator: there's no question but that, long before the first silent films of Charlie Chaplin, the Mack Sennett comedies, the Marx Brothers and cartoon films, the 'bon maître' of Arcueil had invented that bizarre mixture of loony naivety and sour, rambling humour which has since swept the world.

He often used to say: 'It's a sign of the times. Artists have become artisans; amateurs have become artists.'

Marcel Herrand
'L'humour de Erik Satie', *Le Figaro*, 23 November 1937, p. 5

CHARLES KOECHLIN

In another letter Satie asked me [in 1918] to join him and Roussel – and Milhaud and various young composers (those who made up the Groupe des Six) – in a group which would be called the 'Nouveaux Jeunes'. Naturally I accepted. But this group never came to anything, I don't know why; perhaps 'Les Six' preferred not to join up with their 'old' comrades (even though they were on excellent terms with them).

Charles Koechlin
Letter to Rollo Myers, 27 December 1948

FRANCIS POULENC

My meeting with Satie dates from . . . [May] 1917 [when] Diaghilev let off yet another bomb with his Russian Ballet by putting on Erik Satie's ballet *Parade*, with scenery by Picasso. I was conquered! With all the injustice of youth, and although I idolized Debussy, I agreed to disown him a little because I was so eager for the new inspiration Satie and Picasso were bringing us. That was the time when Ricardo Viñes introduced me to Satie. He'd heard tell of me from Georges Auric whom I'd met several months previously at Viñes's house and who'd then become what he has never ceased to be for me: my true brother in spirit. Satie was suspicious of the young Poulenc because he came of middle-class stock, but my admiration for *Parade* seemed so genuine to him that he adopted me completely. An amusing circumstance brought us still closer together a few weeks later. Not expecting to leave so early for the Front, I wanted to study composition seriously. Viñes sent me to Paul Dukas who gave me a very pleasant reception and examined my first attempts with indulgence; but Dukas, since he gave few lessons during the war, thought it better to pass me on to Paul Vidal, the composer of *La Korrigane*, a Breton ballet that used to be well known. He was a tall man with a ruddy complexion. Scarcely had I shown him my *Rapsodie nègre* than he flew into a frightful rage, told me I was playing practical jokes and threatened a portion of my anatomy with his foot if I didn't leave his office 'im-med-iate-ly!' Next day, told of the incident by Auric, Satie sent me the following note:

> Cher ami,
>   I'd like to see you. You seem lost to me but easy to find again. Suggest a date.
>   Who can be giving you such strange advice? It's funny. Never mix your schools: the result is an explosion, which after all is quite natural. What's more, if I'm to give you useful advice, I shall have to know what you plan to do and what you can do. Your application to Vidal was that of an amateur pupil, not an artist pupil. He showed you that himself. He's an old dyed-in-the-wool prima donna who's put you off your stroke. Laugh it off, old chap.
>
> Yours ever,
Erik Satie

Our close friendship dates from that letter [of 29 September 1917].

Francis Poulenc
My Friends and Myself (conversations with Stéphane Audel, trans. James Harding) (London, Dennis Dobson, 1978), pp. 39–40

GABRIEL FOURNIER

Satie often used to come to the rue Huyghens to chat with his painter
friends and also to give us the first performance of a few pages of his
latest piece. His own works aside, that's how I heard him playing pieces
whose curious novelty captivated me: they were 'ragtimes'. I was so
surprised by those syncopated rhythms which I'd never heard before, and
by the left-hand figurations so characteristic of black pianists, that I forgot
to ask him where he'd found this strange, unknown music. With the
benefit of hindsight, my knowledge of jazz now tells me that these private
performances by Satie were of pieces by Jelly Roll Morton, the father of
jazz. I puzzled over this question for years, and asked everyone how Satie
could have got to know this black American music. Then I read Alexandre
Tansman's book on Stravinsky, and learnt that when Ernest Ansermet
came back from America in 1916, he brought back some jazz records for
Stravinsky. This was before *Parade* – Stravinsky was in Paris and was
friendly with Satie, so he would certainly have played these records for
him. I say this was before *Parade*: it was also before *Histoire du soldat*.

It was after *Parade* that I got to know Satie better, when he was sued
by Jean Poueigh, the music critic of *Le carnet de la semaine*, a newspaper
belonging to the politician Dubarry. On the evening of the dress rehearsal
of *Parade* Poueigh came to Satie's box to congratulate him. So Satie was
considerably surprised the following week to read Poueigh's article in
which the ballet was torn to shreds in the most vulgar and wounding
terms. Satie, activated by a perfectly understandable impulse, decided to
give vent to his indignation and surprise in a reply. On an open postcard,
he inscribed the following highly distasteful lines:

> My dearest Sir,
> You're nothing but a bum, and an unmusical bum.
>   Signed: Erik Satie

Jean Poueigh, who lacked a sense of humour, sued Satie for libel and
defamation of character. I was at the hearing and I can still see Satie, his
eyes twinkling, but overcome with emotion and outraged by the injustice
of it all, tiptoeing to the witness box, with his gloved hands holding his
bowler hat in an elegant gesture tightly against his chest and, as always,
with the eternal umbrella hanging over his arm. It was a disgraceful

hearing. The prosecution inveighed against modern art and modern artists as being 'Boches'! Dunoyer de Segonzac, Roger de la Fresnaye, Luc-Albert Moreau, Derain, Apollinaire, they were all 'Boches'! Satie's lawyer replied on their behalf to these outrageous insults, and did so eloquently. But the voice of intelligence, justice and reason had no effect: Erik Satie, the leader of the French school of music, was condemned to a week in prison, without remission.

During the hearing, his friends, crammed into the public gallery, formed a Greek chorus. Our shouts and protests at the appalling farce being played out led to a number of threats of expulsion. We clapped when, in the ensuing silence, we heard mentioned the names of previous artists of repute who had been insulted: Cézanne, Renoir, Degas . . . and the point being made that their genius was truly French.

Through his lawyer [Maître Théry], Poueigh demanded a severe penalty – 'do not forget, members of the Bench, that this postcard is an open postcard, and as a result could be read by anybody, starting with the caretaker and, thereby, exposing him to the ridicule of a whole block of flats; not just that, but a whole street, even a whole neighbourhood, causing real and considerable prejudice to the high reputation of my client, M. Jean Poueigh.'

When the verdict was announced, we redoubled our shouts and the court was cleared. Satie gave us a supplicatory look, apparently urging us to calm down. But it was too late. We were all thrown out into the hall: Jean Cocteau white with rage under his yellowish make-up, Léon-Paul Fargue (who still had a beard in those days), René Lhote, Jacques Rivière, Ricardo Viñes, Louis Durey, his brother René, Pierre Farrey and myself. And we were astounded to see Poueigh's lawyer walking past us with his nose in the air. There was a stir among us and a voice rang out: 'I'll break the bugger's neck!' It was Jean Cocteau, who proceeded to slap his face twice. He was immediately grabbed by the attendants and taken down to the police station in the basement, where we later picked him up in the sort of state you can imagine after some rough handling. His father's chauffeur was terrified when he saw the young master coming towards him without a tie, his shirt in shreds and his hair dishevelled, 'done over' by hands which should never, under any pretext, be laid on a poet.

At the police station, Satie arrived to beg leniency for the troublemakers and for his friend Cocteau in particular. He was truly overwhelmed and was full of apologies – it was all his fault. He was still thanking everyone when the group broke up.

Gabriel Fournier
'Erik Satie et son époque', *ReM*, 214, June 1952, pp. 130–32

ARTHUR HONEGGER
(1892–1955)

Arthur Honegger was born in Le Havre of Swiss parents and came to Paris to study at the Conservatoire in 1911. He participated in the Nouveaux Jeunes concerts during the war and subsequently became a member of Les Six, though he never really fitted in with the aesthetic aims of the group. Despite his similar emphasis on craftsmanship, Satie came to dislike Honegger's music, calling him a 'pure Impressionist' in 1921.

Poueigh, who is among the lower ranks of critics, had poured scorn on Satie's ballet [*Parade*]. The composer proceeded to make fun of him by sending him a series of open postcards in which he addressed him in fairly direct language. It was hilarious listening to the cards being read out indignantly by Poueigh's lawyer and repeated in judgement by the president, who looked distinctly cross at being obliged to read out such epithets. Here, for Toto's amusement, is the third of the cards: 'Mr Jean-Fucker Poueigh, king of the idiots, head of the nitwits, emperor of the asses. Stupid bum. I'm here in Fontainebleau, from where I shit on you with all my might. E. S.'

Naturally Satie was punished, but much more severely than we were expecting. Eight days in prison, 1000 francs in damages and interest and a 100-franc fine. He appealed and it will probably come up in December. According to the newspapers, the public for this consisted of 'the whole artistic world of Montparnasse'. In fact, there were only the Engel-Bathoris, Cocteau, Auric, Fargue, Viñes, Armandie and myself.

Arthur Honegger
Letter to his parents in Zurich, 26 July 1917. Cited in Harry Halbreich, *Arthur Honegger* (Paris, Fayard, 1992), p. 52

ROLAND-MANUEL

Roland-Manuel recounted that he and Satie were walking down the street one day when they passed a *pissotière*. Satie said: 'Excusez-moi, j'ai envie de pisser,' went in, and as he came out again he remarked, 'Ah, que c'est bon de pisser! Si j'étais riche, je pisserais toute la journée!'

Recounted by Roland-Manuel to the pianist Vlado Perlemuter
Information supplied by Roy Howat

VLADIMIR GOLSCHMANN

All in all, *Parade* was a triumph. This was the moment in Satie's life when he became famous not only among musicians but to the general public. The success of *Parade* never changed him. He stayed as unassuming, modest, charming, witty as he always had been, and always generous to young musicians who, from the day they got acquainted with his music, became his devotees. They loved him not only as an artist but as a wonderful human being with a lively sense of humour.

It was not long after the première of *Parade*, which did not bring much financial reward, that Satie told me that he had decided to find pupils. So far he had one: Albert Verley, a great scientist, a chemical engineer who had a factory in the suburbs of Paris where he produced things I know nothing about except that they were needed in the making of perfumes. Verley wrote for piano, for violin, for orchestra and he told Satie that he would like to know a good sightreader who could give him an accurate idea of the way his compositions sounded. 'I have your man,' said Satie. 'Golschmann, who plays piano and violin, who can even reduce your orchestral scores and play them on the piano.' This is how I met Albert Verley. The day he put an orchestral score on the piano stand was musically the turning point in my life. 'Can you play it? Not easy,' said Verley. I went through the score and he exclaimed: 'To read a score that well is amazing; you should have the makings of a fine conductor.' 'That is my most cherished wish,' I exclaimed.

'Alright,' said Verley, 'I will give you 25,000 francs and do whatever you want with it; let us see what you can accomplish.' And this is how I started the Concerts Golschmann in Paris. Without Satie I would never have met Verley. Can I ever forget what I owe to their kind, generous hearts?

Vladimir Golschmann
'Golschmann Remembers Erik Satie', *High Fidelity/Musical America*, 22, August 1972, p. 12

JANE BATHORI
(1877–1970)

> Jane Bathori was a well-known French mezzo-soprano, who studied at the Paris Conservatoire with the Belgian tenor Émile Engel, whom she married in 1908. She made her début in opera, but soon decided to devote her life to concert work and the contemporary French song repertoire. She inspired many composers and gave numerous first performances, including Ravel's *Histoires naturelles* in 1907 (which achieved a *succès de scandale*) and Satie's *Trois mélodies* in 1916. She was also a resourceful concert organiser, and as the wartime directrice of the Théâtre du Vieux-Colombier she helped to popularise the works of Satie and the Nouveaux Jeunes, just as the subsequent success of Les Six owed much to her efforts.

What a strange figure Satie was! I did not know him until I met him at a talk about him given by Roland-Manuel in a Paris salon in 1916.* I had often heard him spoken of about 1890 by a class-mate to whom he had dedicated some of his earliest works,† but she had not understood whom she had to deal with and had not given him the attention that he perhaps deserved; and I was too young to be really curious – otherwise I might have appreciated both the *naïveté* and elegance of his early songs. Our friendship of ten years was too short, but it nevertheless brought me many unexpected pleasures and opened new horizons on that new kind of expression in music which had such a great influence on the young French school after the First World War. Satie was a questing spirit and he would have been glad, as he himself often said, to have followed a young

---

*At the Société Lyre et Palette on 18 April 1916.
†Mlle Jeanne de Bret, to whom Satie dedicated his first *Gymnopédie* in the 1895 edition. He dedicated his Latour setting *Chanson* to her sister Valentine in 1888.

composer capable of showing him a new path; but it happened to be he whom many tried to follow by grouping themselves around him. In 1917 [1916], the Princesse de Polignac, in whose home I sometimes sang and played, told me one day of her great wish to know Erik Satie, whose works she had heard but whom she had never been able to meet. I suggested she should invite him to Versailles one evening to a musical party. This was a great success and the Princess asked Satie to write her a work, leaving him absolutely free to choose its subject, its form and its size. Satie was particularly fond of the dialogues of Plato and he chose three passages in the translation by Victor Cousin – making up a portrait of Socrates. What was so extraordinary about this music was that although apparently so simple, so fluid, without *fortissimi*, without dramatic effects, it achieved an expressiveness of great originality and realism which mounted in intensity to the end and sometimes left the public silent with emotion and admiration.

At the beginning of January 1919, Satie came to my home one Sunday afternoon with a few friends. He brought with him the first part of *Socrate*: Alcibiades, which I sight-read. Valentine Gross, Jean Cocteau, Max Jacob, Roland-Manuel and the Comte Étienne de Beaumont – all were delighted and astonished, all were unable to express their thoughts except by making comparisons which really meant nothing at all, and all were unable to find any language in which to discuss a work which resembled nothing that they had heard before. Satie was the kindest and most amusing of friends, and we passed many happy times together: nevertheless he was not always very easy to get on with and I have seen him on several occasions get very angry over minor failings on the part of his friends.

Jane Bathori
'Les musiciens que j'ai connus' (trans. Felix Aprahamian), *Journal of the British Institute of Recorded Sound*, 15, 1964, pp. 238–9

[For *Socrate*], Satie had envisaged four women dressed in white robes (Directoire style), meeting each other in a salon to reread the translation of Victor Cousin in high-pitched voices. I tried this once in the apartment of a painter [Jean Bonnier], in the avenue de Villiers, but it added nothing and detracted from the emotion. As for Cocteau, he had imagined a bar with soldiers dressed in blue; but that was no better a solution.

Jane Bathori
French Radio broadcast in March 1958 (transcribed in Bibliothèque Nationale
Rés. Vm. 334(4), p. 2)

X

Last years: high society and the theatre

Satie's final period as a composer (from 1918 to 1924) began with the completion of his two most serious works: *Socrate* and the five *Nocturnes* for piano. After 1920 his life revolved around the theatre, and his main desire in his last years was to make his music striking and novel. This was undoubtedly stimulated by his desire to please his high society patrons, who adopted him as the mascot of the avant garde. His entry to the exclusive world of a wealthy post-war côterie eager for fashionable amusement was effected by Comte Étienne de Beaumont and his wife Edith, who began giving lavish masked balls during the summer of 1918, even before the war had ended. As well as commissioning *Mercure*, Beaumont brought the *Parade* team (Cocteau, Satie, Massine and Picasso) together again in 1923 to provide a *tableau vivant* for a ball whose theme was 'Antiquity under Louis XIV'. Satie composed a divertissement entitled *La statue retrouvée* for organ and trumpet, as well as his final song-cycle *Ludions* (to miniature poems by Fargue) for this glittering occasion.

This busy period also saw the launching of Les Six and the École d'Arcueil under Satie's 'umbrella'. Simultaneously, he somehow found the time to increase his journalistic output and to become the only composer of note to be involved in the Dada movement. He presided at the famous trial which condemned André Breton at the Closerie des Lilas in 1922 (after Breton had made a public attack on his friend Tristan Tzara), and he also performed at the uproarious Soirée du Coeur à Barbe in July 1923 when the police were called in to break up the fighting. A similar event occurred after the première of *Mercure* in June 1924 when the opposition was organised by Satie's enemy Auric, and it continued with *Relâche*, which was deliberately designed to provoke the sort of uproar Satie now revelled in as he moved further and further to the left. So, through the theatre, Satie provided exactly the sort of spectacular and scandalous diversion that

high society craved, and in recompense that society effectively
financed Satie's uncompromising artistic path towards the
future, which climaxed in his revolutionary film score for
René Clair's *Entr'acte*.

MOÏSE KISLING

(1891–1953)

Kisling was born in Poland and was a forward-looking painter
who, on occasions, exhibited alongside Picasso, Matisse and
Modigliani. He met Satie in 1916, who dedicated a copy of
the 'Entrée des Managers' from *Parade* to him the following
year, when Kisling also helped set up the studio in the rue
Huyghens at which Satie's Nouveaux Jeunes concerts took
place.

I met him for the first time in 1916 in the apartment of an American
lady, Mrs Sybil Harris, who kept open house on the rue Delambre. All
the Montparnasse artists of the time used to gather there, and Satie and I
soon became friends. I liked his tact, his curiosity about anything new,
and his voice, deep and slow, like his way of walking. Soon he was a
regular visitor to my studio on the rue Joseph-Bara, where he'd sit in a
far corner, only occasionally taking part in the conversation. Every now
and then he'd remind us of his presence with a loud laugh, stifled by his
beard, though the smile continued to show in his eyes.

We often met too at the Dôme or the Rotonde. Planted firmly on the
bench, with his bowler hat beside him, he used to dream rather than
experience the life around him. And he always smoked a cigar, a faithful
companion whose spiralling clouds he used to turn into magic whorls, as
the fancy took him! One could say that everything which came under his
control became material for art. We used to have uninhibited discussions
about everything under the sun. I realised that he was expressing important ideas, but I never thought to write them down, and now that I'm old,
I can no longer remember what they were: I can hear only the musical
outline of his conversation, without the words which he had the knack of
choosing and fashioning to get his message across as clearly as possible.

Even so, amid these vague memories, I do recall one evening when
we had a long discussion about dancing. 'No, no,' Satie was saying, 'the

great thing is to begin at the beginning and not worry about what the end will be! I maintain that you ought to work out the dancers' steps first of all, and then write music to illustrate their movements. The choreographer's thinking only about himself, the ballerina only about how she can get the audience to applaud, and where's the composer in all this? Where are his feelings, his message? Nowhere! His music is plundered and chopped up into bits, and finally the only member of the team who has something to say and who knows what his work is about finds himself keeping his mouth shut, or else telling lies. What a business! But those of us who recognise the music that lies in every movement, we could mechanise our art – since that, it seems, is what everyone's after – and, in this particular market-place, I'd choose the music I myself would impose rather than what other people try and impose on me.' He couldn't help getting excited when we spoke of art: he'd go red and have difficulty keeping his temper, but before it exploded, he'd leave, very dignified, walking almost as slowly as usual.

Moïse Kisling
'Souvenir de Satie', *ReM*, 214, June 1952, pp. 108–9

E.L.T. MESENS

It was around the end of 1920 or the beginning of 1921* that Satie made his first visit to Belgium for the first performances of *Socrate* in Brussels and Gand. The singer Évelyne Brélia, a champion of modern music in Belgium and an excellent interpreter of Satie's works, had promised to introduce me to the 'bon maître'. You can imagine my excitement. In Brussels Satie stayed at the old Hôtel Britannique in the place du Trône, an aristocratic hotel, already out of fashion at that time. He was accompanied by his friends Marcelle Meyer, Pierre Bertin and Georges Auric. The day before the first concert I went to collect Évelyne Brélia at her house. We were five minutes late and when we arrived at the corner of the place du Trône we saw in the distance Satie, with his famous umbrella over his arm, walking up and down the pavement opposite the hotel with Pierre Bertin. Even before introductions were effected, he gave the singer a severe look and said flatly: 'You're late, dear lady!' Then

*Actually in April 1921.

he proceeded to grumble about the two other people who were keeping him waiting. When they too arrived, he had further words of reproach for them. Understandably, I was put out. Then Satie's mood changed abruptly and, with his most charming smile, he inspected me from head to foot. I don't know if he thought I looked ridiculous because, apart from my long hair and a budding beard, I had clothed my 17-year-old self in a Borsalino, a jacket with velvet sleeves, a loosely tied, overlong bow-tie and rust-coloured trousers which did not often see an iron. In fact, I was dressed exactly like Satie himself when he lived in Montmartre. The little group set off and Satie and I brought up the rear. By way of conversation, and to put me at my ease, he said: 'This hotel is very swish, dear boy . . . much too swish for a poor man like me.' Then he devoted himself to me for the entire day, asking his friends if I could stay on for lunch, talking with me for the whole afternoon and arranging for me to be invited, that evening, to a fashionable party. 'There'll probably be music,' he said, somewhat mockingly, 'but we'll manage to find a corner to have a little chat.'

Satie's interest in the young was real and lively. From then on we wrote to each other regularly and I had some of his articles and pieces published in avant-garde Belgian journals of the day. When I came to Paris, I never missed the opportunity of seeing him. He'd arrange a meeting by *pneumatique* outside some café and we'd walk together for hours. It was Satie who took me on my only visit up the Eiffel Tower, pointing out to me the whole of Paris from the topmost platform; and it was he who took me to see the museum of ancient mouldings, which he knew down to the last detail.

He'd been keen on England since his youth, and he like to show off the fact that he had various English friends: 'Do you know that nice Leigh Henry?'* he would ask. 'He's a funny old chap.' But when I mentioned the Satiesque titles that the composer Lord Berners was giving to his works, he looked irritated and snapped: 'He's an amateur-pro-fessional. He doesn't understand.' When I asked him where his third Christian name Leslie came from, he replied: 'It's a Scottish name, from my mother's side,' adding, half pedantically, half jokingly: 'What, don't you know the Leslie clan?'

---

*The editor of the magazine *Fanfare*, to which Satie contributed words and music in 1921–2.

In 1924, Satie came to Belgium again and gave a talk in Brussels, at the 'Lanterne sourde'. He repeated it at Antwerp, at the Cercle Artistique et Littéraire. He gave me the manuscript of his talk as a present. It was beautifully written – as always – in an exercise book in pencil, traced over in ink. On the last pages of the book he'd drawn for his own convenience a rough plan of the main buildings in the centre of Brussels and how to get to them – a typical example of his meticulous character.

On the rare occasions when I showed Satie any musical manuscripts, he was tactful and discreet in the original remarks he made. His advice was decidedly curious, but he never adopted the learned tone, born of knowledge and authority, which composers so often use.

We sometimes touched on painting in the course of our long talks, but we were much happier discussing poetry: poems for setting to music, poems which shouldn't be touched at any price etc. In this area, for the most part, we didn't agree in the slightest.

E. L. T. Mesens
'Le souvenir d'Erik Satie', *ReM*, 214, June 1952, pp. 148–51

Satie was a man of colossal integrity. I don't think I have met very many people as honest as he was. Because he was terribly poor, he always showed himself in Paris as extremely clean: neat shirts with starched fronts, 'soigné' as we say, and morally it was the same thing. Satie was a man who never profiteered. Finally, my mother gave me the money for my first trip [to Paris in 1921], which lasted, with a minimum of money, about a week, and I finished by eating rotten herring fillet which I had to leave on the plate, and I fainted in the tube station. But I had seen Satie and we had spoken and at my second visit I abandoned all my Syndicalist people. I saw Satie nearly exclusively and he took me to the opening of a gallery – Librairie Six – near the Military School in Paris. He took me there to the first exhibition of Man Ray in Paris, whom I met there, and again in the evening with the most beautiful model of Montparnasse. The famous Kiki de Montparnasse was the girlfriend of the American Man Ray, who had just arrived in Paris a week or so before.

At the same time Satie took me to the studio of Constantin Brancusi to a lunch on an enormous white table in stone, which we had difficulty in pushing our legs under – we had to sit sideways to eat. The company was the following: Satie, Brancusi (our host), Marcel Duchamp, myself and, strangely enough, a Napoleonic princess, the Princesse Violette Murat, who was there because she was a friend of that enormous bearded bear. Brancusi was not big, but he was square, with an enormous square beard and hair dropping from all over the place. He made us an enormous roast in his sculptor's oven. I was in a marvellous company.

E. L. T. Mesens
Interview with George Melly on BBC Radio 3, 13 October 1969

LOUISE VARÈSE
(1890–1989)

> Louise Varèse was the wife of the composer Edgard Varèse (1883–1965), whom she married in 1921. She was born Louise McCutcheon in Pittsburgh, and her first marriage was to the poet and journalist Allen Norton, with whom she founded a short-lived Dadaist magazine called *Rogue* in 1916. She received the French title of Officier de l'Ordre des Arts et des Lettres for her translations of Saint-John Perse, Stendhal, Rimbaud, Simenon and others, and she also wrote scenarios and librettos for the theatre.

Satie came to see me [in June 1921] at the apartment a friend had loaned me on the noisy rue Notre-Dame de Lorette and, warned by Varèse, I had provided a bottle of cognac. He was the image of the person Varèse had described to me: pointed beard, derby hat [sic], stick in one hand, gloves in the other, and the most mischievous eyes I have ever seen, behind crooked pince-nez. He stood his cane in a corner by the door, put his gloves in his hat, and sitting down, placed them on the floor beside his chair. Then he said: 'Oui, oui. Et comment va ce brave garçon?' He was full of his recent travels. He had gone to Brussels! Then he talked about *Alice in Wonderland*, which he adored. He wanted to make a ballet of it. Would I write it? He was the only Frenchman, he said, who understood English humor (his mother had been English – or Scottish?) and the only composer whose music 'understood Alice'. I sincerely agreed with him.

Louise Varèse
Varèse. A Looking-Glass Diary (London, Davis-Poynter, 1973), p. 161

HENRI SAUGUET

Darius Milhaud set up a meeting with Erik Satie in his flat on the rue Gaillard. I'd caught glimpses of Satie several times, either at concerts (such as those organised by Jean Wiéner), or at the Boeuf sur le Toit, where everybody involved in the artistic life of Paris used to gather, but I'd never met him, although I was very keen to do so. Milhaud took the decision on his own to bring together the man whom the critics (or 'criti-queueu', as Satie used to say) were in the habit of calling the 'Maître of Arcueil', and a group of young composers in whom Milhaud hoped Satie might take an interest. So it was that late one afternoon Satie responded to Milhaud's invitation and Milhaud introduced to him five composers: Roger Désormière, Henri Cliquet (who had not yet added to his name that of his famous ancestor Pleyel), Maxime Jacob, Jacques Benoist-Méchin and Henri Sauguet. This was the first time the five of us had all been together.

Each of us introduced himself by name. Milhaud's warmth and friendliness saw to it that bit by bit all reserve was dissipated. Then Milhaud unveiled his plan, a sort of plot that he'd thought up on his own, and as he explained it we were as surprised as we were excited.

The world of young composers could not be entirely represented by or limited to the Groupe des Six. We had to show that other composers were coming up who formed a new cohort, looking towards the future. These young people had to have a platform, and the moment had come to organise a concert which would present them to the public.

Since each of us recognised Satie as being the guide sent by Providence, it became the job of the 'Maître of Arcueil' to introduce these new composers. Milhaud seemed not to mind playing this prank on his fellow members of Les Six and Satie, entering into his little game, agreed to take on the task, smiling with a certain amused twinkle above the little beard, and making unctuous, appeasing gestures with his hands which told of a certain embarrassment and shyness. He'd be pleased to do it, he always trusted the young. Milhaud's guarantee was enough for him and he didn't ask to hear a single one of our compositions: that was to come later. 'But,' he added, 'aren't you afraid I may compromise you?' He'd got to the heart of the matter. But then, being compromised is exactly what all truly young artists want, who desire to build rather than grovel, who burn with passion for a cause rather than following the herd. Satie was not only our flag, he was our fetish!

In a state of relaxed, enthusiastic gratitude we surrounded Satie like sons recognised by their father at the end of the play. When it came to naming the little group we'd just formed, I suggested the 'School of Arcueil'. Since there was a 'Maître of Arcueil', we would form his school, as there had been a school of Titian, of Leonardo, of Florence, or of Athens. The suggestion was carried unanimously. Satie said once again: 'That's going to compromise you . . .'

One day when I was with him I washed my hands with the soap provided:

'Fancy your using that stuff!' he said, angrily. 'If you knew what it's made of: sweat, human waste, it's revolting!'

And in fact when he was ill and was taken into the Hôpital St-Joseph, his toiletries included a pumice stone and a dog brush. He claimed he cleaned his face and his body with these, no doubt using his saliva, like a cat and he was like them too in his contemplative, silent, discreet habits – capricious, as well.

Henri Sauguet
'Quelques extraits des souvenirs', *ReM*, 361–3, 1983, pp. 237–9, 242–3

JEAN WIÉNER

One evening the Princesse de Polignac gave a dinner in his honour. At 8.30 all of high society was there, the gentlemen in tails, the ladies covered in diamonds. But the vast drawing-room did not contain only the millionaire tribe; there was also Colette, Anna de Noailles, Paul Claudel, Milhaud, Cocteau, Nadia Boulanger, Forain, Picasso, Diaghilev, Misia and José-Maria Sert, Stravinsky, Aragon, Chanel and a host of other important people. It got to 9 o'clock. The majordomo, with a chestful of medals, came and had a quiet word with the princess, huddled up in her famous armchair and not speaking to anybody. 'Clear off,' she replied in her fine American accent, 'we're waiting for the *maître*.' And the major-domo vanished. It was 9.30; the *maître* still hadn't arrived.

Boni de Castellane, his gardenia in his buttonhole and his hands in lace mittens, seemed to be getting impatient. He waited, by the door. And around 10 minutes to 10 it opened. A footman in short trousers announced: 'Maître Satie!'

And in came 'Monsieur le pauvre', wearing a shabby grey suit. His trouser bottoms, turned up several times, revealed a fair expanse of hairy leg above button boots white with dust, because, of course, he had come from Arcueil on foot. Everyone got up. Satie stopped and looked through his pince-nez. Finding the princess, he went up to her, shook her hand and said: 'But, madame, I didn't know . . . All these important people . . . I just came . . . for a friendly evening!'

Someone told this story to M. Henriquet, one of the proprietors of the Old England chain of shops, and he dropped Satie a line asking him, if he was agreeable, to come and see him so that they could take his measurements, because he wanted to make him a free dinner jacket.

Satie, very flattered, accepted M. Henriquet's offer and, after two fittings, went one morning to pick up the suit. In the shop he looked at himself in the mirror and smiled; and when they brought a box to put the suit in, he said he would wear it. And he made his way, stage by stage, on foot, back to Arcueil, on a spring morning, stopping off at each 'watering-hole' of his acquaintance to show them 'how fine he looked'!

Jean Wiéner
Allegro appassionato (Paris, Belfond, 1978), pp. 101, 103

JACQUES GUÉRIN

Satie often came here, in summer naturally, to spend Sundays at Thimé-court. He was very kind and indulgent with the young, but he was not very indulgent in general. Indeed, he was extremely sharp and there was always some particular hate on the go, some person he'd quarrelled with, and he didn't hide the fact. He even used to use extremely rude expressions. He used to make allusions to the private life of Cocteau and say, 'Cocteau is not an *homme*, he's an *hommelette!*'

He was fond of my mother, who was a very gentle, generous, good person and a good musician, and when Satie came to lunch, as he often did, he sometimes had the idea – without making a fuss about it – of sitting at the piano, which was a Bechstein. Sometimes he played, he even played duets with my mother, and with my brother, who was very musical. Several times, of an evening, there'd be a little musical gathering, with ten people or so, in Satie's honour, to hear him playing his own music; or, when it was more important, my mother would invite Marcelle Meyer, Pierre Bertin's wife, and after dinner she would accompany Paulette Darty singing Satie. Even though her voice was now showing some signs of wear – because she was now around 50, or a bit more – it was still extremely fresh – a natural voice, of an exceptional freshness, charm and grace. I remember, after a concert she'd been singing in at my mother's, Satie heaping praise on her, saying, 'Marcelle Meyer has been impressed by other voices, but she realised, even though she wasn't expecting it, that Paulette Darty was also a musician.'

Satie was very quiet and discreet, he used to talk in a low voice. He didn't say anything of great importance. When he spoke, he always put his hand to his mouth, not to hide his teeth but probably out of a kind of timidity. I think it was another way of concealing himself, because he didn't like to open his heart to people. He'd say short phrases very quietly, smiling and closing his eyes slightly with a look of complicity.

We used to go out to Luzarches every Sunday by car. My mother used to have regular arguments with Satie about whether she could pick him up from Arcueil, after collecting us in Paris. He obstinately refused, and even used to get rather tetchy – 'No, no, I beg you – no, thank you.' It wasn't something you could discuss, because there were times when he could show himself violent and hot-tempered, for all his surface gentleness. All one can say is that his wasn't a simple nature.

And after dinner, at 9 o'clock in the evening, when everyone was thinking about going home, he would refuse over and over my mother's offer of a lift in the car. You wouldn't have thought that at 9 at night it would have been such an infringement of his rules, but he refused, I've never been quite sure why. I think it must have fitted in with his mania for order, which was extreme, as you can see from his handwriting, from his musical manuscripts and from the way he laid out his letters. It was more calligraphy than ordinary writing; there are a few letters written in the ordinary way, but very few. And I think going back home on foot was one of his rules.

Satie, as you know, was a communist. And for the same reason that he was so straight in everything that he did in his life, he might have said to himself, 'I will never go in the car of rich people.' I'm not sure. But what I know is that when he left the house of Mme Dreyfus, he still had three kilometres to walk to get to the station. Why would he want so much to go on foot? I now know why. Because, on the way from the house to the station, there are two bistros, where he would stop and take a little Calvados – a very good old Norman drink!

Satie respected many things that he had no part of. He respected the family, he respected marriage, but that didn't interest him. From time to time he had rude things to say about homosexuals, not because he disapproved of homosexuality – I don't imagine he ever thought about it – but it came to mind whenever he wanted to hurt Cocteau; then, all of a sudden it became a useful weapon!

Jacques Guérin
In conversation with Robert Orledge, Luzarches, 17 September 1993

GEORGE ANTHEIL
(1900–59)

George [Georg Johann Carl] Antheil was an American composer and pianist of German descent. He studied composition with Ernest Bloch and came to Paris in June 1923 at the invitation of Stravinsky. Here he developed a consciously modernistic approach inspired by Futurism and as a reaction to Richard Strauss and Impressionism. His violent, machine-inspired and dissonant sonatas caused a riot when he performed them at the Théâtre des Champs-Élysées on 4 October 1923, and he was soon championed by Joyce, Pound, Picasso and others. Satie was genuinely delighted by his deliberately provocative display and saw him as a kindred revolutionary spirit. As Antheil later discovered, however, this riot was actually organised by Margaret Anderson to use in a 1924 film called *L'inhumaine*, starring Maeterlinck's mistress Georgette Leblanc. Unfortunately, Satie and Milhaud were not captured by the cameras on this eventful night.

One day Margaret Anderson* phoned me and asked whether I'd like to play at the opening of the Ballets Suédois – after Diaghilev's *Ballets Russes* the next most important social event in Paris.

I said I would – as who wouldn't? Everybody of importance would be

*The editor of *The Little Review*.

present on that October 4! As an added attraction (as if I needed any) she mentioned that Satie would be there too.

Satie was a most peculiar little man, working in the daytime as a clerk in a post office, selling stamps,* and in the late afternoon and at night becoming a high and mighty potentate in the decisions of musical France. He had *always* been in the vanguard.

He too was a 'specialist in genius'; and outside of this, a great composer whose marvellous *Socrate* had done more than any other thing to usher in really new and good French music.

When I came out on the stage of the Champs-Élysées Theatre to play on that night of October 4, I noticed that Satie and his friends had three boxes, Satie in the middle box and Milhaud alongside of him. Strong floodlights, strong as battleship searchlights, played upon the stage. I had programmed three sonatas, my *Sonata Sauvage*, *Airplane Sonata* and the new *Mechanisms*. I started with the *Sonata Sauvage*. Someone down in the front row started to catcall, and then someone alongside of him punched him in the jaw; a dangerous bustle of astonishment rustled through the audience.

Another man in the orchestra jumped up and angrily yelled, 'Silence! Silence!' We were now on the edge of a riot.

I finished the second of my programmed sonatas [the *Airplane Sonata*] and looked up at Satie. He was applauding violently; Milhaud seemed to be holding him back; I couldn't tell for sure. Satie seemed to push him away, continued to applaud. Satie, with his amiable goatee, looked like a beneficent elderly goat!

His applause would, I knew, mean everything to the all-powerful group around him.

I now plunged into my *Mechanisms*. Then bedlam really did break loose. People now punched each other freely. Nobody remained in his seat. One wave of persons seemed about to break over the other wave. That's the way a riot commences, one wave over the other. People were fighting in the aisles, yelling, clapping, hooting! Pandemonium!

I suddenly heard Satie's shrill voice saying, '*Quelle précision! Quelle précision! Bravo! Bravo!*' and he kept clapping his little gloved hands. Milhaud now was clapping, definitely clapping. The endorsement of Satie

---

*This is an error on Antheil's part, possibly inspired by the number of letters Satie wrote each day. In fact, he took no paid employment at any time during his life.

made it fairly certain that my career in Paris was a settled matter, at least for the next three or four years.

George Antheil
Bad Boy of Music (New York, Doubleday, Doran, 1945), pp. 107–9

MADELEINE MILHAUD

(b. 1902)

Madeleine Milhaud was born in Paris and married her cousin Darius Milhaud in May 1925. She studied the piano with Marguerite Long and dramatic art with Charles Dullin. She is an accomplished actress, teacher and theatrical producer, though much of her married life was devoted to caring for her husband who suffered prolonged bouts of crippling arthritis. She was made a Chevalier of the Légion d'Honneur in 1947, and since Milhaud's death in 1974 she has been tireless in her campaign to publicise his music.

MM: I met Satie very often after the First World War because he was extremely interested by the concerts of the young composers. So he attended many of them. I saw him playing piano and playing for singers. The first relationship I had with him was when I was in his box with Darius the night of *Mercure* [15 June 1924], the ballet at La Cigale [theatre]. Of course, it was a very interesting evening, because it was a sort of manifestation, because the Surrealists (who were usually very excited) expressed their feelings that night. They began to shout and scream: 'À bas Satie! À bas Satie! Vive Picasso! Vive Picasso!' They hated Cocteau also, and they knew that Satie was friendly with Cocteau and the whole process was quite mixed up. And before the end of the performance, Satie just stood up and left the box, because he wanted to go back to Arcueil and didn't want to miss his train. And the following day he wrote me a very charming little note, because when he got up he was afraid that he had given me a little push, so he apologised to the little lady that he had pushed her, because he had gone out so suddenly from the box.
RN: Did he have any relationship with the Surrealists?
MM: No, in fact Picabia was not a Surrealist, he was a Dadaist more or less. Satie had friends among writers, but he had more friends among the painters. Satie was very friendly with Braque and Derain. I suppose he

met Picasso, because they did work together. The Surrealists were young, and made manifestations about anything, so scandals were part of their youth. But I think Satie was quite indifferent about those things. But he was rather a sentimental man; the letters he wrote to most of his friends are absolutely full of affection and sweetness and he never forgets to 'give my love to your charming mother or father'. I suppose he didn't have any family. I think Satie's life is a mystery and always will be.

I don't think he was happy. I'm pretty sure that when he arrived on stage at the Théâtre des Champs-Élysées after his ballet *Relâche* in a little car with Picabia, in order to take his bow, something like that was for him most delightful. I'm pretty sure he was extremely happy at that moment. But that is really proof of youth, and I'm not sure that he ever really grew up.

I don't think Satie had any influence on Darius, musically speaking. I have the impression that there was a sort of relationship, even a strange relationship, because Darius was much younger than Satie. But sometimes he behaved as if he were much older, because when he took care of Satie, or tried to find him some money, or some American that he could sell his manuscripts to, he would ask for three cheques to be sent instead of one, because Satie would spend the money right away. I think he behaved as if he were his godfather, more than being his much younger friend. But Darius had a great admiration for Satie's honesty and *rigueur*, which he never gave up.

Madeleine Milhaud
In conversation with Roger Nichols, Paris, 9 December 1993

Satie's life has been rather sad and I suppose Satie was rather lonely. He was attracted by young children, by youth, because there was something pure in young people that he liked, that he admired, and that he needed. There was a lack there. He said that he could share with them their joys, their hopes and also their fight. At the same time, he was pleased to find out that they liked him and his company. What was very strange, he added, is that they think that I bring luck, because I never had luck for myself. Which is rather sad and pathetic, in a certain way.

Satie was a most lovable person, but sometimes rather unpredictable, which had a certain charm. The strange thing about Satie is that the way he dressed was completely in contradiction to his face and with his features. He had a face like those little Greek satyrs, with tiny eyes. He had a little beard, very small, and a pince-nez that he needed constantly. He spoke in a very strange way, and he broke the syllables up. That sort of thing seemed a little made up, and in contradiction with what he said, which was absolutely spontaneous. It was about as opposite as his handwriting was contradictory with what he wrote, which was quite fluent. If he laughed, he seemed to be ashamed of that laughter; he would immediately say 'ho, ho, ho, ho' and put his hand in front of his face. But that man who was absolutely anti-bourgeois in his way of thinking and living was like a clerk, dressed in black in a very decent way – a perfect, clean shirt, and a bowler hat. And he *always* carried an umbrella. He *hated* the sun; he *loved* the rain, and he went out with that umbrella if it rained or if it was sunny. And if, by chance, you had spoiled that umbrella, you would never have seen Satie any more. You were his enemy for ever. Cocteau said that one day he met Satie crossing the street under very heavy rain, with his umbrella under his arm!

RN: What was the role of the umbrella? Was it aggressive?

MM: I don't think so, because when he died and three members of his family came to visit Darius, it was a very sunny day and they *all* had umbrellas!

Madeleine Milhaud
In conversation with Roger Nichols, Northcott Theatre, Exeter, 4 June 1987

FRANCIS PICABIA
(1879–1953)

Francis Picabia was a wealthy avant-garde artist of mixed Cuban and French descent whose full name was Francisco Martinez y Picabia de la Torre. He divided his time between Paris and the South of France and was closely involved with the Dada movement in the early 1920s, running the journal *391*, to which Satie was a frequent contributor between 1921 and 1924. André Breton's abortive Congrès de Paris in 1922 marked the end of Dadaism in Paris, but Picabia gave it a brief stay of execution in 1924 with his own offshoot movement called Instantanéisme, of which *Relâche* was the sole artistic product. Picabia adapted its hastily written scenario from another ballet plan by Blaise Cendrars called *Après-*

dîner, but the idea of adding a cinematographic interlude between the acts was his own. Picabia made many enemies, but he and Satie remained close friends.

I've just had a letter from Paris telling me that at La Cigale the other evening Satie had a triumph with the musicians who went to *Mercure*, but it also says (and this is unbelievable) that two pseudo-Dadaists who were there, Louis Aragon and André Breton, conducted a demonstration against the composer of *Parade*! Why? . . . It's probably all part of some political clique, part of their usual little fun and games!

Aragon and Breton often admitted to me that they didn't understand a thing about music; so what's the point of this blackmail and this wild admiration for Picasso? Because the shouts of 'Down with Satie' were mingled with those of 'Long live Picasso!' Picasso really doesn't need defending any more, he was already famous and had found his place when Aragon and Breton were making their first communion!

They shouted: 'Long live Picasso! Down with Satie!' in the same way they say: 'Long live Germany! Down with France!' It serves their little political ends, which consist entirely of publicity whose cheap illumination never goes out or comes on when they want it to!

If their excuse for treating Satie as an old man is that he's 60 years of age, then, for poets, they betray the mentality of wine or cheese merchants, to be judging art by the passage of years. Erik Satie, gentlemen, is younger than you are, what he says is witty and amusing, and he doesn't pontificate with red dye in his hair and rouge on his lips! He loves life, quite simply, he dares to drink, he dares to write his own kind of music, and it's a pleasure for him to do so without asking himself if it will please or displease the left or the right. He dares to live on his own, doesn't forbid himself anything, doesn't forbid anyone anything, unlike those people who surround themselves with a select little côterie to give shelter to ideas as empty as a politician's handshake!

Erik Satie is, in my opinion, the most interesting French composer of our time, and if I'm collaborating with him on this ballet called *Relâche*, it's because that's what I think of him, and because I consider him to be younger and more lively than a lot of young gentlemen who sail through life like so many hot-air balloons!

You, my dear friends, shouted 'Down with Satie!' Your gestures and shouts remind me of the students at Saint-Cyr or the École Polytechnique

who go to Dadaist demonstrations and yell their opposition to the movement like dogs catching sight of the whip!

I seem to recall that Satie refused to have anything to do with your
tedious idea of the Congrès de Paris? . . .

I shout 'Long live Erik Satie!'

Francis Picabia
'Erik Satie', *Paris Journal*, 27 June 1924, p. 1

Relâche is a ballet which is part of the 'ongoing movement'. *Relâche*
consists of two acts, strictly speaking, of a cinematographic act and 'The
tail of the dog'!

Even though I had decided never to write a ballet, Erik Satie persuaded
me to; the single fact that he was writing the music for it was the best
reason I could have.

Erik Satie – with all respect to various right-thinking people, people
who are 'great musicians', people who are 'great critics', people of genius,
of modern genius, naturally – Erik Satie is perhaps the only one who is
still young; young with modesty, young with all the vigour that word
denotes; youth and freshness are so rare these days, when everyone is
mature, so mature they're going rotten! Erik Satie writes French music,
which should please the chauvinists. But no! They prefer American,
Russian or Spanish music, or at least music which derives from those
areas! Erik Satie has too much finesse, he's too simple, too 'I-don't-give-
a-hoot' with respect to 'officialdom' to please them; we'll see sooner or
later, but I'm quite certain I'm not mistaken in saying that Erik Satie is
one of the greatest composers of our time. Sometimes he has amused
himself writing for those idiots who had the effrontery to say that he was
incapable of producing a truly musical work; perhaps it was a mistake to
grant them such proof, but I believe he was simply having fun at their
expense with a nice musical curtsey!

I find the music of *Relâche* perfect. The part accompanying the cinematographic act is a masterpiece, I couldn't ask for anything which fitted
my idea more closely.

Francis Picabia
'Pourquoi j'ai écrit "Relâche" ', *Le siècle*, 27 November 1924, p. 4

Satie's case is extraordinary. He's a mischievous and cunning old artist.
At least, that's how he thinks of himself. Myself, I think the opposite!

He's a very susceptible man, arrogant, a real sad child, but one who is sometimes made optimistic by alcohol. But he's a good friend, and I like him a lot.

Francis Picabia
Letter to the poet André Breton, 17 February 1922 (just after Breton's 'trial' at the Closerie des Lilas). Cited in Michel Sanouillet, *Dada à Paris* (Paris, Jean-Jacques Pauvert, 1965), p. 516

GERMAINE EVERLING
(1886–19?)

At the time she knew Satie in 1922–4, Germaine Everling was the long-standing mistress of Francis Picabia, whom she later married. In autumn 1922 Picabia purchased a villa, La Maison Rose, at Tremblay-sur-Mauldre near Paris, where Satie often visited them during the composition of *Relâche*.

Blaise Cendrars was working at that time for Rolf de Maré and his Ballets Suédois. Cendrars had often spoken of de Maré to Picabia, saying what a nice man he was and the pleasure he got from a collaboration which respected the liberty of the artist. He added: 'You're bound to get on well together.' For his part, de Maré wanted to meet Picabia, but he was away from Paris at the moment when Cendrars was getting ready for one of his long journeys. Before he departed, Cendrars left a ballet project with Picabia with the idea that he should do the décors, and asked him to approach de Maré on his own account.

The two men saw eye to eye immediately. But they weren't particularly keen on Cendrars's scenario [*Après-dîner*]. In the course of their conversation Picabia happened to mention one of his own ideas: a humorous ballet for which he himself would write the scenario and do the décors. De Maré agreed. Satie was chosen to write the score, and Cendrars found himself out of the picture without more ado.

Picabia was happy with the opportunities this offered him and he went immediately to talk to Satie. They had had one or two literary skirmishes in the past, but Satie's separation from the Groupe des Six (among whom he had acted as the 'keeper of souls') helped bring him nearer to Picabia.

The evening he signed the contract with de Maré, Satie as usual drank such an enormous number of glasses of quetsche* that the contents would have filled a two-litre container! In his enthusiasm he kept on repeating: 'My dear fellow! It's really smart! It's going to be astounding!' And from then on he came to le Tremblay every Sunday; he was full of good spirits and confidence, making witty jokes about various of his contemporaries against whom he had complaints. He valued the fact that Picabia understood him and the close collaboration in which they developed their work, and the construction of his music was closely bound up with the painter's line of thought. This was a very far cry from the isolation in which he had so frequently laboured! He used to tell us a joke of the time when he'd been commissioned to write a ballet for the Soirées de Paris.† He went to find the Comte de Beaumont and asked him to let him have the scenario, but the count replied with a grandly mysterious air:

'That's difficult, my dear friend . . . because it's a surprise!'

Germaine Everling
L'anneau de Saturne (Paris, Arthème Fayard, 1970), pp. 153–4 (*AFS*)

CHARLES ÉRARD

Charles Érard was a young Socialist who lived in Arcueil. Soon after they met in 1920, the Socialist Party split up and Satie moved farther towards the left and joined the Communist Party. But he kept in touch with his educated and sympathetic neighbour until his hospitalisation in 1925.

I met Erik Satie at the beginning of 1920. He came to a meeting of the Arcueil-Cachan Young Socialists of which I was a member. We'd asked him to give a talk and he spoke to us about art and artists in a conversational way. I remember his talk vividly: he spoke to us particularly about painting.

'Some time ago,' he said, 'I was walking through the Louvre. In one of the rooms I saw a portrait which, from a distance, seemed to me to be very good. It was a picture by David whom I knew only as the painter of large, boring works. I thought to myself: "So, I'm going senile," and I walked on. But since then, painter friends have told me that David

---

*Alsatian plum brandy.
†*Mercure.*

did in fact paint some very fine portraits. You must never trust your prejudices.'

Later, when I got to know him better, I thought those words could to some extent symbolise his life and work. I met him often and he'd talk to me about his work and projects. One evening, together with a friend, we were sitting outside a café in front of the station at Denfert.* He was working on *Mercure* and he said that the Greek gods seemed to be incarnate in ridiculous characters of our own times. When the time came for the train, the discussion grew more heated with each of us wanting to pay the bill. The waiter intervened at that point, saying solemnly: 'Gentlemen, please, no quarrels here.' Satie reassured him and said to us in a low voice with his wicked smile: 'Let's obey him, he's a Jupiter in his own fashion.'

The last train got us to Arcueil at 1 o'clock. 'It's not late,' Satie said, 'I'd be glad if you'd walk with me a little way.' I remember it was a winter's night and all round us the gas lamps were going out. Satie didn't notice. He spoke to me of a project which was close to his heart: getting the neighbours in his area to listen to some modern music. There had been objections made and he explained his refutation of them. 'They'll understand perfectly well. They're excellent people, and they haven't been turned into academics.' He spoke to me about his ballet *Relâche* and the popular tunes he'd put into it. 'They wouldn't be shocked. "Mesdames, voilà l'navet" and "As-tu vu le cul de la cantinière?",† everybody knows those.' He was never able to have his wish. But it was done after his death, and it went very well.

I saw Satie for the last time in the early months of 1925. He was ill and in pain. I still remember with some feeling how he complained when the draught from a badly fitting door on the tram struck his legs.

It was impossible to be in his company without loving his simplicity and willingness to make allowances. It's true, though, that he only made allowances for those he was in sympathy with. He would speak of the others with biting irony: for example, of those who tried to increase their

---

*Le Lion, a café-tabac in the place Denfert-Rochereau in Montparnasse. This meeting took place in the spring of 1924.

†'Ladies, there's the turnip' and 'Have you seen the canteen-lady's bum?' These songs were probably the reason why Satie described *Relâche* to Milhaud as a 'ballet obscène'.

musical or literary standing by advertising their service in the war, 'boring us witless with their stories of Vardar'.*

Charles Érard
Letter to Robert Caby, 1 July 1929

GEORGES RIBEMONT-DESSAIGNES
(1884–1974)

Georges Ribemont-Dessaignes, the son of a famous gynaecologist, was a leading figure in the Dada movement in Paris after the First World War. He was principally a poet, though he had some musical training and also painted. Like Satie, he was a supporter of Tristan Tzara and a close friend of Picabia, contributing to his journal *391* on numerous occasions. He participated with Satie on the committee that 'tried' André Breton in 1922, and at most of the other notorious Dadaist events.

In the main period of Dada, a discreet collaboration was begun with Satie – Picabia acted as the go-between. That was when I got to know Satie, and I had a number of long and brief conversations with him. The remarkable impression he has left on me is of a man of sparkling wit, possessed of a thousand magic arrows which he kept in a quiver hidden by his beard, bringing to a cruel end this or that music critic whom he persecuted with relentless hatred, and then trampling on him with a delight expressed in his smothered laugh; and at the same time of a timid, reserved person, naively grateful for any mark of consideration or friendship that came his way.

He trusted those who spoke sympathetically of him, and I remember him thanking me one day for some words that had been written about him in the magazine *391*. He didn't understand that these words were ambiguous, and that the real meaning was far from flattering.

Satie is one of those contemporaries of ours who have handled humour in a way that reaches simultaneous extremes of the curious, the caustic and the poetic – using unaccustomed transpositions which take us into the world of the fantastic. One has only to read the titles of his compositions,

*A French battle sector in the First World War.

and especially the indications scattered on them which confirm the kind
of expression he is looking for. I remember one such 'nuance' describing
the spirit in which a phrase of one of his pieces was to be approached: 'I
want a solid mahogany hat.'

Georges Ribemont-Dessaignes
Déjà jadis (Paris, Julliard, 1958), pp. 156, 157 (*AFS*)

YVES DAUTUN

(?1904–?)

> Yves Dautun was a young student when he first met Satie on
> 29 November 1924, the evening of the cancelled première
> of *Relâche*. According to the following account, Satie was just
> as much in the dark as his disappointed audience and the sign
> 'Relâche' [Closed] on the Théâtre des Champs-Élysées was
> no hoax. Like Robert Caby, Dautun frequently visited Satie
> during his final illness, though Satie seems to have distrusted
> him and referred to him disparagingly (to Caby) as 'un
> journaliste'.

Shall I ever be able to forget our first meeting? One wet evening in
November [1924], we were waiting, duped, in front of the closed doors
of the Champs-Élysées. The public dress rehearsal of *Relâche*, Satie's last
work, was postponed: Jean Borlin, the Swede, could not dance.

On the avenue Montaigne stood pale young men with worried looks,
their eyes misty with uncertainty, snobs, beautiful ladies in pearls: the
only public, alas, that Satie knew. The public at large were always sullen
towards him.

We were also there, three or four rather passionate kids, musicophiles
at odds with the Sorbonne. We decided to go and say hello to him.

Through the gloomy doorway, one could see the wings, then the stage.
The lights and the backcloths high in the vaults were swinging gently in
the dim light.

We then saw a little old gentleman, his umbrella under his arm, his
glasses askew: it was Satie. One of us who knew him* walked forward
and made the introductions: Satie, who was very polite and well-meaning,

---

*Probably Robert Caby.

greeted us cordially. And turning towards Milhaud, he said: 'Shall we go *chez* Weber?'*

In the taxi we were all rather crowded together. But we listened to Satie, who told some of 'his' tales, dying of laughter. He passed the evening in enquiring about us and returned with us on foot.

He seemed to me, that evening, really like a modest and clever child, full of gaiety and good nature, with a captivating, joking voice, but very mysterious underneath it all.

Yves Dautun
'Un grand musicien méconnu: Erik Satie', *Le petit Parisien*, 20 August 1929, p. 6

RENÉ CLAIR
(1898–1981)

René Clair (real name René Chomette) was a celebrated film director whose career began with *Paris qui dort* in 1923, and continued with the cinematographic episode between the acts of *Relâche*. This Surrealist fantasy starred many of the famous names in the Parisian avant garde, from Marcel Duchamp to Satie himself, who was filmed firing a cannon from the roof of the Théâtre des Champs-Élysées in June 1924. Clair usually wrote his own scripts and scenarios, but in the case of *Entr'acte* a brief scenario plan was supplied by Picabia. Clair was also an accomplished journalist and actor.

When I met Picabia, he explained that he wanted to have a film projected between the two acts of the ballet, as was done, before 1914, during the interval at café concerts. And as I was the only person in the house concerned with the cinema, I was the one to be called on.

As for the screenplay, Picabia knew only what he had written on a sheet of paper headed 'Maxim's', and great was my satisfaction when, on presenting him with the completed film, I heard him laugh at what I had added. And Satie, that old master of young music, noted down each sequence with meticulous care and so prepared the first composition written for the cinema 'shot by shot', at a time when films were still silent.

*A nearby café.

Conscientious in the extreme, he was afraid of not finishing his work by the agreed date, and sent me friendly and urgent appeals in an inimitable copperplate:

> What about the film? . . . When? . . . Time passes (and does not return). 'Got the jitters' about being forgotten by you . . . Yes . . . Send details of your wonderful work quickly. Many thanks, I am, yours.
>
> E.S.

Time went by, but on the appointed day everything was ready. A short filmed prologue which I had made at the request of the authors, showed them – an unforgettable vision of Satie: white goatee, pince-nez, bowler hat and umbrella – descending from the sky in slow-motion and firing a cannon shot which signalled the beginning of the show. The first part of the ballet was well received and the applause was still going on when a screen came down from the flies. The showing of *Entr'acte* was to begin.

As soon as the first pictures appeared, a murmur composed of titters and confused rumblings arose from the audience: a gentle quiver ran along the rows. In just this way, a storm announces its arrival in the country, and soon the storm broke. Picabia, who had wanted to hear the public shouting, had every reason to be satisfied. Boos and whistles mingled with Satie's comical tunes; he, no doubt, took a connoisseur's pleasure in the sonic re-inforcement which the protestors brought to his music. The bearded ballerina and the camel were appropriately greeted and when the whole theatre felt itself swept away on the Luna Park scenic railway, howls brought the disorder, and our pleasure, to their climax.

Roger Désormière, imperturbable, his hair sticking out and his face impassive, seemed to be conducting the orchestra and unleashing a burlesque tempest with his baton all at the same time. And so, in sound and fury, this little film was born.

René Clair
À Nous la Liberté and Entr'acte (trans. Richard Jacques and Nicola Hayden) (London, Lorrimer Publishing, 1970), pp. 108–11

ANDRÉ BRETON
(1896–1966)

André Breton was a leading poet in his generation. He was
first influenced by Apollinaire and his circle and then played
an active part in the Dada movement in Paris. After 1922,
Breton became one of Satie's bitterest enemies and Satie played
no part in the new Surrealist movement, of which Breton
established himself as leader in 1924. Automatic writing was
anathema to Satie as a systematic composer in the same way
that music of all types was anathema to Breton and most of
his Surrealist colleagues.

Satie was prepared to say that the piano 'like money, is pleasant only for
the person who handles it'. For me, who had broken off relations with
instrumental music the day I was born, this is consoling. A curtain of
thorns – his sharp tongue and his studied mannerisms – hid him from
me and I am all the more sorry to have realised too late, after his death,
what an exceptional person he was.

André Breton
Letter to Robert Caby, 16 June 1955

XI

Final illness and death

ROBERT CABY

When Satie was composing *Mercure*, and *Relâche* too, the choreographers were pressing him, undermining his structure. This upset him terribly and in secret he harboured a bitter grudge against them. Also, in the second part of *Relâche*, we may question certain repeats which he resorted to reluctantly, not having the time to generate other ideas (no doubt he also made this decision out of a move away from rigour, a move he favoured thanks to the ideas of Picabia, whom he admired). Even though he 'adored' commissions, because they provoked him to crystallise his ideas into architecture, he used to think about his works and shape them long in advance. *Socrate* took years to mature inside him.

In this way he composed a string quartet. The *only thing* he regretted in his composing life was that he never wrote it down. He made this admission to me several days before he died, and it upset me considerably. What would I not have done, what would I not have given for this ancient skeleton, as he'd become in his hospital bed, to have had the time to write the wonderful quartet that he must have had in his mind!

You may say, 'Surely he had time in hospital?' Satie's way of living was incompatible with hospitals, however well they looked after him. He was so much in love with real life! And other friends than I have recounted the innumerable demonstrations of this love-cum-humour. In hospital he practically never talked about music in general, or about his own. Such was his modesty. I was perhaps the only person with whom he would talk about it. And I shall never forget the last lesson he taught me: 'I don't regret anything,' he said. 'I have never written a note' (and he sat up to make his point) 'which did not mean something, do you see?'

It was indeed the only time I heard him express a kind of artistic pride – one that was truly justified.

Robert Caby
'Erik Satie à sa vraie place', *ReM*, 214, June 1952, p. 30

I chiefly knew him during his last years and my admiration for him knew no limits. His was a unique personality. He was something else: a child of genius, with the candour and purity that one finds in a child. Because there was a spiritual side to him that was quite extraordinary.

Certainly he worked in Arcueil. He composed parts of *Relâche* there, or at least he verified them at the piano, because at the time when I was so taken with Satie, I went there. I spoke to the concierge . . . a large woman. She then told me: 'Sometimes he works at night at the piano, but he doesn't play loudly. No one says anything, because it's Monsieur Satie, and everyone has great respect for him.' This took place in the year before his death and it's absolutely authentic.

One day, he sensed that he would never leave the hospital again. And he said to me: 'Ah, *mon bon*, when I get out of hospital, we'll go together and a drink a beer in the Terminus at the gare du Nord.' This brasserie still exists today.

Another day, he looked at me and said: 'Have I been too wicked with certain people? With Ravel, Schmitt, and Debussy?' And he cried. Can you imagine? A young boy of 20, who knew so few artists . . . and Satie cried in front of *me*!

One day, he also told me: 'If you want to learn something about me, look carefully at the *Quatre petites mélodies*. They are very different, aren't they?'

After his death, Milhaud, Satie's brother and I finally entered his room. Afterwards, Milhaud said to me: 'You can come and take a bath at my place, because you can't stay like that!' We were completely BLACK! Here it's dirty, I admit, because I live alone, but this is *nothing* by comparison. The state Satie's room got into between 1898 and 1925 was quite unbelievable. We were BLACK with greasy dust. How *could* Satie leave there each morning clean, neat and tidy? After his death certain people talked of a second home or some sort of liaison. But it wasn't true, there *was* no other home. His concierge confirmed this.

Robert Caby
Interview with Robert Orledge, Paris, 13 September 1986

JEAN WIÉNER

At this more affluent time of his life he used to spend most evenings in Paris, but as he insisted on going back to Arcueil, whatever the hour of the night, one or other of us would offer to take him home in a car. He generally accepted the offer but, when we reached a certain spot on the journey, he'd always say the same thing: 'Stop here, my friends. It's an excellent thing to have a little walk before going to bed . . .' and he'd vanish into the night. We would have loved to see 'his house' and 'where he slept', but it remained impossible. We realised why when, after his death and with his brother Conrad overruling our repeated refusals, we had to force the door of that unforgettable rubbish heap.

And then came *Mercure* and *Relâche*. He was on everybody's lips, but you had the feeling he was quickly tired. The cirrhosis which he'd been suffering from for years was becoming more and more troublesome and frequently made him tetchy. He often came to the studio I shared with my small family in the rue La Fontaine. Sometimes he would say he'd 'like a little glass'. So we'd bring him a bottle with just a little champagne in the bottom and leave him for a moment 'to have a rest'.

In the early summer [spring] of 1925 his health took a turn for the worse and we couldn't allow him to go back to Arcueil. I asked my father if he could be given a room at the Grand Hôtel, and he was put in one which faced out over the place de l'Opéra, with the idea of giving him something to look at. But he didn't like it and we had to change hotels. He was no happier in Montparnasse and, as he was beset by fatigue, he agreed to go into the Hôpital St-Joseph where he lived out his last days.

There were some difficult moments. With Désormière, Darius, Cliquet-Pleyel, Caby and one or two others we did our best to please him! He'd often ask us for things that were impossible to find and, when by some chance we did unearth them, they were never what he wanted and he'd throw them back in our faces.

Despite the wonderful patience of the hospital sisters and the good will of everybody, he was rarely at peace. On 1 July he died after agreeing to take the Holy Sacraments, which was unexpected. He had perhaps rediscovered the mysticism of his youth.

Jean Wiéner
Allegro appassionato (Paris, Belfond, 1978), pp. 103–4

HENRI SAUGUET

The scandal and uproar [over *Relâche*] made it into even more of a success, and enthusiastic applause finally drowned the shouts and whistles. There were cries of 'Author! Composer!' and they came on to the stage in Désormière's 5 h.p. car. No one had seen that done before! It was the final triumph, the apotheosis, and also Satie's last public appearance. A few days after that sensational première, Satie fell ill.

He couldn't be looked after in his lodgings in Arcueil, so he had to leave them for ever and go first of all into a hotel bedroom in Paris. He locked himself so securely into this room that it was impossible to get in, because he was too weak to get up and open the door to visitors. Then he invented a system of strings which were tied to his bed and which made it possible for him to work the latch.

He didn't stay there long. Shortly afterwards he went to the Hôtel Istria on the boulevard Raspail, and finally to the Hôpital St-Joseph where the Comte de Beaumont, being a benefactor of the institution, had the use of a bed. And my memories of Satie from this point are of a sick man in a hospital run by nuns. I went to visit him often, or as often as my work allowed, because I didn't have as much time at my disposal as some others.

I saw him get paler, thinner and weaker, but the bright, piercing look in his eye never faltered. He kept his lively, whimsical sense of humour and his sly, tender smile. When the secretary of his publisher Lerolle brought him a bunch of flowers, he exclaimed 'Already,' and gave them to me, no doubt regarding them as an ill omen. Lerolle himself also came to get him to sign contracts for the songs *Ludions* he'd written on poems by Léon-Paul Fargue (the first performance, with Jane Bathori singing, had been given at Étienne de Beaumont's salon, and Stravinsky had admired their perfect word-setting) and for *Relâche*, and suggested waiting to pay him until he was well enough to come to Lerolle's offices in the rue d'Astorg to collect his cheque. Satie replied: 'No, no, my dear friend, at once, at once!' And when he got the cheque he put it on the pile of newspapers which was building up behind his bed. The good sisters removed these immediately after his death, and we only just retrieved the cheque before it was destroyed with the newspapers.

He asked me one day to sort out the large number of presents brought by his visitors; he didn't want to touch them and left them in their packing (I gather that when Braque was dying he did the same). This was the one and only time when he addressed me as 'mon petit Sauguet', although many of my friends called me that as, at 23, I looked barely 18. He passed away peacefully at 8 p.m. on 1 July, after receiving the last rites of the Church (the hospital was run by the Sisters of Saint-Vincent de Paul). His last words were 'Ah! the cows . . .'

What did he die of? Not old age – he was born in Honfleur in 1866, so he hadn't yet reached 60 – but of a kind of pneumonia which he would have survived if he had not at the same time had cirrhosis of the liver, brought on by too much spirits and beer. When he went to a café, he'd pile up the saucers, mixing brandy with glasses of beer.

He was never drunk, at least not in front of me. Instead, he became violent, aggressive, and his eyes raged. It was best on those occasions not to contradict him! All of us were witnesses to one of his fits of anger, which took on cyclonic proportions.

His grave is in the Arcueil cemetery. It was to have been marked by a sculpture of Brancusi, his great friend: the Comte de Beaumont was to pay his fee. But this was never set up or even made, I know. His resting-place is shown by a stone with just the dates 1866–1925 and the name Erik Satie.

Some time later the sale took place, at one of the auction houses in Arcueil, of various items which were found in that famous room. The sale took place in front of a few friends, and some rag-and-bone men and second-hand dealers. So we managed to rescue some of his belongings. Désormière got the copy of Debussy's Baudelaire songs, with the lovely dedication 'to the gentle, medieval composer . . .', Darius Milhaud acquired several portraits (including the one by Zuloaga), while I bought the piece of card he'd put on the door of his room in the rue Cortot in Montmartre (the one he called 'the cupboard' because it was so small), where he lived before coming out to Arcueil: in Gothic lettering and in medieval French it announces 'Maître de chapelle de Messire le Roy . . .' etc. The young Marcelle Meyer was also there – her husband Pierre Bertin had just made his first appearance at the Comédie-Française – and it must have been the first sale she'd ever attended because she kept outbidding herself, shouting 'a hundred . . . two hundred . . . three hundred . . .' to get the things she wanted.

Henri Sauguet
'Quelques extraits des souvenirs', *ReM*, 361–3, 1983, pp. 247–9

MADELEINE MILHAUD

Satie was obliged to move into Paris from Arcueil because he was extremely sick. At the beginning he spent the whole day with Derain, or Braque, or with us. For a few weeks he spent his life in this way. Then we decided for him that he couldn't stay in Arcueil, and Jean Wiéner was able to find a room for him in the Grand Hôtel, which is a very comfortable hotel. So there was Satie in a comfortable room, which he *hated*, sitting all day in front of the looking-glass on the cupboard and watching himself in the mirror, which was absolutely horrible. He had strings attached to his armchair, going directly to the door, so that he wouldn't have to get up to open the door. I think he only stayed there two days, because when we went back to see him, he was no longer there. So we had to try to find out where Satie had vanished to. And we found him in a little hotel in Montparnasse, which was a very noisy, *little* place, extremely gay, the type of place where the women who sit for painters have rooms. There he was lying with a high fever, so we had the doctor come to see him, and the doctor said he had to go into hospital right away. But Satie had never been sick in his life: he didn't know anything about sickness; he didn't know anything about fever; he didn't know anything about temperatures. Everything was absolutely new to him. Including the thermometer. So that when Milhaud tried to shake the thermometer, Satie blew up and said: 'You're going to *break* it!'

I had to make up his suitcase and pack his things, and I'm a very *bad* packer. Milhaud said that he married me because from that moment he didn't have to pack any more, but he soon found out what it meant! So I was terrified. I asked Braque, the painter, who was a big, tall man, to stand between the bed and the suitcase, and so I was able to pack because Satie couldn't see. Then, when we arrived at the hospital, the nun who was supposed to take care of Satie asked for the soap, and I had to tell her that he didn't have any, because in fact he never washed with soap. He scrubbed his skin very carefully with pumice-stone and his skin was as soft as it can be. It seems that the Chinese do that, at least that's what he said.

In fact, I had two commissions. The other was to go and fetch a bundle of his laundry when he was in the hospital. That was a great honour. So I went to Arcueil and picked up the bundle from the concierge and brought it back. And Satie blew up again because there were only ninety-eight handkerchiefs when it seemed that he had given ninety-nine or a hundred to the laundry.

Madeleine Milhaud
Interviews with Roger Nichols, Northcott Theatre, Exeter, 4 June 1987, and Paris, 9 December 1993

DARIUS MILHAUD

Despite his intolerable sufferings, he still retained his own characteristic brand of wit. When [Jacques] Maritain brought a priest to see him, he described him to us next day as 'looking like a Modigliani, black on a blue background'. When M. Lerolle came to see him about publishing *Relâche*, he insisted on being paid at once: 'You never need money so much as when you're in hospital,' he remarked slyly. Hardly had Lerolle paid over the money, than he hid the banknotes between the sheets of old newspapers piled up on his suitcase, together with all sorts of papers and bits of string. Satie refused to allow anything to be thrown away, and loved to accumulate all kinds of odds and ends. Yet, when Valentine Hugo asked him what he would like, he said: 'I've seem some lovely handkerchiefs in the draper's next to the Hôtel Istria, I should like to have some of them.'

As soon as Poulenc heard of his illness, he asked me to beg Satie to see him. Satie was touched by this, but refused, saying: 'No, no, I would rather not see him; they said goodbye to me, and now that I am ill, I prefer to take them at their word. One must stick to one's guns to the last.' For six months, Madeleine and I went to see him every day. When we left him at the end of April to go to Aix, where we were to be married, we feared we should never see him alive again. After a visit to the Middle East from which I returned in very poor health, Madeleine was so alarmed by Satie's condition that she insisted on my going to see him next day in spite of my own feeble state. Alas, we found only an empty bed.

Our poor friend's death created a series of administrative problems, some of which seemed insoluble. To avoid a pauper's grave for him, the law required that a member of his family should be present before the funeral took place: so his brother had to be found at once, at all costs. The news of Satie's death was announced by the Agence Havas in all the provincial and foreign newspapers. That is how his brother Conrad and his nephews came to hear about it. Conrad Satie proved to be a charming man: he was sincerely grieved at not having been able to look after his brother, whom he loved dearly, and with whom he had quarrelled for family reasons that were really quite unimportant. At the funeral, we were astonished to see an aged composer, Alexandre Georges, of whom Satie had never spoken, yet they must have been great friends in former days for the old man to have gone to the trouble of coming as far as Arcueil for the funeral.

Conrad Satie did not know the address of his married sister [Olga] in Buenos Aires. In such a case, the law requires that seals be affixed on the deceased's property and a public sale be held. Before this took place, Conrad obtained permission to take away all his brother's personal papers and correspondence. (He had kept all his letters, as well as the rough drafts of his own replies, even the most insignificant.) Conrad was an exceptionally disinterested and tactful man, and his first thought was for making his brother's work as widely known as possible. He packed into the suitcase, bearing the initials 'E.S.', that Satie had bought for Monte Carlo (in 1923), all the little manuscript albums and separate sheets of music that he could find. He brought them to me, for me to sort out and publish what was worthy of being saved from oblivion.

Conrad asked Désormière, Wiéner, Caby and ourselves to help him go through his brother's effects before the public sale. A narrow corridor, with a washbasin in it, led to the bedroom into which Satie had never allowed anyone, not even his concierge, to penetrate. It was with a feeling akin to awe that we approached it now. What a shock we had on opening the door! It seemed impossible that Satie had lived in such poverty. This man, whose faultlessly clean and correct dress made him look rather like a model civil servant, had literally *nothing* worth a shilling to his name: a wretched bed, a table covered with the most unlikely objects, one chair and a half-empty wardrobe in which there were a dozen old-fashioned corduroy suits, brand-new and absolutely identical. In each corner of the room there were piles of old newspapers, old hats and walking sticks. On the ancient, broken-down piano with its pedals tied up with string, there was a parcel whose postmark proved that it had been delivered several years before: he had merely torn a corner of the paper to see what it contained – a little picture, some New Year's present no doubt. On the piano we found gifts bearing witness to a precious friendship, the *édition de luxe* of Debussy's *Poèmes de Baudelaire*, and *Estampes* and *Images*, with affectionate dedications like: 'To Erik Satie, the gentle medieval musician' or 'To the famous contrapuntist Erik Satie'. Behind the piano, we found an exercise book containing *Jack-in-the-Box* and *Geneviève de Brabant* that Satie thought he had lost in a bus. With his characteristic meticulous care, he had arranged in an old cigar-box more than four thousand little pieces of paper on which he had made curious drawings and written extravagant inscriptions. They spoke of enchanted shores, pools and marshes in the time of Charlemagne. There were frequent allusions to a demon or magician who inhabited a 'cast-iron castle in the Gothic style'. He had also very carefully traced tiny plans of an imaginary Arcueil, in which the Rue du Diable stood near the Place Notre-Dame. Had we not also seen chalked up on the gate of the house opposite (by whom?): 'This house is haunted by the devil'.

Darius Milhaud
'The Death of Erik Satie', in *Notes Without Music* (trans. Donald Evans) (London, Calder & Boyars, 1967), pp. 148–51

VALENTINE HUGO

In June 1925 I often used to go to see Satie at the Hôpital St-Joseph where he lay very ill. The last time I saw him, a few days before his death, I was with Jean Hugo. While he was talking to us, he suddenly pulled back the bedclothes, like Socrates, and showed us how appallingly thin he was. Ever since then, I cannot hear 'The Death of Socrates' without bursting into tears and feeling my heart contract with pity – that death which, on one level, was so like Satie's own. My last visit to him was on the morning of 2 July 1925. I'd gone to the hospital to take him some red roses. There I met Roger Désormière who had also come to see him, and it was while we were climbing up to his room that we were told he had died. We were taken down again and into a totally empty room, cold and clean. In a pine coffin, Satie was laid out, with his mouth wide open. He looked like a dead bird.

I placed the roses on his heart and arranged them to cover the lower part of his face, so as to hide somewhat that despairing mouth.

Désormière and I were so crushed, we couldn't say a word. I really felt I was his *douce petite fille*. I felt such love and admiration . . . it was all so sad . . . sadder still than if I had lost one of my real grandfathers, whom I never knew.

Valentine Hugo
'Le Socrate que j'ai connu', *ReM*, 214, June 1952, pp. 144–5

JEAN HUGO

Satie fell ill in April 1925 and Étienne de Beaumont had him moved to the Hôpital St-Joseph. Valentine often went to see him. She took him *oeufs de Villebon* as well as handkerchiefs, which he always wanted despite the dozens of them piled up in the cupboard in his room. He could still sometimes lose his temper, as he'd done so often in the past.

I too went to see him. He said to me:

'Your father, now, he saw a priest!'

He approved of that, and he too made his confession and took communion.

On the morning of 1 July he dozed off and died in his sleep at 8 o'clock that evening. Valentine and his disciple Roger Désormière saw him next day in the hospital chapel and admired the regularity of his features, no longer concealed by the pince-nez.

The funeral took place in Arcueil on the 6th. I saw the house where he'd lived on the top [second] storey and the ground-floor café Au Rendez-Vous des Bretons, where he'd been a regular customer. The humble country church, the cemetery which looked like nothing in particular, the pine coffin placed almost at ground level in a shallow grave – everything was in keeping with the poverty of the *maître* of Arcueil, with the simplicity of his music and with the humility of his death.

Jean Hugo
Avant d'oublier (Paris, Librairie Arthème Fayard, 1976), p. 190 (*AFS*)

'M. F.'

Those present at Satie's funeral yesterday were: MM. J.-R. Bloch, Jean Hugo, Auric, Mlle Tailleferre, MM. Poulenc, Honegger, Cocteau, Paul Julien, Serge Ferat, Jacques Maritain, M. et Mme Henriquet, MM. Robert Aron, Sauguet, Édouard Dreyfus, Caby, Rouart & Lerolle,

Mme Georges Cocteau, MM. Vladimir Golschmann, Jacques Reboul, M. et Mme Milhaud, Mlle Paulette Darty-Dreyfus, MM. Viñes, R. de Castries, Henri-Pierre Roché, Mme Valentine Jean Victor-Hugo, MM. Pierre Bertin, Alexandre Georges, Mme Picabia, MM. Marcel Herrand, Jean Pierné, Louis Cretté, Boulisset, Marcel Raval, Lucien Vogel, Maxime Jacob, Albert Roussel, René Clair etc.

'M. F.'

'Les obsèques d'Erik Satie à l'église d'Arcueil', *Comoedia*, 7 July 1925, p. 1

RAYMONDE LINOSSIER

(1897–1930)

Raymonde Linossier was a close childhood friend of Francis Poulenc. She studied law and orientalism and practised as a lawyer before specialising in oriental matters at the Musée Guimet between 1923 and her early death (from an intestinal obstruction) in 1930. Her literary and musical interests were wide; she was a frequent visitor at the bookshops of Adrienne Monnier and Sylvia Beach and the author of *Bibi-la-Bibiste* in 1917.

Letter to Francis Poulenc

Monday 6 [July 1925]

Cher enfant,

Forgive me for not writing sooner to give you the details about poor Satie. He was buried this morning in Arcueil, in a simple rustic cemetery, where the coffin was lowered straight into the earth – a deal coffin stained red to imitate mahogany.

I saw the poor old thing on Wednesday, on the morning of the day he died. I went into his room and found him asleep, with his face greatly altered since my last visit and covered in flies that did not even wake him, so sound was his sleep. Naturally, I did not want to wake him, and I left. Then I spoke to the nun who was looking after him and she told me of the profound change that had taken place over the last few days. While expecting the end, she had no idea of just how close it actually was. It appears that he slept the whole day and died in the evening – I believe without regaining consciousness. The next day Madeleine Milhaud found his room empty.

For some days he had been living on nothing but champagne and paregoric. Now that he is dead I will tell you about that horrifying visit that so upset me. Without any warning, I found myself in the presence of a man whose mind had gone and who rambled on deliriously for two hours. This disintegration of what had once been our *bon maître* was terrible to behold.

He had been so happy to see me. He wanted me to come back; but because he was sleeping, I was unable to see him again.

His brother [Conrad Satie] learnt of his death through the caretaker of his factory who asked him if he knew the Monsieur Satie whose funeral preparations were reported in the newspaper.

The burial in Arcueil was fine. No doubt many people were unable to attend, and only the smart, leisured, homosexual set was well represented. But the setting was pleasant and the good people of Arcueil – his café companions and others – followed the funeral procession. It would have been a pity to see Satie, after his death, taken over by that fashionable milieu for which he always showed such contempt. Darius was there, looking impressively upset. Auric, stricken, had the same hangdog expression he wore at the première of *Les Matelots*, and was very close to tears. Cocteau sobbed rather noisily. Valentine was made up to the nines. Forgive me, but I could not help looking at the ceremony through Satie's eyes.

As to the flowers, I did not ask Cocteau's advice, firstly because I did not understand your telegram about this and secondly because I could not see what advice he could possibly give me.

I feared, and rightly so, that people would not turn up because of the holidays and the remoteness of Arcueil. I also feared that the funeral might be a rather poor affair and I wanted *le bon maître* to be treated as a *maître* and not as a penniless musician. So I sent on your behalf a very beautiful wreath (salmon pink roses and hydrangeas in the same colour) and I must tell you that what came from elsewhere barely covered the catafalque and that your wreath and mine were the only decorations that graced the church, apart from a piece of black cloth behind the altar. The only official wreaths were from the Swedish Ballet – in as bad taste as their performances, from Rouart & Lerolle, and from Les Amis du Vieil Arcueil. There was also a touching artificial violet tribute costing about

25 francs with a ribbon bearing the message: 'To Monsieur Satie – the tenants'. He must have been greatly loved there. The *patissière* wanted to know all the details of his death.

To answer your questions – he had definitely been given the sacraments as he was at Saint-Joseph's, a religious hospital, where he had already taken communion, which enabled the nuns to give him the last rites.

As for the manuscripts, I don't really know anything. His brother arrived on Saturday and no one had gone into the room in Arcueil after the death. I will phone Darius [Milhaud] tomorrow to hear his news and to put your question to him.

These, *mon vieux*, are all the details I can give you. I was very sad at the passing of this man who was always so friendly – even affectionate – to me. The particular kind of tenderness he showed towards me right until the last moment, and from our very first meeting seven or eight years ago, touched me – I might even say flattered me – deeply. And there were many reasons for our getting on so well. I was struck by this thought this morning, seeing some of his friends from Arcueil.

Raymonde Linossier
From Francis Poulenc, *'Echo and Source'. Selected Correspondence 1915–1963* (trans. and ed. Sidney Buckland) (London, Gollancz, 1991), pp. 76–7

CONRAD SATIE

Impressions written (in the third person) on 6 July 1925, after his brother's funeral:

Satie used to say: 'I have great confidence in the good Lord; when I'm dead He will do with me absolutely whatever He likes.'

A friend relates that ten months ago he saw him down ten black coffees with liqueur brandy in one evening. I never saw him drink more than three in a row.

His brother is there, robust, correct. He says: 'I haven't seen him for a year. After my wife's death I told him I didn't want to see anyone and he granted this wish all too freely, since his death took me by surprise.'

The church of Arcueil, not far from the grandiose aqueduct, is old and small. The nave is filled with friends. The priest chants the Mass in a timid voice; perhaps he is afraid of this musical audience. The little choirboy who carried the heavy silver crucifix fidgets and can't sit still. In the side chapel a marriage is taking place at the same time, four people all told whose gestures recall Henri [Douanier] Rousseau.

The little funeral procession wends its way through the little town . . . Brancusi's eyes are moist. A few weeks ago he tried to revive Satie by bringing him yoghurt and chicken soup every day that he had made himself at home, and Satie did show some improvement, but it did not last.

Darius Milhaud is losing a friend who loved him dearly.

We move away from the burial vault. I hear Satie's bantering voice saying to God: 'Just give me time to put on a petticoat, and then I'm yours.'

He was so alive.

Conrad Satie
Cited in Ornella Volta, *Satie Seen Through his Letters* (trans. Michael Bullock) (London, Marion Boyars, 1989), pp. 210–11

Index